Shaping the Journey

Shaping the Journey

Wesley, Merton, Mulholland,
and the Spiritual Formation Movement

DANIEL ETHAN HARRIS

WIPF & STOCK · Eugene, Oregon

SHAPING THE JOURNEY
Wesley, Merton, Mulholland, and the Spiritual Formation Movement

Copyright © 2025 Daniel Ethan Harris. All rights reserved. Except for brief quotations in critical publications or reviews, no part of this book may be reproduced in any manner without prior written permission from the publisher. Write: Permissions, Wipf and Stock Publishers, 199 W. 8th Ave., Suite 3, Eugene, OR 97401.

Wipf & Stock
An Imprint of Wipf and Stock Publishers
199 W. 8th Ave., Suite 3
Eugene, OR 97401

www.wipfandstock.com

PAPERBACK ISBN: 979-8-3852-5130-8
HARDCOVER ISBN: 979-8-3852-5131-5
EBOOK ISBN: 979-8-3852-5132-2

All Scripture quotations, unless otherwise indicated, are from New Revised Standard Version Bible, copyright © 1989 National Council of Churches of Christ in the United States of America. Used by permission. All rights reserved. friendshippress.org.

For Kara.
Thank you. I love every day that has you in it.

Contents

Acknowledgments xi

Introduction 1

Chapter 1: Mulholland and the Spiritual Formation Movement in Historical Context 17

Chapter 2: Wesleyan Pietistic Evangelicalism's Contribution to the Spiritual Formation Movement 44

Chapter 3: Mertonian Contemplative Monasticism's Contribution to the Spiritual Formation Movement 83

Chapter 4: Points of Synthesis Between Wesley and Merton in Spirituality and Theology 116

Chapter 5: Mulholland's Contribution to the Spiritual Formation Movement as a Confluence of His Wesleyan and Mertonian Influences 145

Appendix: Key Figures, Organizations, and Influencers of the Spiritual Formation Movement 187

Bibliography 201

Index of Names and Subjects 221

Index of Scripture References 231

Acknowledgments

I WILL FOREVER BE grateful for the opportunity I never thought I would have to do this research, and I feel immense gratitude for the relationships that have made it possible and sustained me through the process. B. H. Carroll Theological Seminary's PhD program was the setting for this project, and the experiences there repeatedly exceeded my expectations as a student, from my first conversation with Dr. Karen Bullock through Dr. Greg Tomlin's identification of me as the unusual Methodist student in a Baptist school who really likes to write about a Catholic. The encouragement from both of them was tremendously meaningful. Perhaps the greatest gift from the school has been the unforeseen opportunity to study under the supervision of Dr. Gordon T. Smith, whose work I already regarded highly, and I am thankful that the regard is now paired with a relationship that has been meaningful and enjoyable. I have benefited from the knowledge and coaching skill of Dr. Jen Harrison, whose work has been key in helping me get this project away from being stuck and now up to the finish line.

I am grateful to Lynne Mulholland for her interest in and support of the project, which opened the door to support from the organizations in which she and Bob were involved that made critical resources available to me, including Asbury Theological Seminary and the Upper Room through Johnny Sears and Donna Bryant. This research is also a fruit of the long and profound impact of the Transforming Center on my life, and in this case, the impact has taken the form of support for this project from Dalene Strieff and Ruth Haley Barton.

The impetus for beginning this work is directly tied to two of my most meaningful friendships: with my pastor, Steve Brooks (whose new nickname can be "a disciple whom Dr. Bob loved") and Dr. Robert Pelfrey. The conversations about the project with other friends have been invaluable, particularly Dr. David Wallace, A. J. Perea, Anthony Shelton, Jerry Lee, Mark Anderson, and the two remaining "HBs": Dr. Daniel J. Miller and Dr. Gerard Booy.

The demands of my other work responsibilities would have made this impossible without the support of my mother and brothers, Cathy, Jason, and Adam, and the constant and highly competent help of my good friend, Allen Modisette, whom I deeply value and respect.

I will never forget the conversation with my wife, Kara, when she surprised me by saying, "You should just do the PhD." God's goodness is abundant to me in my life with her, of which this academic work is only one of the many things she makes possible and enjoyable. The central joys in our lives are our children, Ethan and Mia. I am thankful that all three of them have put up with my endless stacks of books, and I enjoy all of the jokes about how I've put so much effort into writing things in which their friends will never have any interest whatsoever. I love my family, and I hope that this project serves to help me be who God has created me to be for them.

Introduction

STEVEN L. PORTER BEGINS the first issue of the *Journal of Spiritual Formation and Soul Care* subsequent to the death of M. Robert (Bob) Mulholland Jr. (1936–2015) with the statement, "Somewhere in my mind there is a vaguely defined short list of the founders of the spiritual formation movement and M. Robert Mulholland Jr. is on it."[1] Porter then quotes Fred Sanders, who states that Mulholland "was a major figure in the spiritual formation movement, and an early anchor to hold the movement firmly to biblical standards."[2] This research argues that the spiritual formation movement (SFM) represents a confluence of the approaches to theology and spirituality of John Wesley (1703–1791) and Thomas Merton (1915–1968) and that this confluence is represented in Mulholland's foundational contribution to the movement.

Identification of Mulholland's contribution as foundational to the SFM implies that a "movement" exists that can be referred to as the SFM. Evidence for this is presented throughout the coming chapters. Chapter 1 analyzes the dramatic increase in usage of the term "spiritual formation" by North American Protestants, beginning in the 1970s and accelerating rapidly in the 1980s. Also, as presented in each of the chapters, it is evident that this shift in terminology is accompanied by parallel shifts in theology and spirituality among those connected to the SFM, as the recovery of the theological emphasis on sanctification through theoretical and practical guidance on spiritual disciplines are hallmarks establishing movement as substantial beyond changes in semantics.

Consideration of the Wesleyan and Mertonian influences on the SFM through Mulholland is given in detail in the following chapters. To

---

1. Porter, "In Memoriam," 2. Mulholland's death was on December 20, 2015. See Barton, "Dr. M. Robert Mulholland."

2. Porter, "In Memoriam," 2.

introduce this, it is pivotal to the project's thesis that the quotations above are accurate and that Mulholland's contribution was foundational to the movement rather than peripheral. Evidence for this claim is seen early in what is described in chapter 1 as the SFM's organizational phase through Mulholland's role as faculty in the opening session of the first Upper Room Academy for Spiritual Formation (URA), which occurred May 17–22, 1983.[3] Throughout the five days, Mulholland gave five lectures on "The Place of Scripture in Spiritual Formation."[4] Rueben P. Job was in his final two years as world editor of The Upper Room and participated in the academy. He requested that Mulholland's lectures be transcribed and published "as quickly as possible."[5] The lectures became Mulholland's *Shaped by the Word: The Power of Scripture in Spiritual Formation*, first published by Upper Room in 1985, in a revised edition in 2000, an anniversary edition in 2023 (marking forty years since the first URA lectures), and was the first book written by a Protestant with "spiritual formation" in its title to be reviewed in an academic journal.[6] Mulholland taught as faculty in the URA seventeen more times in the ensuing thirty years, including five more courses on The Place of Scripture.[7]

After the URA had been conducting academies for twenty years, Doble Research Associates surveyed URA clergy alumni, and The Place of Scripture course and engagement with Mulholland emerged among the most meaningful experiences of participants.[8] The Doble report notes, "As many as eighty percent of the pastors said the faculty presenters were extremely important to them. . . . The names of various faculty members were mentioned from time to time, especially the name of Bob

---

3. For background on the academy's development and structure, see Sears, "Contemplation," 73–76.

4. Mulholland, "Place of Scripture," Session 1.

5. Mulholland, *Shaped by the Word*, 12–13. Job was elected a United Methodist bishop in 1984. See Gilbert, "Bishop Job."

6. Weisgram, "Review," 616.

7. This is according to records of the URA provided by Donna Bryant, email message to the author, August 22, 2019. The other courses Mulholland taught for the Academy were Spirituality of the New Testament (ten times) and Sustaining Life in the Spirit: New Testament Communities and Our Communities (two times).

8. Doble, "Academy," 1, 10–11, 15, 17. The report indicates The Place of Scripture as one of the two most helpful courses among the sixteen in the Academy curriculum. Although other faculty sometimes taught the course, Mulholland's teaching can legitimately be seen as a contributor to the high degree of satisfaction with the course in the survey, since all five of the academies in which he taught the course were within the twenty years covered by the survey and *Shaped by the Word* became a required text for URA participants.

Mulholland."[9] Consideration of this level of professional and interpersonal impact beginning with the opening session of the first URA, in combination with his publications on spiritual formation, decades of teaching and administration at Asbury Theological Seminary (ATS), and his later teaching at Transforming Center retreats[10] is demonstrative of Porter's and Sanders's identifications of Mulholland as one of the central founders of the SFM.

DELIMITATIONS AND OPPORTUNITIES FOR FURTHER RESEARCH

In order to clarify aspects of the SFM that this project seeks to explore and others that are not addressed herein, it is helpful to summarize a perspective on the SFM's origin that has become evident in the research process but which is beyond the scope of this book's argument and can, therefore, be a significant topic for further research. While multiple organizations have contributed to the SFM, it has no unifying structure nor official leaders and its beginnings are likewise not unified by any single person, location, or institution. Rather, the beginning of the movement can be observed as concurrent developments within three clusters. First, a Northwestern cluster centers around Regent College of Vancouver, BC, its founding principal, James M. Houston,[11] and professor of spiritual theology Eugene H. Peterson, who later occupied Regent's spiritual theology professorship named in Houston's honor. Second, a Southeastern cluster centers on the Upper Room of Nashville, Tennessee, and ATS of Wilmore, Kentucky. While multiple early contributors to the SFM were associated with one or both of these organizations, the SFM's lasting foundational contribution of widest impact from this cluster is from Mulholland.[12] Third, a Western cluster centers on Renovaré, its founder Richard J. Foster, and Dallas Willard who was Foster's close friend and a

---

9. Doble, "Academy," 10–11.

10. See Mulholland, "Sake of Others." He was the primary teacher of the "For the Sake of Others" retreats of the Transforming Center six times, from May 1–3, 2011 through July 26–28, 2015, which was his final public teaching before his death, and it was during the 2015 retreat that he and Barton recorded "Spiritual Transformation."

11. Regent College, "James M. Houston."

12. Steve Harper and Maxie Dunnam also made significant contributions to both of these institutions, although their impacts are primarily among Wesleyans in the SFM, whereas Mulholland's is broader.

frequent teacher at Renovaré events. While these clusters are not mutually exclusive (for example, Foster lectured at ATS multiple times and was part of the advisory group that led to the founding of the URA) nor strictly geographical (for example, Peterson pastored in Baltimore, Maryland, during the early years of the SFM before joining the faculty at Regent in 1993, and Foster moved from Southern California to Kansas before founding Renovaré),[13] the early contributions to the movement can be traced to one of these three clusters and the network of relationships each of them represents.

The identification of these clusters for the delimitations of this research is to highlight that while the following chapters seek to explore the prevalence of themes across SFM literature, such as sanctification, pietistic *ecclesiola in ecclesia*, and solitude, this book's focus on Mulholland is naturally concentrated on the second (Southeastern) cluster, meaning that the other respective foundational contributions of Houston, Peterson, Foster, and Willard are not considered in depth here. Further research will be valuable on each of the three clusters and the degree to which they did or did not develop independently of one another.

Additionally, conceiving of these three clusters as the relational centers from which the SFM developed delimits this research regarding the work of two other critical influences on the movement through the respective works of two Roman Catholic priests whose decades of work in North America concurrent with the SFM had direct influence upon it: Henri J. M. Nouwen and Adrian van Kaam. Nouwen's works remain tremendously popular among evangelicals in the SFM,[14] whereas van Kaam's name is little known among most readers of the SFM's literature although he established an institution and resources in which early students of the SFM could participate in advanced studies.[15] While van Kaam had significant influence on some of the SFM's intellectuals[16] and

---

13. All of the geographical descriptors are loose rather than precise. For example, Regent is only Northwestern in relation to the other two, not in its own Canadian geography. ATS and the Upper Room are relatively close to each other in Kentucky and Tennessee. Renovaré was founded when Richard J. Foster was a professor at Friends University in Kansas, but the friendship he established with Dallas Willard began in Southern California and Renovaré became headquartered in Denver, Colorado. Nevertheless, the loose geographical descriptors are indicative of the three relational networks.

14. See Johansen, "What a Friend," 32–46.

15. See the section on van Kaam's Institute of Formative Spirituality in chapter 1.

16. Van Kaam's influence on the SFM is more observable in the Southeastern cluster

Nouwen's writings are vastly influential on the SFM, neither became directly involved in these relational clusters from which the SFM developed nor participated directly in their respective institutions. Substantive examination of the influences of Nouwen and van Kaam on the SFM apart from its three originating clusters from their concurrent Catholicism is another topic for further research.

RESEARCH WARRANT

Although previous research exists on other movements that developed from within shared historical contexts as that of the SFM,[17] particular organizations associated with the SFM,[18] and the works of some of the other founding contributors to the SFM,[19] prior research does not address themes across the SFM as a whole, nor is there other research into Mulholland's works beyond dealing with singular titles.[20] Additionally, Wesley and Merton are established as two of the most influential voices in Christianity since the Reformation by the evidence of the quantity of scholarly inquiry into their respective works, with hundreds of dissertations and monographs available on each. However, a void exists of comparative study between them. While there are clear distinctions in context and content between Wesley's pietistic evangelicalism and Merton's contemplative monasticism, the possibility of complementarity between their emphases in theology and spirituality is worthy of substantive inquiry. This research seeks to contribute to these present voids of research on the SFM, Mulholland's works, and comparative study between Wesley and Merton.

The SFM is explored in this project as a movement that adopted paradoxical characteristics from multiple spectrums in the development

---

than the other clusters, as evident in the *Upper Room Dictionary of Spiritual Formation* (*URDCSF*). Further consideration of van Kaam in relation to the SFM is included in chapter 1.

17. See Markofski, *New Monasticism*. While the SFM and New Monasticism developed from similar histories and share some overlap in contributors, the movements are distinct. The similarities and differences between the two movements call for future research.

18. Reside, "Renovaré"; Wesley, "Impact of Completion."

19. Black, *Theology of Dallas Willard*; Moon, *Becoming Dallas Willard*; Collier, *Burning in My Bones*; Pfaff, *Light and Fire*.

20. Williams is critical of Mulholland's *Shaped by the Word* in the first and last chapters of her master's thesis. See Williams, "Role of Scripture."

of Christian history: for example, it is evangelical yet also monastic; it is ascetical yet also mystical; it emphasizes regular participation in highly relational small groups yet also urges immersive experiences in solitude. Students of Christian history and spirituality will be quickly aware that the SFM is not the only movement in Christianity to adopt paradoxical emphases, nor these particular emphases. Another noteworthy instance of a similar combination of emphases is the Finkenwalde Seminary led by Dietrich Bonhoeffer.[21] Finkenwalde was evangelical in a sense described in chapter 1 of this book yet also directly influenced by monasticism,[22] strongly emphasized both the "day together" in community and the "day alone" in solitude,[23] and guided participants in the practice of spiritual disciplines,[24] thus sharing core characteristics with the SFM. Accordingly, Bonhoeffer's work is influential within the SFM,[25] although the historical context in which it emerged in Nazi Germany in the 1930s was distinct from the context in which the SFM developed in North America in the 1960s–1980s. It is, therefore, viewed as influential on the SFM rather than part of it.

DEFINING SPIRIT, SPIRITUALITY, SPIRITUAL FORMATION, AND SPIRITUAL THEOLOGY

Whereas "spiritual formation" is the term most central to understanding Mulholland's contribution to the SFM and the influences of Wesley and Merton therein, the term is used inconsistently in both popular and academic discussions. For clarity in usage in this project, it is best understood in relation to the closely related terms of "spirit," "spirituality," and "spiritual theology."

Willard draws on Judeo-Christian and classical Greek traditions to identify the human "spirit" as synonymous with the will and the biblical meaning of "heart." He writes,

---

21. For an overview, see Bonhoeffer's *Life Together*, its editorial introduction by Geffrey B. Kelly, and editors' afterword by Gerhard Ludwig Müller and Albrecht Schönherr in Bonhoeffer, *Life Together*, 1–140.

22. Bonhoeffer, *Life Together*, 12, 20.

23. Bonhoeffer, *Life Together*, 48–92.

24. Bonhoeffer, *Life Together*, 93–118.

25. See Dahill, *Reading from the Underside*; McGarry, "Con-Formed to Christ," 226–42; Rios, "Bonhoeffer and Bowen Theory," 176–92; Burkholder, "Bonhoeffer's Account," 70–91.

> Within the invisible dimension of the person, and right at its conscious center, lies the *human* spirit. "God is Spirit," the creative will that creates and governs the universe, and "spirit" is the creative element in human nature, the "image of God in man." The human spirit is primarily what we today call "will," the capacity of choice and resolution, and what biblically and traditionally is called "heart." It is the radical source of our life: of the stream of actions and influences and contributions we make to our shared, visible world and its history.[26]

In this sense, it follows that all humans are spiritual beings, regardless of whether or not their lives include any theistic beliefs or religious practices, and the degree to which one's life is or is not integrated in alignment with his or her spirit is that person's "spirituality." Sandra M. Schneiders writes, "Spirituality as lived experience can be defined as conscious involvement in the project of life integration through self-transcendence toward the ultimate value one perceives."[27] However, a person still has a spirituality even if they do not have "conscious involvement" in such integration. Ronald Rolheiser describes this universality of spirituality:

> At a very basic level, before anything explicitly religious need be mentioned, it is true to say that if we do things which keep us energized and integrated . . . we have a healthy spirituality. Conversely, if our yearning drives us into actions which harden our insides or cause us to fall apart and die then we have an unhealthy spirituality. Spirituality is about what we do with that incurable desire . . . within us. Everyone has to have a spirituality.[28]

"Spiritual formation," then, includes all of the factors that shape a person's spirit and spirituality, and, like spirituality, spiritual formation is also a universal dynamic of human life. Mulholland comments,

> *Spiritual formation is the primal reality of human existence.* Every event of life is an experience of spiritual formation. Every

---

26. Willard, *Great Omission*, 104 (all italics in quotations are original unless otherwise indicated). See also Willard, *Renovation of the Heart*, 27–44; Black, *Theology of Dallas Willard*, 100–103. O'Rourke identifies this as a prevalent understanding of Willard's, described by her as "one of the keys to reading any of Dallas' works" ("Spirit," 237).

27. Schneiders, "Christian Spirituality," 1. Highlighting the same emphases, Kenneth J. Collins observes, "Though there are obviously a variety of spiritualities in existence . . . there is nevertheless a common thread that unites them all—the elements of *transcendence* and of personal *integration*." See Collins, "Introduction," 13–14.

28. Rolheiser, *Holy Longing*, 18.

action taken, every response made, every dynamic of relationship, every thought held, every emotion allowed: These are the minuscule arenas where, bit by bit, infinitesimal piece by infinitesimal piece, we are shaped into some kind of being.... Human life is, by its very nature, spiritual formation. The question is not *whether* to undertake spiritual formation. The question is *what kind* of spiritual formation are we already engaged in?[29]

Willard's description is parallel to Mulholland's:

> Spiritual formation, without regard to any specifically religious context or tradition, is *the process by which the human spirit or will is given a definite form, or character*. Make no mistake, it is a process that happens to everyone. The most despicable as well as the most admirable of persons have had a spiritual formation. Their spirits or hearts have been formed. We all become a certain kind of person, gain a specific character, and that is the outcome of a process of spiritual formation understood in general human terms.[30]

Therefore, spirituality and spiritual formation are universal dynamics of human life within which distinctively Christian applications of each term can be specified. For example, Walter Principe describes his understanding of both the general and specifically Christian meanings of spirituality: "Spirituality . . . points to those aspects of a person's living a faith or commitment that concern his or her striving to attain the highest ideal or goal. For a Christian this would mean his or her striving for an ever more intense union with the Father through Jesus Christ by living in the Spirit."[31]

Likewise, Mulholland and Willard each offer definitions of Christian spiritual formation that describe the ideal of the process.[32] Mulholland

---

29. Mulholland, *Shaped by the Word* (2000), 25–26. This passage has minor edits from the respective passage in the first edition, which predates Willard's parallel description by fourteen years. See Mulholland, *Shaped by the Word*, 27–28. See also a similar passage in Mulholland, *Invitation to a Journey*, 23–24.

30. Willard, *Great Omission*, 104. Willard similarly states, "We could forget the phrase 'spiritual formation,' but the fact and need would still be there to be dealt with. The spiritual side of the human being, Christian and non-Christian alike, develops into the reality that it becomes, for good or ill. Everyone receives spiritual formation, just as everyone gets an education. The only question is whether it is a good one or a bad one." See Willard, "Spiritual Formation in Christ," 69.

31. Principe, "Toward Defining Spirituality," 51.

32. In these descriptions, Mulholland and Willard avoid the ambiguity that comes when the same term as for the universal process is used in reference to a distinctively

succinctly describes the inward and outward dynamics of the process: "Christian spiritual formation is the process of being conformed to the image of Christ for the sake of others."³³ Similarly, Willard states,

> Christian spiritual formation, in contrast [to that which all humans are always undergoing], is *the redemptive process of forming the inner human world so that it takes on the character of the inner being of Christ himself*. In the degree to which it is successful, the outer life of the individual becomes a natural expression or outflow of the character and teachings of Jesus. But the external manifestation of Christ-likeness is not the focus of the process, and when it is made the main emphasis the process will be defeated, falling into crushing legalisms and parochialisms. "Until Christ is formed in you" (Galatians 4:19) is the eternal watchword of Christian spiritual formation, fortified by the assurance that "the letter [of the law] kills, but the spirit of the law gives life" (2 Corinthians 3:6).³⁴

As discussed in the chapters of this book, there is no emphasis more central to the literature of the SFM than the practice of spiritual disciplines. This has led some writers to identify Christian spiritual formation *as* such practices, thereby making Christian spiritual formation a subset of Christian spirituality. For example, Gerald G. May writes, "Spiritual formation is a rather general term referring to all attempts, means, instructions, and disciplines intended towards deepening of faith and furtherance of spiritual growth."³⁵ Similarly, in his paper from a recent

---

Christian description of a person's development. Sometimes, this is because "spiritual formation" is a form of shorthand for the specifically Christian application, as in Mulholland, *Invitation to a Journey*, 12–17; Willard, *Great Omission*, 53–67. At other times, it is because the universal application is not considered, such as in Dunnam, *Alive in Christ*, 26; Tracy et al., *Upward Call*, 12; Greenman, *Life in the Spirit*, 24. Often, in scholarly discussions of spiritual formation, a descriptor is added to distinguish the distinctively Christian versus the universal applications of the term, such as "Christian spiritual formation," "spiritual formation in Christ," or "spiritual transformation."

33. Mulholland, *Shaped by the Word* (2000), 25. Compare with the slight variations in the definition in Mulholland, *Shaped by the Word*, 27; Mulholland, *Invitation to a Journey*, 12; Mulholland, *Invitation to a Journey*, expanded ed., 16.

34. Willard, *Great Omission*, 105.

35. May prefaces his definition, along with his accompanying definitions of "soul," "spiritual guidance," and "spiritual direction" by stating he does "not propose the definitions . . . as absolute or theologically final," but that they clarify his usage in the text (May, *Care of Mind*, 6). Similarly, Evan B. Howard writes, "Christian spiritual formation in general refers to the intentional and semi-intentional processes by which believers become more fully conformed and united to Christ, especially with regard to maturity of life and calling. As a field of study, *spiritual formation explores particularly the means*

conference titled "Shared Spaces and Shifting Contexts: A Conference on the Study of Spirituality and Spiritual Formation," Glen G. Scorgie comments, "Hopefully, going forward there will be greater rapprochement between two frequently siloed spheres of endeavor: the academic study of Christian spirituality, and the more explicitly practical, applicational work of Christian spiritual formation and soul care."[36] Scorgie elsewhere comments,

> The popular term spiritual formation properly signals the importance of soul crafting and positive change in individual believers. It is through disciplined, attentive dependence on the impulses of the indwelling Holy Spirit that believers are privileged to participate in the renewing work of God within them. Yet *formation should probably not be treated as a synonym for the totality of Christian spirituality, because the latter is a broader reality.* Whenever formation is dislocated from its proper relational context and neglectful of the necessary divine impulses, it becomes a mere portfolio of spiritual disciplines and another grinding self-improvement project.[37]

This reflects Bernard McGinn's observation that the contemporary subject of spirituality, including Christian spirituality, is primarily anthropological in its focus, as "the greatest stress [is] on spirituality as an element in human nature and experience."[38] It is understandable, therefore, that those whose conceptions of Christian spiritual formation

---

by which growth toward maturity is fostered in Christian life." See Howard, *Brazos Introduction*, 472 (emphasis added). In a later publication, however, Howard's description of spiritual formation is less limited to the emphasis on means: "Christian spiritual formation [is] a Spirit- and human-led process by which individuals and communities mature in relationship with the Christian God (Father, Son, and Holy Spirit) and are changed into ever-greater likeness to the life and gospel of this God." See Howard, *Guide*, 18.

36. Scorgie, "Patterns of the Wind," 24. The conference occurred November 18–19, 2021, at Oblate School of Theology in San Antonio, Texas.

37. Scorgie, "Overview," 28 (emphasis added). Howard concurs: "While there are similarities between these two ideas [spiritual formation and spirituality] . . . spirituality appears to be the broader idea, embracing spiritual formation as a vital part of its horizon" (*Brazos Introduction*, 24).

38. McGinn comments, "Despite [the] nuanced theological options, the majority of definitions today can be described as variants of 'anthropological' understandings" ("Letter and the Spirit," 32). Later in the same volume Schneiders clarifies that although she had favored an anthropological approach to the study of spirituality, describing it as anthropological is "potentially misleading," and she now prefers to articulate her approach as "hermeneutical" instead. See Schneiders, "Hermeneutical Approach," 49. See also Scorgie, "Patterns of the Wind," 33–36.

focus on human "attempts, means, instructions, and disciplines" (as in May's description above) would understand Christian spiritual formation within the "broader reality" of Christian spirituality. While there is agreement that the interplay between human and divine is the crux of any religious understanding of spiritual formation, understanding its Christian application as a subset of spirituality is an expected result of what this project views as a reduction of Christian spiritual formation to an anthropological focus on the practices of spirituality.

To highlight the distinction, it is helpful to notice the variant descriptors in definitions of Christian spiritual formation. Jeffrey P. Greenman's valuable definition accords with the descriptions above from May and Scorgie, identifying Christian spiritual formation as a *human response*: "Spiritual formation is *our continuing response* to the reality of God's grace shaping us into the likeness of Jesus Christ, through the work of the Holy Spirit, in the community of faith, for the sake of the world."[39] Although Greenman states that he is seeking to offer a "theologically oriented definition,"[40] the weight of his statement remains anthropological with its identification of spiritual formation as a response from people.

This project, however, understands Christian spiritual formation as essentially theological in its focus with inextricable connections to anthropological foci such as ecclesiology, sociology, psychology, and spirituality. The theological locus of Christian spiritual formation is reflected in the biblical emphases that the term "spiritual formation" conveys and the humanly *receptive* nature of descriptors frequently used in definitions of Christian spiritual formation. Discussions of spiritual formation in Christianity are developed from the basis of a variety of New Testament terms describing formation, such as the Pauline texts: "My little children, for whom I am again in the pain of childbirth until Christ is *formed* in you," "those whom he foreknew he also predestined to be *conformed* to the image of his Son," "be *transformed* by the renewing of your minds."[41] While this project (accordant with much of Christian theology) emphasizes that humans have an irreplaceable role to play in this kind of formation, the terminology itself emphasizes that conformation to the image of Christ is not something one can possibly do to oneself. Rather,

---

39. Greenman, "Spiritual Formation," 24 (emphasis added).

40. Greenman, "Spiritual Formation," 24.

41. Respectively, Gal 4:19, Rom 8:29, and Rom 12:2. These three passages are cited repeatedly in SFM literature, and are cited together in Barton, "Biblical Perspective," 241.

Christian spiritual formation occurs by God's transforming grace and human receptivity to that grace. This receptivity is reflected in several of the definitions of spiritual formation by contributors to the field:

- "Christian spiritual formation is the process of being *conformed* to the image of Christ for the sake of others."[42]
- "Spiritual transformation is the process by which Christ is *formed* in us for the glory of God, for the abundance of our own lives and for the sake of others."[43]
- "Spiritual formation . . . is the ongoing process of the triune God *transforming* the believer's life and character toward the life and character of Jesus Christ—accomplished by the ministry of the Spirit in the context of biblical community."[44]
- Christian spiritual formation "is defined as an interactive process by which God the Father *fashions* believers into the image of his Son, Jesus, through the empowerment of the Holy Spirit by fostering development in seven primary life dimensions (spirit, emotions, relationships, intellect, vocation, physical health, and resource stewardship)."[45]
- Spiritual formation is "the *transformation* of the person into Christlikeness."[46]

Therefore, the theological orientation of Greenman's definition could be increased if, rather than identifying Christian spiritual formation as continuing human *response* to God's grace, it is identified as the *effect* of God's grace when received by humans.[47] Although 1 Cor 15:9–10 does not use the language of formation as in the other Pauline texts cited

---

42. Mulholland, *Shaped by the Word*, rev. ed, 25 (emphasis added).
43. Barton, "Biblical Perspective," 240–41 (emphasis added).
44. Pettit, *Foundations*, 24 (emphasis added).
45. Chandler, *Christian Spiritual Formation*, 19 (emphasis added).
46. Foster and Helmers, *Life with God*, 10 (emphasis added).
47. Although this proposes a change in Greenman's language, it accords with his stated intent. He writes, "By using the term *response* I want to emphasize that spiritual formation is not self-generated. . . . Spiritual formation in its best sense . . . is primarily a matter of God's own initiative and God's vital action. . . . Spiritual formation necessarily involves intentional action and commitment, yet we recognize that divine grace is not opposed to human effort, but rather is opposed to earning divine favor." See Greenman, "Spiritual Formation," 24–25. Greenman cites this as "a key theme" in Willard's writings ("Spiritual Formation," 25).

above, it does epitomize this sense of the theological primacy of God's grace in a person's transformation while also acknowledging the necessity of human reception: "For I am the least of the apostles, unfit to be called an apostle, because I persecuted the church of God. But by the grace of God I am what I am, and his grace toward me has not been in vain. On the contrary, I worked harder than any of them—though it was not I, but the grace of God that is with me." Greenman's definition could, therefore, be modified to the following: "Spiritual formation is [the process] of God's grace shaping us into the likeness of Jesus Christ, through the work of the Holy Spirit, in the community of faith, for the sake of the world."[48]

Locating Christian spiritual formation on the theological side of the interrelationship between God's grace and human response not only clarifies the language of human receptiveness in Christian spiritual formation but also clarifies spirituality as an anthropological *expression* of the human will. In this light, another Pauline text encapsulates the interrelationship between this project's understandings of spirit, spirituality, and spiritual formation. Philippians 2:12–13 states, "Therefore, my beloved . . . work out your own salvation with fear and trembling, for it is God who is at work in you, enabling you both to will and to work for his good pleasure." Paul's readers are encouraged to "work out" [in their spirituality] what God is "working in" [as their spiritual formation] so that they will be able to "will" [in their spirits] what God wills and act accordingly.

This interrelated understanding of the human spirit, Christian spirituality, and Christian spiritual formation is an apt summary of this project's *spiritual theology*, which, in relation to these terms, is understood as the most comprehensive and inclusive of the others. Simon Chan states, "Generally, spirituality refers to the kind of life that is formed by a particular type of spiritual theology. Spirituality is the lived reality, whereas spiritual theology is the systematic reflection and formalization of that reality."[49]

If, as argued here, Christian spiritual formation is essentially theological in its focus on what God "works in" human lives, it remains to be emphasized that it is not only the human spirit—nor even primarily the human spirit—into which the study of Christian spiritual formation

---

48. Greenman, "Spiritual Formation," 24.

49. Chan, *Spiritual Theology*, 16. See also Chan, "Spiritual Theology," 52–57; Peters, "On Spiritual Theology," 5–26.

appropriately inquires. To further specify Christian spiritual formation as essentially theological, it is essentially both pneumatological and Christocentric, studying the process of how God's Spirit forms the human spirit in the image of Christ.[50] Gordon T. Smith comments, "In the Spirit, we increasingly come to union with Christ. In and by the Spirit, we come to know Christ more fully, love Christ more deeply, and, to serve Christ with greater generosity. Christ is formed within us."[51] Similarly, Leopoldo A. Sánchez M. utilizes the image of sculpting to elaborate on much of what has been described here regarding Christian spirituality and Christian spiritual formation: "Like a sculptor who molds a mass into its desired shape, the Spirit's sanctifying work lies in shaping Christ's image in persons. A theology of the Spirit strives at fostering the sanctified life in others by making them participants by grace in the Spirit's manifold ways of forming persons after the 'image' or 'likeness' of Christ."[52]

CHAPTER SUMMARIES

"Chapter 1: Mulholland and the Spiritual Formation Movement in Historical Context" argues through historical analysis that the SFM represents an essentially non-fundamentalist expression of evangelicalism by exploring the nature of twentieth-century, North American evangelicalism and the variety of developments within it. The emergence of the SFM is situated in three phases from the 1960s through the 1980s alongside concurrent contrasting developments in North American evangelicalism, including the rise of the Religious Right and the Church Growth Movement (CGM).

"Chapter 2: Wesleyan Pietistic Evangelicalism's Contribution to the Spiritual Formation Movement" claims that the varieties of pietism that

---

50. Willard writes, "Spiritual formation may be thought of as a shaping by the spirit or by the spiritual realm, and by the Holy Spirit and other spiritual agencies involved in the kingdom of God, especially the Word of God. We speak of spiritual formation here because the means (or agency) that does the shaping of the human personality and life are spiritual." See Willard, "Spiritual Formation in Christ," 71. While Willard equates the human spirit with the heart and will, his general definition of "spirit" is "unembodied personal power." See Willard, *Spirit of the Disciplines*, 64. Also, Gordon D. Fee notes the impoverishing irony that much discussion of Christian spirituality has been separated from pneumatology. See Fee, "On Getting the Spirit," 36–44.

51. Smith, *Welcome, Holy Spirit*, 116. See also Pinnock, *Flame of Love*, 149–84. For a distinctively Wesleyan exploration of this theme, see Jones, *God the Spirit*, 77–88.

52. Sánchez M., *Sculptor Spirit*, xv.

John Wesley encountered and participated in through the Anglican religious societies of his upbringing, the Moravian pietism central to the years surrounding his Aldersgate experience, and his synthesis of their dynamics in his early Methodist system of societies, classes, and bands is reflected in the SFM's emphasis on small groups based on a combination of guidance in the practice of spiritual disciplines and mutual relational knowledge.

"Chapter 3: Mertonian Contemplative Monasticism's Contribution to the Spiritual Formation Movement" outlines Merton's search for solitude throughout his adult life and argues that his writings are the most influential source of the emphasis on solitude that became widespread in the literature of the SFM but was uncommon in earlier pietistic evangelicalism.

"Chapter 4: Points of Synthesis Between Wesley and Merton in Spirituality and Theology" claims that there is a high degree of compatibility in spirituality between Wesley's early Methodism and Merton's monasticism and in theology between their respective understandings of and approaches to sanctification. The chapter presents their mutual opposition to quietism as an application of the points of synthesis and completes the project's description of the SFM as a non-fundamentalist, pietistic evangelical expression of non-quietist contemplative mysticism.

"Chapter 5: Mulholland's Contribution to the Spiritual Formation Movement as a Confluence of His Wesleyan and Mertonian Influences" argues that Mulholland's contribution to the SFM is reflective of both his "accents": his non-fundamentalist, pietistic evangelical Wesleyan accent and his non-quietist, contemplative mystical Mertonian accent. The chapter establishes the prevalence of Wesleyan and Mertonian influence on the SFM through Mulholland's foundational contribution by analyzing the theology and spirituality of his major spiritual formation and biblical studies works.

Through these chapters, this project seeks to further the clarity of today's Christian spiritual theology regarding what it means to "work out" in spirituality what God graciously "works in" through spiritual formation.

CHAPTER 1

Mulholland and the Spiritual Formation Movement in Historical Context

In 1985, M. Robert Mulholland Jr. published his first book on spiritual formation, and the opening paragraph of the first chapter includes the following statement: "There is an awakening in the church to the need for spiritual formation as an essential part of growth into Christian wholeness."[1] Eight years later, his second book on spiritual formation began with a statement that was similar yet also indicated the development of that awakening into a movement: "Spiritual formation has become one of the major movements of the late twentieth century."[2] As demonstrated in the sections below, the SFM was in its early years when he published the first statement in *Shaped by the Word* and was well underway when the second statement appeared in print in 1993 in *Invitation to a Journey*. These two texts not only offered these observations relative to the SFM, but the books also became foundational contributions to the movement by grounding emphases of the SFM in New Testament exegesis and theology.[3]

---

1. Mulholland, *Shaped by the Word*, 17. In the revised edition, the statement is given increased emphasis as the first sentence of the first chapter and slightly modified: "There is an awakening across the church to disciplined spiritual formation as an essential part of growth into Christian wholeness." See Mulholland, *Shaped by the Word* (2000), 15.

2. Mulholland, *Invitation to a Journey*, 11.

3. This will be elaborated upon later in the chapter, but Mulholland's background as a New Testament scholar and skills in exegesis were critical to the impact of the books on the SFM, and this is evidenced by comments from reviewers. For example, *Invitation to a Journey* is described as "profoundly biblical" in Wheatcroft, "Review," 45. *Shaped by the Word* is described as "part of the 'balm' so needed today for the healing of our spirits and our corporate wounds" caused by misuse of the Bible in Thornton, "Review," 655.

This chapter first explores the pietistic evangelicalism in which the SFM is rooted and the fundamentalist evangelicalism to which it arose as a response. Second, the latter twentieth-century historical context of North American Christianity, which includes the development of the SFM, is examined. Finally, the chapter establishes Mulholland's influence on the SFM as foundational to the trajectory of the movement.[4] These considerations contextualize the remainder of this project's claim that Mulholland's contribution to the SFM is most clearly understood in light of the two major influences on his work: the pietistic evangelicalism of Wesley and the contemplative monasticism of Merton.

HISTORICAL CONTEXT

As evident below, although the SFM's emergence relied on non-Protestant sources, the movement originated among North American Protestants.[5] Further, Mulholland and others who were early participants in and contributors to the SFM predominantly came from evangelical traditions.[6]

---

4. Accordingly, this chapter frequently references others (particularly Willard, Foster, and Hinson) who contributed to the emergence of the SFM in addition to Mulholland, while the focus narrows to Mulholland toward the end of this chapter and throughout chapter 5.

5. This chapter's exploration of the development of North American Protestantism, evangelicalism, and the SFM is intentionally presented in a non-linear structure in order to locate general characteristics of evangelicalism elsewhere than in the current intensity of associations between evangelicalism and conservative politics in the United States, although these associations are mentioned. For important historical explorations of such associations and their development, see Markofski, *New Monasticism*, 29–158; Fitzgerald, *Evangelicals*; Du Mez, *Jesus and John Wayne*. None of these projects mention the SFM.

6. See the appendix of this book for key figures and organizations in the SFM from 1970–1989. See also Black, *Theology of Dallas Willard*, 2-48; Reside, "Renovaré," 105–52; Black and Reside each summarize scholarship on the development of American evangelicalism from its origin in the eighteenth century into its contemporary forms in the twenty-first century, with Black concluding that this historical lineage is the context from which the SFM emerged. Reside's conclusion is similar, except that he focuses on one specific organization within the SFM, Renovaré. Black's summary is unique, as it is the only such prior research to specifically identify the SFM (*Theology of Dallas Willard*, 40–42). While Black's focus on Willard's theology and Reside's focus on Renovaré are complementarily informative for this research, the present book requires other aims since Mulholland was never directly involved with Renovaré and this project seeks in part to address a void that Black indicates he is not attempting to fill when he states that he is not attempting to define or localize the SFM (*Theology of Dallas Willard*, 40). See also Markofski, *New Monasticism*, 29–158. While Markofski does not mention the SFM, his focus on the New Monastic Movement is relevant. Along with the Emerging

Accordingly, it is essential to explore the North American evangelical tradition from which the SFM emerged.

The SFM in Relation to Emphatic and Historical Descriptions of Evangelicalism

Attempts to define and describe evangelicalism have been numerous among historians and theologians, leaving some to conclude that evangelicalism qualifies as an "essentially contested concept."[7] The contested nature of the concept, however, does not mean that the term "evangelical" is left meaningless, nor that there is a lack of substantive tradition to which the term refers. Two reasons for this are particularly relevant to the task of situating the emergence of the SFM. The first is emphatic, relating to shared emphases among evangelicals, and the second is historical, relating to eras in evangelical history.

First, the SFM sufficiently reflects evangelical emphases to be attractive and meaningful to many evangelicals, even while it arose as a countermovement to dominant evangelical expressions of the time.[8] David W. Bebbington's quadrilateral of evangelical priorities has become the standard description of evangelical emphases,[9] constituting a broad evangelical "family resemblance."[10] Bebbington identifies "the four qualities that have been the special marks of Evangelical religion" as "*conversionism*, the belief that lives need to be changed; *activism*, the expression of the gospel in effort; *biblicism*, a particular regard for the Bible; and

---

Church Movement, the New Monastic Movement could be characterized as a close cousin of the SFM within what is sometimes labeled "post-evangelicalism," although such an examination is beyond the scope of this research. For descriptions of post-evangelicalism, the Emerging Church Movement, and the SFM, see Black, *Theology of Dallas Willard*, 38–56.

7. Abraham, *Coming Great Revival*, 7–10, 71–79; Olson, *Westminster Handbook*, 1; Dayton, "Some Doubts," 245; Dorrien, *Remaking of Evangelical Theology*, 3. The term is from Gallie, *Philosophy*, 157–91.

8. Watson and Scalen, "Dining with the Devil," 177. Watson and Scalen do not refer to the SFM but to Renovaré, a major organization in the SFM. Black translates their reference to Renovaré to refer instead to the SFM. See Black, *Theology of Dallas Willard*, 40.

9. Bebbington, *Evangelicalism in Modern Britain*, 2–3; See Noll et al., *Evangelicals*, 123–87. In an editorial note earlier in the book, Marsden refers to Bebbington's quadrilateral as "now canonical" (Marsden, "Evangelical Denomination," 20).

10. Abraham, *Coming Great Revival*, 9.

... *crucicentrism*, a stress on the sacrifice of Christ on the cross."[11] These four evangelical emphases are evident in the literature of the SFM, while the sense in which they are evident as adaptations of their expressions elsewhere in evangelicalism highlights the essentially contested nature of the tradition.[12]

Second, these emphases of evangelical tradition must be combined with understanding of their varying historical expressions in order to contextualize the SFM as both emphatically evangelical yet antithetical to some other expressions of evangelicalism. As William J. Abraham notes,

> What holds the various expressions together as one tradition is not one agreed set of doctrines; rather unity resides in family resemblance. Despite differences of emphasis and expression, there is sufficient common appearance for both outsiders and insiders to identify a single evangelical tradition within the Christian tradition as a whole. It is this, not detailed agreement in essentials, that justifies the descriptive use of the label. But beneath the description there is an intense informal contest about its very soul and substance. The tradition itself is essentially contested; from one generation to another various figures arise who either launch new models of the tradition or so skillfully develop old models that differences in definition become commonplace. To see this is to be liberated from naive readings of the past and to be summoned to greater efforts of analysis and expression for the future.[13]

Therefore, it is critical to note that describing people, organizations, or movements as evangelical involves "distinct though occasionally overlapping meanings" during and in reference to different historical eras.[14] Although there is no consensus, three frequently-mentioned historical

---

11. Bebbington, *Evangelicalism in Modern Britain*, 2–3.

12. See Black, *Theology of Dallas Willard*, 57–86, which demonstrates that these four emphases are present in the SFM through the foundational contribution of Willard. The four emphases are also evident in Mulholland's contribution. As examples: for conversionism, "If Christ Is," 26–34; for activism, *Invitation to a Journey*, 40–44; for biblicism, see "Biblical Spirituality," 209–14; for crucicentrism, see *Revelation*, 412.

13. Abraham, *Coming Great Revival*, 9–10.

14. Olson, *Westminster Handbook*, 3–6. Olson's list of seven meanings is beyond but inclusive of the three historical periods and their respective meanings summarized here. He identifies usages associated with: (a) the apostolic good news; (b) the Protestant Reformation; (c) the evangelical party within Anglicanism; (d) the Great Awakenings; (e) fundamentalism; (f) post-fundamentalist evangelicals; and (g) contemporary popular and journalistic usage, whether within or beyond Christianity.

eras to which the term can refer are summarized by Abraham: "the Reformation, led by Luther and Calvin, the evangelical revival of the eighteenth century . . . and modern conservative evangelicalism."[15] Gary Dorrien labels these three usages, respectively, as "classical evangelicalism," "pietistic evangelicalism," and "fundamentalist evangelicalism."[16]

Each of these historical distinctions provides a critical point of reference for situating the SFM. In reference to the "classical evangelicalism" of the Protestant Reformation, while the SFM arose among Protestants, the non-Protestant sources from which the SFM draws (represented in this research by Mertonian contemplative monasticism) cause it to sometimes be accused of being too Roman Catholic to be legitimate in the sense of classical evangelicalism.[17] In reference to the "pietistic evangelicalism" of the eighteenth century and its subsequent history in the first half of the nineteenth century, the SFM represents an attempt to recover the emphasis on sanctification that was widely present in that era's theology and spirituality (represented in this research by Wesleyan pietistic evangelicalism) but which came to be de-emphasized in much of later evangelicalism.[18] In reference to the "fundamentalist evangelicalism" from the late nineteenth century to the present, as argued below, the SFM emerged as an expression of inherently non-fundamentalist evangelicalism. More specifically, the impetus of the SFM centers on the lack of emphasis on sanctification in two major movements in conservative evangelicalism in the decades after the fundamentalist–modernist controversy of the 1910s and 1920s: neo-evangelicalism and the CGM.

---

15. Abraham, *Coming Great Revival*, 73. See also Dayton, *Variety of American Evangelicalism*, 47–48; Dorrien, *Remaking of Evangelical Theology*, 2–3.

16. Dorrien, *Remaking of Evangelical Theology*, 2–3. He comments, "Modern evangelical theology has been dominated by third-type fundamentalists, many of whom have called for restoration of first-type confessional orthodoxy; but much of the creative ferment in evangelical theology today is being stirred by thinkers from the pietist traditions" (6). Dorrien also identifies a possible fourth type as "postconservative or even progressive" evangelicalism (*Remaking of Evangelical Theology*, 6, 185–209).

17. See Williams, "Review," 189–90 for an example of this criticism in an otherwise positive review of *Invitation to a Journey*: "Mulholland's work shows an acquaintance with some of the best thinking on spirituality, but it is disappointing in its uncritical acceptance of Roman Catholic categories and presuppositions." Williams makes the accusation without specifying what those categories and presuppositions are. See also a defense of the SFM against this accusation in Porter, "Sanctification," 132–34.

18. The SFM is not an attempt to recreate pietistic evangelicalism's emphasis on sanctification as much as it is an attempt to further that era's theology and spirituality of sanctification in light of a reincorporation of sources beyond Protestantism.

The SFM in Relation to Turning Points in Evangelical History

Randall Balmer summarizes the history of evangelicalism in the United States from the eighteenth through the twentieth centuries as a chronological series of four turning points.[19] The first is a soteriological shift from predominantly Calvinist to Arminian theology and evangelistic practice amid the burgeoning American ethos between the first and second Great Awakenings. Balmer primarily associates the Calvinist soteriology of the first Great Awakening with Jonathan Edwards and George Whitefield and the Arminian soteriology of the second Great Awakening with Charles G. Finney.[20] Second, Balmer identifies an eschatological shift from postmillennialism to premillennialism in the national devastation following the Civil War.[21] This shift toward premillennialism was based on the teaching of John Nelson Darby and was popularized by Dwight L. Moody and Cyrus. I. Scofield.[22] Third is a social shift from cultural engagement to fundamentalist retreat beginning in the early twentieth-century response to the spread of modernism.[23] Balmer characterizes this shift as initially evident in the separatism characteristic of figures such as J. Gresham Machen or Bob Jones Sr., and later, in the "neo-evangelicals" like Carl F. H. Henry and Billy Graham who maintained much of fundamentalism except its separatism and therefore reengaged society from the newly-created evangelical subculture.[24] Fourth, Balmer identifies a political shift from withdrawal to proximate engagement in the last quarter of the twentieth century as many of the heirs of fundamentalism contributed to "the rise of the Religious Right" by identification of evangelicalism with American cultural and political conservatism, commonly associated with

---

19. Balmer, *Making of Evangelicalism*. Balmer discusses each of the four turning points respectively in the book's four chapters.

20. Balmer, *Making of Evangelicalism*, 9–25. The characterization of Finney as Arminian is ubiquitous but debatable, as explored below in this chapter. See Caldwell, *Theologies*, 58–68, 171–96.

21. Balmer, *Making of Evangelicalism*, 27–42.

22. Balmer does not mention Scofield, but the 1909 publication of the *Scofield Reference Bible* was critical to the dissemination of Darby's premillennial teaching. See Hummel, *Rise and Fall*, 129–39; Dorrien, *Remaking Evangelical Theology*, 29–32; Witherington, *Problem with Evangelical Theology*, 111; Marsden, *Fundamentalism and American Culture*, 150.

23. Balmer, *Making of Evangelicalism*, 43–58. Marsden explores this shift in detail in *Fundamentalism and American Culture*, 177–247.

24. Marsden, *Fundamentalism and American Culture*, 289–93.

evangelical leaders such as Jerry Falwell, Pat Robertson, Tim LaHaye, and James Dobson.[25]

In Balmer's characterization, each of these four turning points had persisting influence on subsequent developments in evangelicalism. In his view, the prevalent soteriological understanding never returned to Calvinism,[26] postmillennialism never again became the dominant form of eschatology, the subculture created in response to the fundamentalist-modernist controversy persists and has become socially strengthened, and evangelicals have remained highly politically engaged since the rise of the Religious Right.

Therefore, the four critical junctures that Balmer claims formed American evangelicalism were all active dynamics in the tradition when the Religious Right and the SFM were both originating within evangelicalism in the 1970s and 1980s. While it is plausible that some evangelicals participated in the beginnings of both movements, there are no clear links between the two.[27] Not only is this non-identification of the SFM and Religious Right the case regarding the Religious Right's explicit political

---

25. Balmer, *Making of Evangelicalism*, 59–76. For a more recent perspective, including the effects of the 2016 US presidential election of Donald Trump, see Noll et al., *Evangelicals*, 216–78.

26. Scholars disagree over whether evangelicalism after the Great Awakenings has been more predominantly Reformed or Arminian. For example, see Balmer, *Making of Evangelicalism*, 24–25, where he states, "In recent years, Calvinists have tried to stage a comeback on two fronts, both theological and historical. . . . Such efforts largely come to naught, however, at the grass roots. Finney's pragmatism and his brand of Arminianism carried the day among evangelicals—in the antebellum period and ever since. At least as understood at the popular level, the revivalist's plea to come to Jesus or Billy Graham's invitation to 'make a decision for Christ' makes little sense in the Calvinist and Edwardsean scheme of revival, where even the repentant sinner must await the visitation of grace." A seemingly opposite characterization is in Dorrien, *Remaking of Evangelical Theology*, 159: "The evangelical establishment was led and controlled by Reformed-oriented conservatives who gave little consideration to the notion that modern evangelicalism had much to learn from the spiritual descendants of Finney, Moody, or even John Wesley. . . . Billy Graham's revival preaching called unbelievers to 'make a decision for Christ,' but Graham was careful not to cross the border into wilder Arminian territory. Through Graham's ministry and such institutions as Wheaton College, Inter-Varsity Christian Fellowship, and *Christianity Today*, the evangelical movement succeeded in creating a significant transdenominational image and ethos, but Reformed evangelicals either dominated or controlled most of these institutions. Their conception of ecumenical evangelicalism assumed a Reformed center."

27. For example, of the names listed in this book's appendix, none are mentioned as participating in the current narratives of the development in the Religious Right in Balmer, *Making of Evangelicalism*; Du Mez, *Jesus and John Wayne*; Fitzgerald, *Evangelicals*; nor Fea, *Believe Me*.

alignment, but it is also consistent in relation to the dynamics of the previous three turning points that were still persistent as the two movements began. The SFM is expressly ecumenical rather than separatist, drawing from sources across the Christian tradition in the decades following the ecumenical movement and the Second Vatican Council (Vatican II).[28] Likewise, the SFM does not emphasize premillennialist eschatology. Rather, Mulholland's combination of his formational and exegetical approach in his contribution on interpretation of the book of Revelation was evangelical yet expressly amillennial and non-dispensationalist.[29]

The relation of the soteriological shift to evangelicalism's disparate expressions in the Religious Right and the SFM in the late twentieth century requires further clarification. As the earliest and, therefore, longest enduring of Balmer's four turning points, the soteriological shift shaped the subsequent eschatological, social, and political transitions.[30] Balmer's characterization, however, of the transition as being from Calvinism with Whitefield and Edwards to Arminianism with Finney—whose brand of Arminianism Balmer claims to have remained dominant thereafter—needs reexamination.

A leap from Calvinism to Arminianism was unnecessary for Finney because of the significant shift in the understanding of the role of human agency in the process of salvation that took place within Calvinism itself in the theology of Edwards through what Robert W. Caldwell III has termed Edwards's "voluntarist accent."[31] Caldwell describes this development of Reformed theology as Edwards's attempt "to unite freedom, responsibility, inability, and sovereignty into one consistent system"[32] by claiming that "sinners possess both a moral inability to choose Christ and a natural ability to repent and believe."[33] Finney's early revival theol-

---

28. See Sears, "Contemplation," 68–79.

29. Mulholland, *Revelation: Holy Living*, 304–11; Mulholland, *Revelation*, 578–79.

30. Although in a different sense of soteriology than the evangelicals involved would have used (which generally centers on the eternal destinations of heaven or hell after death), the eschatological, social, and political shifts can all be seen as having soteriological dynamics: premillennial eschatology is a theology of being saved from the ever-increasing influence of evil in the world; fundamentalist separatism is a spirituality of salvation from the perceived apostasies of modernism and liberalism; the political engagement of the Religious Right reflects a sense of need for salvation from the attacks of secularism on the evangelical subculture.

31. Caldwell, *Theologies*, 58–68.

32. Caldwell, *Theologies*, 67.

33. Caldwell, *Theologies*, 74.

ogy, then, drew neither from Arminius nor Wesley but from his native Reformed tradition and Edwards's development of it. Finney's further development was to maintain the Edwardsian notion of ability but deny Edwards's concept of inability.[34] Understanding the "voluntarist accent" in Edwards clarifies Finney's soteriology as "not technically Arminian" but "a progressive, some might say extreme, version of the Edwardsian theological tradition."[35]

This provides an explanation for why the theology of the SFM resonated not only with those from Arminian traditions but also with broader evangelicalism.[36] If the divide between Reformed and Arminian soteriologies were as wide as Balmer implies, the SFM would have primarily drawn from evangelicals from either one camp or the other. In contrast, the SFM's development among Methodists, Presbyterians, Baptists, Quakers, and evangelicals of other traditions suggests a different soteriological shift that would influence the subsequent development of evangelicalism, including the Religious Right and the SFM, and that soteriological shift has to do with the widely divergent evangelical views of sanctification. Before exploring this further, it is important to clarify the SFM's identity as an inherently non-fundamentalist expression of evangelicalism.

The SFM as an Expression of Inherently Non-Fundamentalist Evangelicalism

If it is true that the beginnings of the Religious Right are traced to fundamentalist leaders who sought "to reassert fundamentalist influence in mainstream American life,"[37] and that "while not all persons associated with that phenomenon called themselves fundamentalists, the ethos of the movement was embued by fundamentalist values,"[38] then the mutually distinct lists of the early leaders of the Religious Right and the SFM

---

34. Caldwell's chapter on Finney (*Theologies*, 165–96) is very helpful in this clarification.

35. Caldwell, *Theologies*, 195.

36. As examples, Mulholland's Methodism was clearly an Arminian tradition, but that is not the case for the Presbyterianism of Peterson, the Quakerism of Foster, the Congregationalism of Houston, nor the Baptist background of Willard.

37. Olson, *Westminster Handbook*, 78.

38. Olson, *Westminster Handbook*, 78.

are one reflection of the SFM's nature as an expression of inherently non-fundamentalist evangelicalism.

As evident in the SFM, some of the streams of American evangelicalism whose roots trace through the pietistic evangelicalism of the Great Awakenings continued to maintain the evangelical emphases of conversionism, activism, biblicism, and crucicentrism without adopting the general theological, ecclesiological, and social characteristics displayed in fundamentalist evangelicalism.[39] First, regarding theological characteristics, what came to be known as the "five points of fundamentalism" were "the inerrancy of Scripture, the Virgin Birth of Christ, his substitutionary atonement, his bodily resurrection, and the authenticity of the miracles."[40] Abraham comments that these five points "constitute a firm core of the [fundamentalist] tradition, but they are but part of the total agenda,"[41] as other beliefs are evident as prevalent characteristics in fundamentalist orthodoxy. Roger E. Olson summarizes the continuing theological commitments of fundamentalism beyond the five points "to what they consider to be the fundamentals of Christianity, including biblical inerrancy, often (perhaps not always) young earth creationism and anti-evolutionism, dispensationalism, and rejection of critical biblical scholarship."[42]

Second, the ecclesiology of the early fundamentalists strongly emphasized "biblical separationism."[43] Olson describes this as "the hallmark of fundamentalism" beginning in the 1930s as conservative Christians were urged by their leaders "to abandon all churches and religious

---

39. One example of such a group, in addition to the SFM, includes black Christians in North America. See Tisby, "Black Christians," 262–72.

40. Marsden, *Fundamentalism and American Culture*, 147. Marsden notes that premillennialism later came to substitute as the fifth point rather than authenticity of the miracles.

41. Abraham, *Coming Great Revival*, 13.

42. Olson, *Westminster Handbook*, 79. Similarly, Abraham describes three additional elements of fundamentalist theology: a premillennialist view of history with "the present time being very close to the return of Christ," a literal interpretation of every part of the Bible, and an understanding of creation that "held that the human world is so corrupt that it can only get worse and worse. The present world is really under the sway of the devil; the most God does is preserve a pure remnant; in due course he will move in to act in judgment to clear up the present unspeakable mess that pervades the institutions of Christendom and the world at large" (Abraham, *Coming Great Revival*, 13–14).

43. Olson, *Westminster Handbook*, 78.

organizations even indirectly 'tainted' by liberal thinking."[44] Over time, the separatist ecclesiology of some fundamentalists lessened, particularly with the influence of leaders such as Henry and Graham, but emphases such as inerrancy and premillennialism remained.[45]

Third, the social stance of fundamentalism, whether strictly separatist or intensely politically engaged through the Religious Right, has remained staunchly oppositional to perceived threats to its religious and cultural conservatism. George M. Marsden observes,

> When in the mid-1970s the Religious Right entered the national consciousness as a politically active movement, some of its early core leadership was drawn from separatist fundamentalists, of whom Jerry Falwell and Tim and Beverly LaHaye were fairly typical. As a political coalition, however, the new Religious Right soon drew in many conservative evangelicals who were militant, or fundamentalistic on cultural issues.[46]

Parallel to the persistent effects of Balmer's four transitions into the years when the Religious Right and the SFM began, these theological, ecclesiological, and social characteristics of fundamentalism were not only present but heightened during the 1970s and 1980s. For example, each of the books perhaps most associated with premillennialism, inerrancy, and the SFM were published within eight years of one another: on premillennial eschatology, Hal Lindsey published *The Late Great Planet Earth* in 1970;[47] on inerrancy and resistance to critical biblical scholarship, Harold Lindsell published *The Battle for the Bible* in 1976;[48] and Richard J. Foster published the book sometimes credited with launching the SFM, *Celebration of Discipline*, in 1978.[49]

44. Olson, *Westminster Handbook*, 78.
45. Marsden, *Fundamentalism and American Culture*, 290–91.
46. Marsden, *Fundamentalism and American Culture*, 291.
47. Dorrien describes Lindsey's book as "one of the best-selling books of all time" and "a dispensationalist primer" (*Remaking of Evangelical Theology*). See Hummel, *Rise and Fall*, 233–47.
48. Olson comments on the impact of Lindsell's book, "It helped propel the entire Southern Baptist Convention—America's largest Protestant denomination—into a twenty-year convulsion. Almost overnight evangelical organizations and institutions rushed to include inerrancy in their doctrinal statements" (*Westminster Handbook*, 62). Meanwhile, Mulholland's 1977 dissertation employed multiple forms of higher criticism in biblical interpretation. See Mulholland, "Markan Opponents of Jesus."
49. Foster's book is credited with launching the SFM in Smith, "Techniques Without Transformation," 44. Greenman describes the book's publication as a "clear marker" of the SFM's birth. See Greenman, "Spiritual Formation," 23.

Douglas M. Strong uses the fundamentalist views on inerrancy to illustrate the divergence that emerged between pietistic and fundamentalist evangelicalism, as he states that in the mid-nineteenth century, "American evangelicals . . . were not held together primarily by their affirmation of correct doctrine coming from a perfect Bible as much as by their commitment to a sanctified life coming from a personal Jesus."[50] The drastic diminishment of emphasis on sanctification is a soteriological shift in evangelicalism of equal significance with the other four identified by Balmer, and it is the minimization of sanctification in the dominant evangelical expressions of the middle and late twentieth century that provided the impetus for the SFM to begin.

The SFM as a Response to the "Sanctification Gap" in Finney, Neo-Evangelicalism and the CGM

In 1973, Richard F. Lovelace published an article that would become highly influential in the SFM titled "The Sanctification Gap."[51] The frequent allusions to the seven-page article in SFM literature are epitomized in Porter's editorial introduction to the inaugural issue of the *Journal of Spiritual Formation and Soul Care*, which states, "It is in the aftermath of this 'sanctification gap' . . . that this journal has come to fruition."[52]

Lovelace's article recounts that he initially had no interest in Protestant theology following his conversion from atheism to Christianity because it "seemed as supernatural as a Sears Roebuck Catalogue."[53] He states that later, however, "I did find evangelical Protestants who understood the dynamics of spiritual life, whose spirituality commanded my respect . . . and who had biblical answers for the troubles in my soul."[54] Yet, he says, "I was amazed to find that most Protestants were ignorant of the body of tradition which seemed to me to be the living heart of the Reformation heritage."[55] He continues,

---

50. Dayton and Strong, *Rediscovering an Evangelical Heritage*, 14.

51. Lovelace, "Sanctification Gap," 363–69. The influence of the article on the SFM is evidenced by at least twelve citations of the article in the first fifteen volumes (2008–2022) of the *Journal of Spiritual Formation and Soul Care*. See also references to Lovelace's concept in Coe, "Approaches to the Study," 37; Chan, "Spiritual Theology," 55.

52. Porter, "Inaugural Issue," 5.

53. Lovelace, "Sanctification Gap," 364.

54. Lovelace, "Sanctification Gap," 364.

55. Lovelace, "Sanctification Gap," 364.

> There seemed to be a sanctification gap among Protestants, a peculiar conspiracy somehow to mislay the tradition of spiritual growth and to concentrate on side issues. "Liberals" sought to commend Christianity to its cultured despisers, and to apply its ethics to social concerns. "Conservatives" specialized in personal witnessing activity, sermons on John 3:16, and theological discussion of eschatological subtleties. Other sectors of the church argued over issues of real substance, but with such rancor or confusion that one wished that some attention had first been given to sanctification.[56]

Lovelace locates the beginning of the sanctification gap in the nineteenth-century revivalists who "modified the Puritan system by allowing easier standards of initial conversion."[57] Lovelace argues that this was especially true of Finney, whose "ultimate simplification" was his "call for instantaneous commitment and instantaneous conversion."[58] In this respect, Balmer's assessment of Finney's lasting influence is accurate.[59] This aspect of Finney is persistent into the neo-evangelicalism of Graham and the seeker-sensitive evangelistic approaches of the CGM, while significantly divergent from the understanding of and approaches to conversion in Finney's evangelical predecessors such as Edwards and Wesley.[60]

However, although Lovelace traces this "ultimate simplification" of conversion to Finney, the beginnings of the sanctification gap are evident with more clarity in later evangelicalism's adoption of Finney's early approach to conversion combined with its widespread denial of his later emphasis on sanctification.[61] Finney wrote in 1839 that, earlier

56. Lovelace, "Sanctification Gap," 365.

57. Lovelace, "Sanctification Gap," 366.

58. Lovelace, "Sanctification Gap," 366.

59. See Balmer, *Making of Evangelicalism*, 25. He states, "Finney assured all Americans that they controlled the mechanism of salvation, and the evangelical tradition has never been the same. . . . The message they propagate is simple, straightforward, and utterly indebted to Charles Finney. Come to Jesus. Make a decision for Christ. You control your own spiritual destiny."

60. For comparisons of Edwards, Wesley, and Finney on conversion, see Smith, *Beginning Well*, 85–98; Smith, *Transforming Conversion*, 67–79.

61. See Smith, *Beginning Well*, 99, where he elaborates, "Most evangelicals bought into only half of the Finney conversion package. Finney himself acknowledged that he presented conversion as easy; but he compensated for this by calling for a further work of sanctification, along similar lines to the experience advocated in the Holiness movement. Many streams of evangelicalism reject such a 'second crisis,' though they have accepted Finney's notion of a 'first crisis,' the initial salvific event. The consequence

in his life, his mind was "occupied almost exclusively with that class of truths that were calculated to work the conviction and conversion of the unrepentant."[62] He continues, "In the midst of my efforts, however . . . we have overlooked in a great measure the fact that converts would not make one step of progress unless they were constantly urged with means as well adapted to their sanctification and growth in grace, as were the means for their conversion."[63] He then mentions his struggle after revisiting churches in which he had previously held revivals:

> I was fully convinced that converts would die, that the standard of piety would never be elevated, that revivals would become more and more superficial and finally cease, unless something effectual was done to elevate the standard of holiness in the church. . . . I have felt as strongly and unequivocally pressed by the Spirit of God to labor for the sanctification of the church as I once did for the conversion of sinners.[64]

In the years just prior to this letter from Finney, he had been reading Wesley's *A Plain Account of Christian Perfection*,[65] and the section just quoted of Finney's letter is reminiscent of a comment in Wesley's journal:

> I was more convinced than ever, that the preaching like an Apostle, without joining together those that are awakened, and training them up in the ways of God, is only begetting children for the murderer. How much preaching there has been for these twenty years all over Pembrokeshire! But no regular societies, no discipline, no order or connexion; and the consequence is, that nine in ten of the once-awakened are now faster asleep than ever.[66]

However, as similar as Finney's comment is to Wesley's, it is in contrast to Billy Graham's response to criticism about a lack of support for converts after his crusades:

---

has been a wide-spread emphasis on easy conversion without an attendant emphasis on sanctification. Tragically, then, those outside the Holiness movement have often viewed holiness, spiritual maturity, and the work of the Holy Spirit as entirely incidental or secondary within the Christian experience."

62. Finney, "Letter to Readers," 17.
63. Finney, "Letter to Readers," 18.
64. Finney, "Letter to Readers," 19–20. For further detail on latter Finney's understanding of sanctification, see Smith, "Doctrine of the Sanctifying," 92–113.
65. Smith, *Revivalism and Social Reform*, 103.
66. Wesley, *Works* (Jackson), 3:144.

We were challenged many times about what happens to the converts when the crusade is over. Apparently the brethren who made these statements had no faith in the Holy Spirit. The work of regeneration is the work of the Holy Spirit. The work of follow-up is the work of the Holy Spirit. The same Holy Spirit that convicted these people of sin is able to follow them.... We did all we could in follow-up, but ultimately all converts are in the hands of the Holy Spirit. *He is more than able to nurture them toward maturity.*[67]

Scot McKnight observes that Finney's early emphasis on persuasive techniques in evangelism persisted into Moody, Billy Sunday, and Graham, while Finney's later emphasis on sanctification was present in Moody, somewhat lessened in Sunday, and noticeably absent in Graham and neo-evangelicalism.[68] McKnight argues, "The gospel of the mid-twentieth century reduced the Reformation's soteriology into four or five crisp claims.... That gospel is also divorced from moral transformation, which . . . undercuts everything preached from Wesley to Moody and Sunday."[69]

Graham's defense against accusations of lack of follow-up for new converts not only indicates the kind of deemphasis on sanctification which E. Glenn Hinson characterizes as "overloading the front end of the spiritual life,"[70] but the position from which Graham made the statement (not as a pastor, but as a parachurch evangelist) suggests an individualism and minimized ecclesiology in Graham's understanding of conversion,

---

67. Graham, *Hear My Heart*, 52. This was originally part of an April 3, 1957, address to the National Association of Evangelicals in Buffalo, New York. See "Lost Chord," 26. It is noteworthy that Graham seems to indicate that evangelists are indispensable in the task of evangelism, while no one except the individual person and the Holy Spirit is needed for the task of sanctification.

68. McKnight, *King Jesus Gospel*, 85–93. McKnight identifies further examples of what is characterized in this project as examples of the sanctification gap in neo-evangelicalism (which he calls "post-fundamentalist evangelicalism"): "Those who want to criticize revivalism are taking dead-aim at Youth for Christ's Four Spiritual Laws, the gospel of Billy Graham's crusades, James Kennedy's *Evangelism Explosion*, and the reduction of the gospel to gospel tracts. They are claiming that in the middle of the twentieth century, American post-fundamentalist evangelicalism went astray and we are suffering for it even today" (*King Jesus Gospel*, 93). McKnight makes this case, although he is careful to imply that this generalized accusation against revivalism is not true until neo-evangelicalism, specifying Bright and Graham as "the real target of the contemporary aversion to revivalism" (*King Jesus Gospel*, 92).

69. McKnight, *King Jesus Gospel*, 93.

70. Hinson, *Baptist Spirituality*, 31–44.

salvation, and sanctification.[71] While Graham made his historic impact from a parachurch position, he paved the way in the 1950s and 1960s for an ecclesial iteration of similar dynamics[72] in the 1970s and 1980s in the CGM.[73]

As Graham is the primary figure of neo-evangelicalism, that of the CGM is Donald McGavran, whose background was not in American fundamentalism but in missions in India.[74] McGavran's ideas developed into the core of the CGM theory, and he was strongly influenced by a missionary colleague, J. Waskom Pickett. Alan G. Padgett comments that if McGavran is the father of the CGM, Pickett is the "ideological 'grandfather.'"[75] The origin of the sanctification gap in the CGM is evident in a comparison of the approaches of these two.

---

71. For a contrasting view, see Smith, *Beginning Well*, 33–39. He states, "In a genuine Christian conversion, through an encounter with Christ we become part of the community of those who are called (*ekklesia*) and who, in response to that call, become one in Christ. There is no such thing as an isolated Christian; a conversion to be properly Christian includes incorporation into a community of faith" (*Beginning Well*, 34). Similarly, McKnight focuses his criticism on "individual conversion absent ecclesial formation and context" (*King Jesus Gospel*, 89).

72. Ed Stetzer writes that an emphasis on "numerical growth" over "spiritual growth" has been "one of the most pervasive" criticisms of the CGM, reflecting a similar criticism as that leveled against Graham's lack of follow-up with converts. See Stetzer, "Evolution of Church Growth," 91. Stetzer qualifies this as an "alleged emphasis," although he does not directly refute it in the article.

73. Abraham begins an assessment of the theory of the CGM with a clarification that while "evangelism and church growth are not exactly identical . . . they are intimately connected." See Abraham, *Logic of Evangelism*, 71. Noll comments on fundamentalists' resistance to Graham's evangelistic strategy of cooperation with non-evangelical Christians, identifying "a clear distinction between separatistic and intentionally narrow fundamentalism and more open, intentional outgoing evangelicalism. . . . [This distinction] draws a straight line from Graham to Bill Hybels, Rick Warren, and Tim Keller." See Noll, "Where We Are," 48.

74. Later figures more widely known than McGavran include Hybels and Warren. Although their model of seeker churches is not identical with the CGM, their approach is sufficiently aligned with the CGM to be included with it for the sake of this project's thesis regarding the SFM. For varying opinions on the relationship between Hybels, Warren, and the CGM, see Watson and Scalen, "Dining with the Devil," 172–73; Stetzer, "Evolution of Church Growth," 94–96; Towns, "Rise and Decline," 168–70; For more on McGavran's relationship to and critiques of fundamentalism, see Marsden, *Reforming Fundamentalism*, 237–44.

75. Padgett states, "A careful reading of Pickett's three books published in the thirties, one of which he co-authored with McGavran and others, exhibits most of the features of the Church Growth paradigm, in embryonic form at least. It is also clear that this early missionary literature from India suffers from few of the problems . . . of the Church Growth movement as it developed under the hands of McGavran. In

McGavran states that when he first read Pickett's *Christian Mass Movements in India*, his "eyes were opened,"[76] and Pickett's emphasis on careful sociological research for the purpose of evangelism strongly influenced McGavran and the future CGM.[77] However, a stark dissimilarity between the two is evident regarding the relative urgency of evangelism (equivalent to McGavran's "discipling") and sanctification (which McGavran describes as "perfecting"). McGavran states, "Antigrowth concepts arise from confusing perfecting with discipling. . . . A perfecting which . . . decreases concern to win kindred to eternal life betrays the Gospel."[78] This compartmentalization of ecclesial mission not only deemphasizes sanctification, service, and social action to the point where justification of their neglect can seem to appear reasonable, but it further ingrains concepts of evangelism and conversion that are disjoined from obedience, transformation, and other aspects of a Christian's experience prior to death.[79] McGavran's separation of evangelism and sanctification is in contrast to their inherent unity in this perspective from Pickett:

> The mission or church that encourages a group of people to embrace Christianity accepts a definite and heavy responsibility. It is not in the position of the professional evangelist in Western countries who conducts a "revival" or "mission" and at its conclusion departs, feeling that his work is done. . . . Not many have taken the attitude of an independent "Pentecostal" missionary who said his responsibility was to get people converted and baptized with the Holy Ghost and that he could then leave them without concern and give his time to others. But many have failed to comprehend that the amount and quality of care given to a group of converts after their baptism is a major element in determining not only what they are to become, but

---

particular, Pickett did not divide social justice from evangelism, and training in obedience (sanctification) from conversion (justification)." See Padgett, "Church Growth Movement," 140.

76. McGavran, "My Pilgrimage in Mission," 55.

77. Padgett, "Church Growth Movement," 144–45.

78. McGavran, *Understanding Church Growth*, 146–47; See also Padgett, "Church Growth Movement," 144–46.

79. Willard later came to call this kind of separation "the great omissions from the Great Commission." See Willard, "Discipleship," 25 (later republished as an appendix in Willard, *Spirit of the Disciplines*, 258–65) and the comment on it in chapter 2 of this project. Advocacy of evangelism that remains united with sanctification is a theme of SFM literature. As examples, see, Smith's concept of "transforming conversion" particularly in *Transforming Conversion*, 1–19; also, Willard's concept of "discipleship evangelism" in *Divine Conspiracy*, 304–5.

whether others are to be won to Christ by the demonstration of his power in them or are to be kept away from Christ by their failure.[80]

The SFM has consistently emphasized understandings of salvation and mission more reflective of Pickett's approach than those in the statement above by McGavran, but McGavran's ideas were pervasively influential on the CGM. The SFM's attempt to address the sanctification gap in the dominant expressions of evangelicalism of its time (Graham's neo-evangelicalism and McGavran's CGM) by the recovery of previous dynamics from pietistic evangelicalism is thoroughly reflected in this passage from Willard, which clearly resonates with Pickett's sentiment:

> A fundamental mistake of the conservative side of the American church today . . . is that it takes as its *basic* goal to get as many people as possible ready to die and go to heaven. . . . Now the project thus understood and practiced is self-defeating. It implodes upon itself *because* it creates groups of people who may be ready to die, but clearly are not ready to live . . . . As a result they actually fall short of getting as many people as possible ready to die, because the lives of the "converted" testify against the reality of "the life that is life indeed" (*ontos zoas*, 1 Timothy 6:19). The way to get as many people into heaven as you can is to get heaven into as many people as you can—that is, to follow the path of genuine spiritual transformation or full-throttle discipleship to Jesus Christ. When we are counting up results we also need to keep in mind the multitudes of people (surrounded by churches) who will *not* be in heaven because they have never, to their knowledge, seen the reality of Christ in a living human being. Charles Finney used to say that the Christian minister is frequently in the position of a lawyer who states to the court the case he intends to prove . . . and then calls his witnesses . . . who contradict in their testimony (their life) every point he said he would prove.[81]

With the SFM thus generally situated relative to the contested tradition of American evangelicalism, the remainder of this chapter examines the SFM's emergence more particularly and Mulholland's place within it.

---

80. Pickett, *Christian Mass Movements*, 246. See also Padgett, "Church Growth Movement," 146.

81. Willard, *Renovation of the Heart*, 238–39.

THE EMERGENCE OF THE SFM AND MULHOLLAND'S PLACE WITHIN IT

The beginning of the SFM is evidenced in the 1970s and 1980s, as reflected in examination of usage of the term "spiritual formation" in publishing (see figure 1). Prior to the 1970s, the term "spiritual formation" was almost exclusively used by Roman Catholics, generally in reference to one aspect of preparation of candidates for the priesthood.[82] The term began to be adopted by some Protestants through the 1970s, began to appear more frequently in publishing through the 1980s (with a shift in primary focus from only clergy to clergy and laity), and its usage escalated rapidly through the 1990s and into the twenty-first century. For example, in the thirty-eight years from the first mention of the term "spiritual formation" in the title of an academic journal article in 1943[83] through 1980, the term was used in the titles of ten journal articles. During the following equivalent period (1981–2018), 446 such articles utilized the term in their titles.[84] Similarly, through the fifty-nine years following a 1927 review of *Ecclesiastical Training: Being a Short Treatise on the Spiritual Formation of Aspirants to the Priesthood*,[85] there was not any other review published in an academic journal of a book with the term "spiritual formation" in the title. In contrast, during the subsequent thirty-three years (1986–2018), the pace jumped from one title reviewed per six decades—one per 720 months—to an average of more than one title reviewed per three months. Again, a similar trend can be observed with book titles. From 1926–1979, one book was published about every three years with the term in the title, with only eleven such books from 1926–1969 and nine in the 1970s. Since 1980, there have been an average of almost eight such books per year.[86]

---

82. Exceptions can be found to both of these generalizations, although the infrequency of the exceptions establishes the generalizations. For an example of the infrequent Roman Catholic usage beyond training for priesthood, see Gallagher, *Catholic Action*. For examples of Protestant usage prior to the 1970s, see Patterson, *Heartening Word*, 38; Taylor, *Remnant in Relation*, 388. The pre-1970s usages by Protestants, however, are very few and do not appear to have meaning consistent either with the Roman Catholic usage nor with one another.

83. "From Other Lands," 456–57.

84. The numbers of journal articles and book reviews in this paragraph are based on the respective searches of the Atla Religion Database with AtlaSerials PLUS completed on October 18, 2022.

85. Janssen, "Review," 250–51.

86. These numbers are based on English print books with "spiritual formation" in

36 SHAPING THE JOURNEY

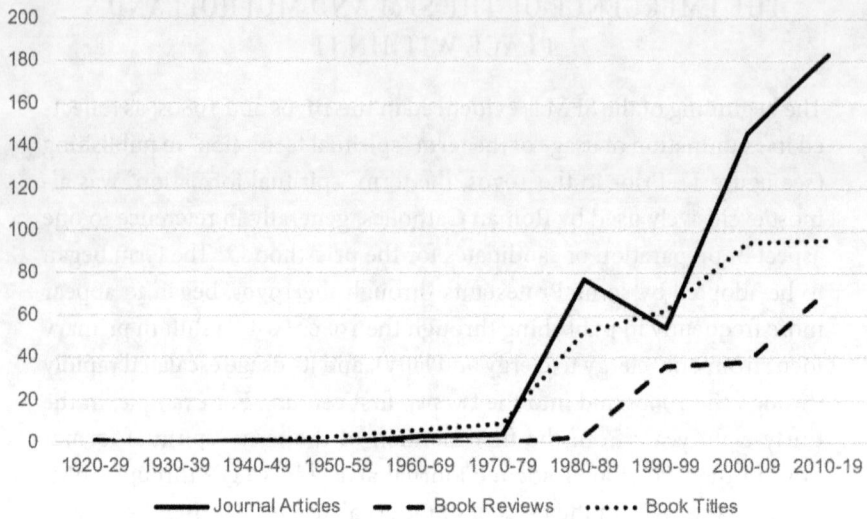

Figure 1: Books, Journal Articles, and Book Reviews with "Spiritual Formation" in the Title by Decade

To understand the drastic increase in usage of the term, three related immediate antecedents to the SFM need to be explored: Vatican II, the Ecumenical Institute of Spirituality (EIOS), and the Institute of Formative Spirituality (IFS). First, Vatican II (1962–1965) placed major emphasis on the spiritual formation of candidates for the priesthood, resulting in the Council's "Decree on Priestly Formation (*Optatam Totius*)." The impact of the decree and its usage of the term is reflected in a later reference by Pope John Paul II:

> The essential content of spiritual formation specifically leading toward the priesthood is well expressed in the Council's Decree (*Optatam Totius*): "Spiritual formation . . . should be conducted in such a way that the students may learn to live in intimate and unceasing union with God the Father through his Son Jesus Christ, in the Holy Spirit."[87]

Along with Vatican II's emphasis on spiritual formation in the training of clergy, another emphasis of the Council that served as a critical

---

the title in all works listed in WorldCat, http://www.worldcat.org, as of October 18, 2022.

87. John Paul II, *Shepherds*, 124. Ellipsis in original, with the referenced passage of *Optatam Totius* found in a slightly different translation in Abbott, *Documents of Vatican II*, 444–45.

forerunner to the SFM was its ecumenical emphasis, which resulted in the "Decree on Ecumenism" (*Unitatis Redintegratio*) and begins with the following words: "Promoting the restoration of unity among all Christians is one of the principal concerns of the Second Sacred Ecumenical Synod of the Vatican."[88] Gregory Baum reflects on the impact of the Council's decree:

> The reaction of Catholics and Protestants to the Decree on Ecumenism was enthusiastic. The new openness transformed the culture of North America. Protestant prejudice against Catholics widely spread on this continent was replaced by the spirit of mutual respect and cooperation. The tensions in families over mixed marriages and the barriers preventing spontaneous Catholic-Protestant friendships disappeared rapidly. Theological education changed: Catholics and Protestants read one another's books. Catholic bishops held meetings with representatives of the other Churches to find ways of cooperating and making joint statements on issues of peace and justice.[89]

Vatican II propelled existing ecumenical efforts in momentous ways. Two examples of relationships formed between Protestants and Roman Catholics that would become influential on the SFM center on friendships Merton began developing in 1960 with faculty at two neighboring Protestant seminaries in Kentucky: Howard F. Shipps and E. Glenn Hinson. Shipps was a professor of church history at ATS in Wilmore, Kentucky, and met Merton on a visit to the Abbey of our Lady of Gethsemani in Trappist, Kentucky (Gethsemani), for a retreat. Merton commented on the visit in his journal:

> In the afternoon, went with the three men from Asbury—Dr. Stanger, Dr. Shipps, and Fr. Hallman, up to the woods behind the lake and we talked theology. . . . It was a good animated discussion in which no one tried to dictate anything to anyone and I had the feeling that the talk was not a matter of words or formulas but of really seeking truth. . . . I am convinced of the great value of such encounters and that all that is needed is for *me* to do less talking. For all those who have come so far I feel a very deep respect and affection and I believe it is mutual. I value their friendship and this is not just a conventional phase: it is important for the wholeness of my own life—it enables me to

---

88. Abbott, *Documents of Vatican II*, 341.
89. Baum, "Ecumenism at Vatican II," 28.

be friends with a hidden part of myself, which I can only find if I give my friendship to *them*. Everywhere, all Christians should be making this same discovery.⁹⁰

Stanger was soon to become ATS's president, and Shipps continued to develop a friendship with Merton. This resulted in Merton's visit to ATS's campus on January 10, 1962,⁹¹ and a memorial service for Merton led by Shipps in ATS's chapel in January 1969.⁹² Thus, by the time Mulholland joined ATS's faculty in 1979 and Maxie Dunnam became president in 1994, interest in Merton among some of the seminary's evangelical Wesleyan scholars was already long-established.

Hinson also met Merton in 1960 when he began taking students from his church history courses at The Southern Baptist Theological Seminary in Louisville, Kentucky to visit Gethsemani.⁹³ Merton visited Hinson on Southern's campus during an errand to Louisville soon afterward, and a friendship developed through correspondence and Hinson's repeated visits with students. In 1973, Hinson published the first academic article by a Protestant with the term "spiritual formation" in the title,⁹⁴ and he elsewhere credits his adoption of the term to his friendship with Merton: "My gradual recovery of the language of 'spiritual formation' owes a lot to my friendship with Thomas Merton.... I kept taking students to Gethsemani every semester until Tom's death in 1968.... He invited me to klatches he held in his hermitage.... He sent me books and mimeographed materials. With all of that I could not help picking up a new language."⁹⁵

---

90. Merton, *Turning Toward the World*, 16–17. The identity of "Fr. Hallman" is uncertain. There were three Hallmans on the faculty of ATS in 1960 (Nyle DuFresne Hallman, Roy Hallman, and Willard Roy Hallman). It is unclear which of these three may have gone with Stanger and Shipps that day, and for a member of ATS's faculty, it is much more likely that the title was incorrectly written as "Fr." rather than "Dr." Dates relating to faculty and administration positions at ATS are found in Kinghorn, *Story of Asbury*, 465–72.

91. See Merton, *Turning Toward the World*, 194. Stanger was executive vice president of ATS at the time, and was president from May 1962 until 1982. He is credited with the "establishment of a formal Spiritual Formation program" at the seminary and was president during the hirings of Reginald Johnson, Steve Harper, and Mulholland. See Kinghorn, *Story of Asbury*, 277.

92. For an audio recording of the memorial service, see Shipps, "Service in Memory."

93. Hinson, *Miracle of Grace*, 124–25.

94. Hinson, "Spiritual Formation," 73–85.

95. Hinson, email message to the author, November 8, 2019. Although the specific term does not appear frequently in Merton's writings, one instance does reveal Merton

The second antecedent movement critical to the emergence of the SFM was much smaller than Vatican II in number of participants but directly related to Vatican II through Douglas V. Steere. Steere participated in Vatican II as an observer-delegate from the Society of Friends, and during a break from the Council sessions in 1963, he and Godfrey Diekmann discussed the idea that would become the EIOS.[96] Hinson comments, "From its first meeting [in 1965][97] at St. John's Abbey in Collegeville, Minnesota, the institute has brought together a roughly equal number of Roman Catholic and Protestant scholars to talk about the horizons of spirituality as it impinges on all aspects of life."[98] About eighteen to twenty-five participants gathered annually for the EIOS from 1965–2007.[99] These participants eventually included Hinson, Dunnam, and Tilden Edwards.

At the time he began participating in the EIOS, Dunnam was world editor and publisher at the Upper Room in Nashville. Johnny Sears writes that the impression that the EIOS left on Dunnam after his early participation was significant enough for him to return to the Upper Room and describe it to his colleague Danny E. Morris: "They didn't talk about evangelism, church growth, missions, or even 'coming to Christ.' They talked about spiritual formation: ways and means by which persons not only grow, but mature in Christ."[100]

By 1978, Morris had assembled an ecumenical group (which included Steere, Dunnam, Edwards, Foster, and others) to help him develop what eventually became the URA.[101] Morris's efforts came to fruition when the URA held its first session in May 1983, in which Mulholland taught a course on The Place of Scripture in Spiritual Formation.[102] The

---

as an exception to the generalization that Roman Catholic usage applied to the training of clergy rather than a dynamic in the lives of everyone. Merton wrote in 1955, "One of the first duties of society to the men who compose it is to enable them to receive the spiritual formation they need in order to live by the light of a prudent and mature conscience." See Merton, *No Man*, 46.

96. Hinson, *Love at the Heart*, 182–91.

97. Hinson, *Love at the Heart*, 189.

98. Hinson, *Spirituality in Ecumenical Perspective*, xiii.

99. Sears, "Contemplation," 72.

100. Morris's description is cited in Sears, "Contemplation," 73, but originates from an unpublished paper, given by Morris to Sears, titled "I Remember When We Were Introduced to the Concept of Spiritual Formation."

101. Sears, "Contemplation," 75.

102. Sears, "Contemplation," 75–76. Records from the URA list an abbreviated

Academy's launch was soon after Dunnam published *Alive in Christ: The Dynamic Process of Spiritual Formation*, the first book by a Protestant to have spiritual formation in its title and apply the concept to all people rather than in the characteristically Roman Catholic sense relating to the preparation of clergy.[103] By that time, Tilden Edwards had founded the Shalem Institute for Spiritual Formation,[104] and Foster later founded Renovaré in 1988.[105] The SFM's origins can be traced primarily to this set of relationships and the efforts that sprang from it.

However, a remaining significant antecedent to the SFM is the IFS, founded by Adrian van Kaam at Duquesne University in 1963.[106] Described as "the father of formation science,"[107] van Kaam worked to develop a scholarly understanding of how all people undergo spiritual formation in the course of life (consistent with the general usage of the term in the SFM), as opposed to spiritual formation only being a seminary emphasis in preparation for ministry. The IFS offered a PhD in formative spirituality and published academic journals from 1980–1994 under the titles *Studies in Formative Spirituality* (1980–1993) and *Journal of Spiritual Formation* (1994). Although van Kaam uses "formative spirituality" more often than "spiritual formation," his usages of the terms are similar.[108] In addition to providing a scholarly foundation for the concepts of spiritual formation, a significant contribution of the IFS to the SFM is the teaching and writing of van Kaam's mentee, Susan Muto. Muto taught alongside van Kaam in the IFS and its successor organization, the Epiphany Association, published extensively, and taught courses

---

version of the title as Place of Scripture. Over time, the title of the course in the URA's curriculum changed to Attentiveness to the Word: Spiritual Formation and Scripture.

103. Dunnam, *Alive in Christ*. An earlier example of a book by a Protestant with the term in the title but with application limited to the training of clergy is Hoyer, *Toward a Program*.

104. Tilden Edwards founded Shalem in 1978, according to Benefiel, *Soul at Work*, 312. Of the SFM contributions listed in this chapter, that of Edwards and Shalem are the least characterized as evangelical.

105. Reside, "Renovaré," 88–91.

106. Van Kaam, *Life Journey*, 225. The original name was the Institute of Man, and was renamed as the Institute of Formative Spirituality in 1979.

107. Zirlott, "Van Kaam."

108. For direct connection of van Kaam's work to the term "spiritual formation," see Beasley-Topliffe, "Formation, Spiritual"; Beasley-Topliffe, *Surrendering to God*, 125–34; Wilhoit, "Only God's Love, 168–81.

on spiritual formation in multiple seminaries, including as a colleague of Mulholland at ATS.[109]

In light of these considerations, it becomes possible to construe a location of the SFM within the following parameters:

First was an ecumenical *pre-SFM relational phase* in the 1960s, including Merton's developing friendships with Shipps and Hinson (and, through them, contact with faculty and students at ATS and The Southern Baptist Theological Seminary), Steere's participation in Vatican II, the resulting EIOS, and the founding of the IFS.[110] Then, a *transitional phase* in the 1970s as Protestants began to adopt the terminology of spiritual formation while still essentially applying it to preparation for a ministerial role (as reflected in Hinson's 1973 "The Spiritual Formation of the Minister as a Person"). Finally, an *organizational phase* in the 1980s, including the launch of new initiatives (including the URA in 1983 and Renovaré in 1988), transitions within existing organizations (particularly Protestant seminaries that began to offer designated courses in spiritual formation—including ATS's 1984 renaming of its Department of Prayer and Spiritual Life to Department of Spiritual Formation[111]), and the beginning of extensive publishing of books and journal articles on spiritual formation. As reflected in figure 1 above, this organizational phase has continued well into the twenty-first century.

Mulholland's contribution to the SFM is foundational in light of his role as an author and teacher in organizations affiliated with the SFM early in this organizational phase: as faculty at ATS from 1979–2009, as faculty at least eighteen times with the URA from its initial session in 1983 until the thirty-fourth two-year academy in 2013,[112] and as an author whose

---

109. See Kloepfer, "Muto."

110. This phase is indicative of how, although the SFM is a movement among Protestants, it could not have happened without relationships and influences from Roman Catholicism.

111. This transition was led by Steve Harper, who was a professor of spiritual formation and Wesley studies at the time. Howard notes, "In 1964, Asbury Seminary received a grant to found the first Department of Spiritual Formation," and then adds in a footnote, "It was originally named the Department of Prayer and Spiritual Life, but director Steven Harper renamed it in 1984 in light of what he saw developing in the study and practice of spirituality." See Howard, *Guide*, 7. Harper confirms, "It's true that we changed the name in 1984, but the term 'spiritual formation' was already being used, thanks to folks like Richard Foster, Susan Muto, and others. The name change was to more clearly connect what we were doing to the larger spiritual formation emphasis taking place at the time." Harper, email message to the author, November 11, 2019.

112. This number is according to URA records provided to the author by Johnny

books and journal articles have become frequently referenced in the field. His writings of particular significance for the early SFM are *Shaped by the Word* (which came from his lectures at the opening session of the URA, was first published in 1985, and was the first book by a Protestant with spiritual formation in the title to receive a review in an academic journal[113]) and *Invitation to a Journey*. Mulholland's contribution is critical within the SFM both because of his relatively early involvement in the organizational phase of the movement and, significantly, because among the names of the early SFM contributors listed in this chapter, Mulholland is the only one whose area of scholarship was biblical studies.[114] This is particularly critical since debates about views of inerrancy were at a peak around the same time in evangelicalism,[115] and Mulholland's contribution as a New Testament scholar allowed the SFM to be a legitimate option for the biblicism of non-fundamentalist evangelicals in the 1980s and afterward.

CONCLUSION

The SFM arose from within the contested tradition of evangelicalism as an expression of inherently non-fundamentalist evangelicalism, developing from a transitional phase in the 1970s into an organizational phase in the 1980s at the same time as reassertions of fundamentalist evangelicalism through the development of the Religious Right and heightened intensification of debates about fundamentalist views of inerrancy and eschatology. The shift from pietistic evangelicalism's emphasis on sanctification to fundamentalist evangelicalism's reduction of that emphasis resulted in the often-referenced concept of the "sanctification gap," which

---

Sears and Donna Bryant of the Upper Room. Another significant SFM organization in which Mulholland taught repeatedly is the Transforming Center, although his activity there is beyond the context described in this chapter, as he did not begin teaching there until 2011.

113. Weisgram, "Review," 616; Thornton, "Review," 655–57.

114. This claim could be contested because of the influence of the works of Eugene H. Peterson on the SFM. This project maintains the claim, however, because, first, Peterson was not active in the organizations associated with the SFM during the early years of its organizational phase. Second, although Peterson engaged in scholarly work and held a position as professor of spiritual theology at Regent College, he finished doctoral coursework in Semitic languages at Johns Hopkins University but did not write a dissertation. See Peterson, *Pastor*, 15–23.

115. See Dorrien, *Remaking of Evangelical Theology*, 138–46.

contributors to the SFM have sought to fill by rediscovery of sources in the Christian tradition within and beyond evangelicalism. Mulholland's early contribution to the SFM through his publishing and teaching at ATS and the URA was particularly critical for the development of the movement because of his training as a New Testament scholar, which was unique among early SFM contributors.

CHAPTER 2

Wesleyan Pietistic Evangelicalism's Contribution to the Spiritual Formation Movement

SEVEN YEARS AFTER LOVELACE published the forerunner to the literature of the SFM in his 1973 "The Sanctification Gap," Willard identified a parallel void as the "great omissions" in an article that would become one of the SFM's foundational writings:[1]

> Obedience and training in obedience form no intelligible doctrinal or practical unity with the salvation presented in recent versions of the gospel. A different model was instituted in the Great Commission Jesus left the church. . . . But in place of Christ's plan, historical drift has substituted: "Make converts (to a particular faith and practice) and baptize them into church membership." This causes two great omissions from the Great Commission to stand out. Most important, we *start* by omitting the making of disciples or enrolling people as Christ's students. . . . We also omit the step of taking our converts through the training that will bring them ever increasingly to do what Jesus directed. These two great omissions are connected. Not having made our converts disciples, it is impossible for us to teach them how to live as Christ lived and taught. That was not a part of the package, not what they were converted *to*.[2]

---

1. Willard, "Discipleship," 24–25, 27. Willard's concept later came to be referred to in the singular—"Great Omission"—and became frequently referenced in later SFM literature, including being the namesake for a collection of Willard's essays: Willard, *Great Omission*.

2. Willard, "Discipleship," 24–25. Emphasis in original.

However, neither Lovelace nor Willard was the first among evangelical scholars of the later twentieth century to utilize language of a lacuna to identify a related void in North American Protestantism. In 1967, Donald G. Bloesch began an essay titled "The Crisis of Piety" by stating, "It cannot be denied that modern Protestantism is troubled by the demise of genuine piety."[3] The article continues:

> It must be recognized that the crisis of piety is directly related to the dissipation of faith and the growing secularization of modern culture. The weakening of faith has many causes, but certainly the de-emphasis of the spiritual life in contemporary theology (both neo-orthodox and secular) is a contributing factor. Faith cannot live apart from prayer and devotion, and the church has not been able to fill this spiritual vacuum.[4]

In a section of the essay under the heading "Learning from Pietism," Bloesch argues that his fellow Protestants of the time needed to re-learn lessons taught by their pietist predecessors:

> We learn from such spiritual giants as [Philip Jakob] Spener, John Wesley, [Count Nicholas Ludwig von] Zinzendorf, and Richard Baxter that spiritual disciplines are very necessary in the life of the Christian. Such disciplines as prayer, devotional reading, and fasting are not to be regarded as means of earning our salvation, but they can be seen as means by which we continue in the salvation purchased for us by Jesus Christ.... Albert Day rightly contends that the disciplines of the interior life are the lost dimension in modern Protestantism.[5]

---

3. Bloesch, "Crisis of Piety," 3. Bloesch did not originate the phrase "crisis of piety." See Zeller, "Protestantiche Frömmigkeit," 85–116; Illg, "Johann Arndt," 309–27. Illg summarizes Zeller's view: "Winfried Zeller developed the *Frömmigkeitkrise* thesis in the 1950s, arguing that Lutheran scholastic theology one-sidedly emphasized the objective facts of salvation while neglecting the practice of piety, as it argued about true theology and engaged in various confessional conflicts" ("Johann Arndt," 322–23). However, Illg cites Axmacher, *Praxis Evangelorium*, 306–14, and Matthias, "Gab es eine Frömmigkeitkrise," 27–36 as examples among "a number of scholars who have [more recently] objected to the piety-crisis thesis, arguing persuasively that it did not exist" ("Johann Arndt," 323). The resolution of that debate does not impact Bloesch's point about twentieth-century North American Protestantism, which is the context relevant to this research. Also, Olson and Collins Winn include Bloesch as an "exemplar" of "contemporary appropriations of the Pietist impulse." See Olson and Collins Winn, *Reclaiming Pietism*, 161–66.

4. Bloesch, "Crisis of Piety," 5.

5. Bloesch, "Crisis of Piety," 8. Bloesch does not include a citation to the reference to Day, but Day's comments in *Discipline and Discovery* align with Bloesch's summary.

Since the observations of Bloesch, Lovelace, and Willard contributed to the trajectory that became the SFM, and Bloesch's point about the centrality of spiritual disciplines came to be a characteristic emphasis of the movement, understanding of the SFM is increased by attentiveness to the subject indicated by Bloesch: learning from the pietists. Therefore, the component of this project's aim that explores Wesley's influence on the SFM through Mulholland highlights the importance of understanding the nature of pietism as experienced by Wesley, Wesley's adaptation of pietism, and the eventual reflections of Wesleyan pietistic evangelicalism in the SFM.

THE NATURE OF PIETISM AS EXPERIENCED BY WESLEY

Commenting on distinctions between classical and pietistic evangelicalism as they came to be expressed in the twentieth century, Dorrien summarizes,

> [Classical] evangelicalism is grounded in and seeks to sustain the doctrinal heritage of the continental Reformationist tradition, especially the Reformed tradition.... Pietistic evangelicalism deviates substantially from the languages of absolute divine sovereignty, forensic justification, and literalistic inerrancy developed in the Reformed and Lutheran traditions, giving heightened evangelical emphasis to experiences of conversion, sanctification, spiritual regeneration, and healing. Though evangelicals from the Pietist traditions generally see themselves as belonging to the heritage of the Reformation, they also tend to follow the eighteenth-century Pietists and Puritans in viewing the "classical" tradition as experience deprived. American evangelicalism in the nineteenth century was dominated by groups in this category, especially various Baptist and independent church groups, Methodists, Wesleyan Holiness groups, Oberlin perfectionists, Campbellite restorationists, and New School Presbyterians.[6]

Day begins the book by stating, "*We, Protestants, are an undisciplined people.* Therein lies the reason for much dearth of spiritual insight and serious lack of moral power. Revolting, as we did, from the legalistic regimens of the medieval church, we have forgotten almost completely the necessity which inspired these regimens, and the faithful practices which gave Christendom some of its noblest saints." See Day, *Discipline and Discovery*, 9.

6. Dorrien, *Remaking of Evangelical Theology*, 3.

Dorrien's observation notes the prevalence of pietist influence on American evangelicalism, which chapter 1 established as the religious context from which the SFM emerged. This retrospective view from late twentieth-century evangelicalism toward its earlier traditions concurs with the background of pietism as described by Justo L. González, who identifies pietism as one of three responses (along with rationalism and spiritualism) in the seventeenth and eighteenth centuries to the dogmatism, violence, and usurpation of religion by political agendas that resulted following the cultural, political, and religious upheaval of the sixteenth-century Reformation.[7] González comments on the period,

> Dogma was often substituted for faith, and orthodoxy for love. Reformed, Lutheran, and Catholic alike developed orthodoxies to which one had to either adhere strictly or be counted out of the fold of the faithful. Not all, however, were content with such orthodoxies.... The Methodists in England, and the Pietists on the Continent organized groups of believers who, while not severing their ties with the established churches, sought to cultivate a more intense and personal faith and piety.[8]

Scholarly descriptions of the boundaries of pietism vary,[9] but Roger E. Olson and Christian T. Collins Winn identify ten "hallmarks" of pietism, which they clarify are not "unique to Pietism except in terms of the emphasis they receive among Pietists."[10] These hallmarks are as follows:

> (1) embrace and acceptance of orthodox Protestant Christian doctrine, broadly defined; (2) experiential, transformative Christianity; (3) conversion, the regeneration of the "inner person"; (4) conversional piety—a strong devotional life and a personal relationship with God through Jesus Christ crucified and risen; (5) visible Christianity—holy living and transformed character; (6) love of the Bible understood as a medium of an immediate relationship with God; (7) Christian life lived in community; (8) world transformation toward the kingdom of

---

7. González, *Reformation*, 173–75.

8. González, *Reformation*, 174–75.

9. For an overview of scholarly lists of characteristics of pietism, see Olson and Collins Winn, *Reclaiming Pietism*, 82–84; Kisker, *Foundation for Revival*, xix–xxiv; Yeide, *Studies in Classical Pietism*, 12–35. Additionally, varying but comparable lists of characteristics of pietism are offered by Arnold, "Pietism"; Chan, "Pietism"; and Hanson, "Pietism."

10. Olson and Collins Winn, *Reclaiming Pietism*, 84.

God; (9) ecumenical, irenic Christianity; and (10) the common priesthood of true believers.[11]

As Olson and Collins Winn argue, these ten hallmarks describe pietist ethos and practice reflective of the core of the pietist movement of Spener and August Hermann Francke and afterward. Further, some scholars, including Harry Yeide Jr. and Johannes Wallmann, identify a specific form of the seventh trait identified by Olson and Collins Winn ("Christian life lived in community") as the singular "external distinguishing mark of Pietism":[12] pietist identity and practice as *ecclesiola in ecclesia*[13] through various forms of groups, such as Spener's *collegia pietatis* and Francke's *collegium philobiblicum*, designed for renewal of the existing church from within, as opposed to groups that seek to be faithful by separation from existing churches. Yeide accordingly defines pietism as "an *ecclesiola* movement in which a great premium is placed on divinely initiated experiential religion as the foundation for renewal actions."[14] He identifies five characteristics as "the marks of the *ecclesiola*," emphasizing that "the decision to organize for renewal" of the church is "the center" of the movement:[15] (1) focus on the existing church as the locus of the need for renewal; (2) organization around at least one specialized function, such as Bible study, missions, or welfare service; (3) interest in modernization beyond specifically religious contexts, such as natural sciences; (4) inclusivity often beyond the church body of which the *ecclesiola* seeks to renew, both geographically—as in missionary expansion beyond a national church—and ecumenically in cooperation

---

11. Olson and Collins Winn, *Reclaiming Pietism*, 84–85. Olson and Collins Winn clarify that their list of hallmarks is descriptive of pietism's relatively consistent "center," rather than its more diverse "circumference" (*Reclaiming Pietism*, 83).

12. Wallmann counters arguments that Arndt should be seen as the father of pietism, stating, "Nowhere does Arndt press for a closer union of the pious. The concept of community (*ecclesiola in ecclesia*) essential to Pietism is foreign to Arndt. He knows nothing of the private assemblies alongside public worship that since Spener became the external distinguishing mark of Pietism" ("Johann Arndt," 35). Similarly, the primacy of *ecclesiola in ecclesia* among the marks of pietism forms Yeide's thesis in *Studies in Classical Pietism*.

13. This book follows Yeide's example in referring to the pietist pattern of *ecclesiola in ecclesia* (little church within the church) with the shortened term of *ecclesiola* or its plural, *ecclesiolae*.

14. Yeide, *Studies in Classical Pietism*, 144 (emphasis added).

15. Yeide, *Studies in Classical Pietism*, 30.

with other traditions; and (5) the sense that renewal of the church would lead to transformation of the world.[16]

While Olson and Collins Winn note that "early Methodism displayed virtually all of the common hallmarks of the Pietist ethos,"[17] and Yeide considers early Methodism a "self-evident" instance of the *ecclesiola*,[18] Yeide and many other scholars see early Methodism as a movement influenced by and with similarities to classical pietism rather than an iteration of it.[19] This distinction highlights the importance of understanding pietism as one, but not the only, essential element within Wesleyanism[20]

16. Yeide, *Studies in Classical Pietism*, 31, 141–42.

17. Olson and Collins Winn, *Reclaiming Pietism*, 129.

18. Yeide, *Studies in Classical Pietism*, xii.

19. For example, see Nagler, *Pietism and Methodism*, 160–75. He concludes, "Pietism was not only anticipatory in the content of its message, but exerted perceptible influences upon Methodism. . . . But . . . Methodism may be regarded as a distinct English movement slightly modified" (*Pietism and Methodism*, 179). See also Brown, *Understanding Pietism*, 159–60. He states, "The Great Awakening in America, like its Wesleyan English counterparts, has been identified as another wave of Pietism. Though it is more accurate to label these later movements with more precise historical designations, German Pietism and its literature were no doubt influential in the revivals" (*Understanding Pietism*, 160). In a later article, Brown elaborates and refers to pietism and the Wesleyan revival as "sisters, or . . . at least, first cousins." See Brown, "Wesleyan Revival," 8. Works that present Wesley as directly pietist, even if still beyond the "classical pietism" of Spener and Francke, include Olson and Collins Winn, *Reclaiming Pietism*, 128–29 and Kisker in *Foundation for Revival*, xix, xxvi, 162–64, 173 and "John Wesley's Puritan," 271–75. Kisker comments that Wesley's "Pietism linked him to certain Reformed Puritans, to Reformed Pietists, and to Reformed Methodists. But the conflict between the Calvinists, Methodists, and Wesley remained—a family squabble between Pietism with a moderately reformed theological grid and Pietism overlaid with a more catholic Anglican theological grid" ("John Wesley's Puritan," 280).

20. For general assessments of the pietist influence on early Methodism, see Olson and Collins Winn, *Reclaiming Pietism*, 108–31. Nagler summarizes his study on pietism and Methodism by stating, "The German movement anticipated the theological message of the English revival in many of its most important characteristics" (*Pietism and Methodism*, 176), and "the chief aims of both movements are thus seen to have been virtually identical, the greatest variations arising from the methods employed to attain the end" (*Pietism and Methodism*, 178). He concludes, "Whether Wesley would have experienced the new birth, the most significant part of his connection with Pietism, if he had not met the Moravians lies without the realm of knowable facts, but that he did experience it under their tutelage will always remain a monument to their devotion and faithfulness. They were largely instrumental in helping him break away from the legalistic type of piety, and this break was necessary to the transformation of Sacramentarian Oxford Methodism into the great evangelical revival" (*Pietism and Methodism*, 180). While this chapter focuses on Anglican and Moravian pietism as major influences on Wesley for the purpose of identifying their reflection in the SFM, this is not meant to imply that he did not also have other significant influences, which would certainly

and serves to further contextualize Wesleyan pietistic evangelicalism's eventual influence upon the SFM. A maxim quoted by Yeide from James Luther Adams regarding the study of pietism is helpful toward this end: "By their *groups* shall ye know them."²¹ Accordingly, attention to "their groups" is the main course of inquiry for this chapter, primarily regarding the pietists, Wesley's Methodists, and, consequentially, the SFM.

THE METHODIST "ORDER" AS ADAPTATION OF PIETIST *ECCLESIOLAE*

David Lowes Watson characterizes the progression that led to the Wesleyan expression of *ecclesiola in ecclesia* as developing from the "disciplined churchmanship" of Anthony Horneck's Anglican religious societies, through the "spiritual nurture" of the Moravian bands begun by Zinzendorf at Herrnhut and as continued into their intersection with Wesley by August Spangenberg and Peter Böhler, to the "Methodist order" of United Societies, class meetings, and band meetings.²² As described below, the differing Anglican and Moravian avenues of pietism both impacted Wesley and contributed to his conception of approaches to spirituality and ministry most conducive to sanctification. The Anglican pietism that was "part of John Wesley's world for as long as he could remember"²³ through the religious societies, the Moravian pietism that furnished "models for both personal spiritual renewal and corporate organizational developments"²⁴ primarily through the bands, and the

---

include Puritanism and mysticism.

21. Yeide, *Studies in Classical Pietism*, 144.

22. David Lowes Watson, *Early Methodist Class Meeting*, 67–91. This project accepts, rather than argues for, Horneck, Zinzendorf, Spangenberg, and Böhler as pietists, although scholars disagree about which names beyond Spener and Francke are genuinely pietist. Zinzendorf, Spangenberg, Böhler, and Johann Albrecht Bengel are considered as pietists in Olson and Collins Winn, *Reclaiming Pietism*. Horneck is considered less frequently in literature on pietism than the others. For example, his name is not mentioned in Olson and Collins Winn. For Horneck as pietist, see Kisker, *Foundation for Revival*, particularly his chapter 7, "Anglican Pietism," 173–204 and also Kisker, "John Wesley's Puritan," 272–73. See chapter 4 of this project for an exploration of early Methodism as an "order."

23. Watson, *Pursuing Social Holiness*, 22. See also Watson, *Early Methodist Class Meeting*, 72–73.

24. Heitzenrater, *Wesley and the People*, 84. Heitzenrater's comment is focused on the impact of Böhler on Wesley but also applies to the general Moravian influence on him.

Methodist order of societies, classes, and bands to which Wesley devoted most of his lifelong leadership can be seen as a dialectic framework with Anglican pietism as a thesis, Moravian pietism as an antithesis, and the Methodist order as the synthesis.

The Anglican Pietist Thesis: Discipline as Means to Holiness in the Religious Societies

First, the Anglican religious societies serve as a *thesis*, positing "real holiness of heart and life"[25] as the *telos* with spiritual discipline as the critical means. Wesley's experiences of the disciplined approach of Anglican pietism are traceable to Anthony Horneck and the religious societies he began in London, through Wesley's childhood at Epworth, and into his early ministry in Oxford and Georgia.

Anthony Horneck's Religious Societies: Although Anthony Horneck (1641–1697) died six years before Wesley's birth, he is the source of Wesley's earliest encounter with pietist influence through the movement he founded of religious societies, which later became a significant part of the environment in which Wesley was raised in his father's parish in Epworth. Horneck was a German immigrant to England who became an Anglican priest in 1664. Following a near-deadly illness in 1671, and in the context of spiritual crisis in the nation and Church of England, Horneck began gathering young men who heard him preach into societies for the cultivation of their piety.[26] He then drafted rules to guide such groups, which became the foundation for the movement of Anglican religious societies.[27]

---

25. Woodward, *Account of the Rise*, 108.

26. Kisker, *Foundation for Revival*, 67–68.

27. There are two extant versions of Horneck's rules for the societies: Kidder, *Life of the Reverend*, 13–16; Woodward, *Account of the Rise*, 108–14. Both are included as appendices in Kisker, *Foundation for Revival*, 108–12. Both lists claim Horneck as their source. Kisker comments, "Both Kidder and Woodward published their works in 1698, so it is not possible to identify which of the cited lists of rules is older. . . . It is quite possible that early on there were variations among different societies, even those overseen directly by Horneck. . . . Thus, both sets of rules, at least in part, may go back to Horneck himself. The tenor of both sets is, in any case, very similar" (*Foundation for Revival*, 70). Although the difference in terminology does not appear to be significant, it is noticeable that Horneck's lists are sometimes referred to in Kidder and Woodward as "rules," and other times as "orders." For consistency with Wesley's "General Rules," the SFM's emphasis on "rule of life," and similarities discussed in a later chapter between Benedictine and Methodist traditions as religious orders, this project refers to

Horneck fashioned the societies as *ecclesiolae* from their beginning by requiring that membership be limited to confirmed Anglican men at least sixteen years of age, that each society choose a member of the Anglican clergy to direct them, only prayers from the *Book of Common Prayer* be used, and the members of the society receive holy communion (implicitly, by participation in Anglican liturgy) at least once per month.[28] The stated purpose of the societies was that the men could "encourage each other in practical holiness, by discoursing on such subjects as tend thereunto; observing Holy Scriptures as their rule, and praying to God for his grace and blessing."[29] The number of participants in societies varied, ranging from very few to sometimes having more than thirty members.[30] This is reflective of the conversational nature of the group meetings as prescribed in Horneck's rules, in which the members discussed Scripture and other religious writings, sang psalms, prayed together, and sought to promote holiness among one another while intentionally avoiding discussion of potentially divisive theological or political issues.[31] In addition to these prescriptions for membership and the content of weekly society meetings, Horneck's rules stipulated guidelines for moral social conduct and individual practice of spiritual disciplines, including prayer

---

such lists as "rules." Although space is not devoted in this project to an exploration of Spener's *collegia pietatis*, Kevin M. Watson makes an important point about the continuities and discontinuities from them to Horneck's societies: "Both were voluntary associations that demanded loyalty to the established church from their membership. . . . Both . . . were primarily focused on mutually supporting one another's efforts to grow in piety. However . . . the Religious Societies were more intentionally guided by rules that emphasized a disciplined practice of the means of grace as the key to the 'holy and serious Life' the members committed to strive after. . . . The *collegia pietatis* were more focused on 'fraternal admonition and chastisement' as the most helpful path to the direct experience of the grace of God." See Watson, *Pursuing Social Holiness*, 22.

28. See Kidder, *Life of the Reverend*, 13–15, rules two, three, six, seven, nine, and fifteen; Woodward, *Account of the Rise*, 108–111, rules two, eight, and ten. Kidder's list has stronger emphasis on the necessity of being led by clergy. See also Kisker, *Foundation for Revival*, 70–71.

29. Woodward, *Account of the Rise*, 109, rule three.

30. It is not evident whether Horneck limited the number of members in a society. However, Woodward writes that societies had been formed in various parts of England "and even as far as Dublin in the Kingdom of Ireland, where from three or four persons, with which they began, they are now increased to nine or ten societies, containing about three hundred persons" (*Account of the Rise*, 55).

31. Kidder, *Life of the Reverend*, 14, rules four and five; Woodward, *Account of the Rise*, 109, rule four. See also Kisker, *Foundation for Revival*, 71–72.

seven times per day "if possible," reading and reflection on Scripture, self-examination in the evening, and fasting at least once per month.[32]

Religious Societies at Epworth: The model of Horneck's religious societies continued to spread after his death, due in part to the Society for Promoting Christian Knowledge (SPCK). Part of the aim of the SPCK was to continue the spread of the religious societies, including by distribution of Josiah Woodward's account of their history.[33] As rector of the Anglican parish in Epworth, Samuel Wesley became familiar with Woodward's writing on the religious societies and desired to begin one in Epworth that closely emulated Horneck's model. In 1702, about fifteen months before John Wesley's birth, his father formed a society among some of the men of his parish that he designed to be "the same in substance with [Horneck's] in London, only differing as our circumstances did."[34]

There are clear continuities between Horneck's rules and those established for the Epworth society, as in Samuel Wesley's first rule, which reads as if it could have been a description of Horneck's societies: "Every week at set hours, when 2, 3, or more do meet together for this intent, first, to pray to God; secondly to read the Holy Scriptures, and discourse upon religious matters for their mutual edification; and thirdly, to deliberate about the edification of our neighbor, and the promoting it."[35] Modifications of Horneck's rules included that the Epworth society was limited to twelve members with a new society to begin if membership approached that number, women were expressly forbidden from membership rather than only assuming male-only membership as in Horneck's rules, and prescriptions for moral conduct and spiritual discipline were

---

32. Examples of rules of moral conduct included "transact all things peaceably and gently," "be just in all their dealings," "consider the dangerous snares of gaming . . . shunning all unnecessary resort to such houses and taverns, and wholly avoiding lewd playhouses." See Kidder, *Life of the Reverend*, 15–16, rule eighteen, and Woodward, *Account of the Rise*, 111–13, rules nine and ten.

33. Woodward's *Account of the Rise* was first published in 1698, one year after Horneck's death. Kisker comments that the SPCK "functioned as a kind of clearinghouse and parent organization for the various local Religious Societies" (*Foundation for Revival*, 148–49).

34. Wesley, "Account of the Religious," 90. The document is also included as an appendix in Kisker, *Foundation for Revival*, 215–20. Samuel spent time in debtor's prison in 1705, and David Lowes Watson notes that it is unclear whether the Epworth societies survived until his return (*Early Methodist Class Meeting*, 72).

35. Wesley, "Account of the Religious," 91, rule one.

presupposed in the lifestyles of Epworth society members rather than expressly stipulated.[36]

During John Wesley's childhood, in the winter of 1711–1712, Susanna Wesley "formed a quasi-religious society"[37] in the Wesley family's home at the rectory at Epworth while her husband, Samuel, was in London for the Church of England's governing convocation.[38] Susanna described the gatherings as "purely accidental,"[39] due to a combination of factors relating to Samuel's absence. First, Susanna began leading John and the other children in family devotions on Sunday evenings, and then neighbors began participating while attendance in Sunday morning services under Samuel's substitute (a "Rev. Inman") was declining. Charles Wallace Jr. comments, "Such a practice, which involved reading prayers and a sermon and discussing devotional topics, would not have been exceptional had it remained within the family. However, word got out, and neighbors began attending in considerable numbers."[40] This is evident in Susanna's comment in a letter to Samuel dated February 1712: "We used to not have above twenty or twenty-five at evening service, whereas now we have between two and three hundred, which is many more than ever came before to hear Inman in the morning."[41]

While there were some fundamental differences between the preceding societies and these large groups gathered in the Epworth rectory, such as the absence of written rules, membership, or the lack of limitations on participants (particularly notable through Susanna's leadership as a woman), there were also similarities. For example, the meetings supplemented rather than competed with the parish worship schedule, and the content of the gatherings resembled the aim of and utilized the same means toward edification as the previously existing tradition of religious societies. In her defense of the meetings to her husband, Mrs. Wesley's description aligned her actions with that tradition: "We meet not on any worldly design. We banish all temporal concerns from our society; none is suffered to mingle any discourse about them with our

---

36. Wesley, "Account of the Religious," 90, 92, rules four, seven, eight, and nine.
37. Kisker, *Foundation for Revival*, 155.
38. For an overview of these events, see Wesley, *Susanna Wesley*, 13–14, 78–83.
39. Wesley, *Susanna Wesley*, 80.
40. Wesley, *Susanna Wesley*, 78.
41. Wesley, *Susanna Wesley*, 82.

reading or singing; we keep close to the business of the day, and as soon as it is over, they all go home."[42]

Thus, at nine years of age, John Wesley experienced this quasi-society in his home, and while he would also eventually adapt his father's model of smaller societies into the structure of the Methodist class meetings, his United Societies would resemble those of his mother more than those of his father or Horneck.[43]

John Wesley's "Little Societies"[44] *in Oxford and Georgia:* Scott T. Kisker comments, "Perhaps the most prominent reinterpretation of the Religious Societies was the Holy Club experiment at Oxford,"[45] of which Wesley was the central leader from 1729–1735. The group "adopted the general approach of the religious societies, though they were even more disciplined in their practice of the Christian life."[46] Initially, the group was essentially "a small study group or literary society made up of persons with pietist inclinations"[47] as they gathered multiple evenings each week to discuss classical literature and the Greek New Testament. Over time, more emphasis on spiritual discipline was added, and then significant time and energy was devoted to ministry to prisoners and the poor.[48]

Along with these reflections of the tradition of the religious societies, there were also marked differences. Wesley's "little society" at Oxford

---

42. Wesley, *Susanna Wesley*, 81. David Lowes Watson comments, "Her use of the word *society* to describe these gatherings cannot have been without significance in view of her husband's previous work" (*Early Methodist Class Meeting*, 73).

43. Wallace comments, "[Susanna's] son John, future organizer of the Methodist movement, may not have sensed the controversy, but he was surely present at the Sunday evening services. His own society and class meetings, innovations that he likewise did not intend to rival the official church worship, may have had an unconscious model in his mother's earlier experiment. Summing up her life at the time of her death, he was ready to place her in the same category as her many male clerical relatives and grant her the biblical title a 'preacher of righteousness'" (Wallace's comments appear in Wesley, *Susanna Wesley*, 78–79).

44. Wesley used "little society" to refer to the groups at Oxford and Georgia multiple times. For example, see his preface to the first extract from his journal in Wesley, *Works* (Jackson), 1:4 and 1:30. This is not meant to imply that these were the only groups he referred to as "little" societies because he used the term with some frequency to refer to various groups. For example, he also used the term for the Fetter Lane Society (see entry for May 1, 1738, in Wesley, *Works* [Jackson], 1:92).

45. Kisker, *Foundation for Revival*, 156.

46. Watson, *Pursuing Social Holiness*, 16.

47. Heitzenrater, *Mirror and Memory*, 72, 85.

48. Heitzenrater notes that the group eventually expended "more energy in acts of social concern throughout the city than in acts of corporate devotion within the walls of the university." See Heitzenrater, *Mirror and Memory*, 64–65.

was drastically different from the experience of hundreds attending his mother's quasi-society at Epworth, including a reversion to exclusive male participation due to its context among the community of university students and tutors. However, although much smaller than his mother's group, Wesley's experiment at Oxford was similar to hers relative to its more permeable boundaries than the previous religious societies. Although there was an extremely high level of commitment expected of participants, there was no process for membership nor written rules.[49]

Even without a set of rules drawn specifically for the group at Oxford, Wesley and the other participants were guided in part by distribution of copies of an anonymous work that deepened Wesley's view of the potential of societies: *The Country-Parson's Advice to His Parishioners*. The majority of the book contains "general directions how to live a holy and Christian life," including guidance on prayer, meditation, spiritual reading, and "conferring with other Christians."[50] Wesley later noted that he and the small group of others at Oxford "approved and followed the advice."[51]

John S. Simon connects the influence of *The Country-Parson's Advice* on Wesley at Oxford to the central role that societies would play in Wesley's ministry in Georgia (and thereafter). He states,

> [The book] made a deep impression on his mind at Oxford.... Its well-known suggestion as to the formation of "Societies"... became one of Wesley's fixed ideas: he was not committed to the precise form they should assume, but he was convinced that, apart from the ordinary public services of the Church, it was expedient that opportunities should be provided for the more serious parishioners to assemble in private and informal meetings in which they might pray, sing, search the Scriptures, and

---

49. For a description of how spiritual disciplines were commended among the Oxford Methodists, see Heitzenrater, *Wesley and the People*, 57.

50. *Country-Parson's Advice*, 61–215. John S. Simon claims that the book "was highly prized and widely distributed by the members of the Holy Club." See Simon, *John Wesley*, 137. It is possible that Simon's claim is exaggerated, as he does not provide evidence of its wide distribution at Oxford. He seems to be making his claim, however, on the fact that Wesley gave the book primacy thirty years after reading it at Oxford and that the Oxford group tried to enact the book's advice. See Wesley, *Works* (Jackson), 13:387–88. Heitzenrater also attributes Wesley's institution of the covenant renewal service to *The Country-Parson's Advice*. See Heitzenrater, *Wesley and the People*, 185.

51. Wesley, *Works* (Jackson), 13:388.

help each other by religious conversation. He lost no time in forming such a society in Savannah.[52]

Wesley's *ecclesiola* efforts in Georgia combined elements of his previous experiences at Epworth and Oxford. Similarly to his father, Wesley utilized these societies as elective ministries within the parish where he was appointed as priest. However, more like his mother's group, he welcomed women, did not limit the number of participants, and did not have a membership process nor written rules. The high frequency of meetings and level of expectation of participants were reflective of the Oxford society.

Therefore, as Simon concludes in his study of Wesley and the religious societies, the "relationship between the 'Religious Societies' and the 'United Societies of the People called Methodists' was so close that the latter cannot be understood without an intimate knowledge of the former."[53] During this period of Wesley's life, 1725 until his 1738 return from Georgia, writers from the "holy living tradition" exerted profound influence on him and others involved in the religious societies[54] and "served to strengthen a concept of spiritual self-discipline as the means of finding God through personal holiness."[55] Underlying these organizational particulars of the religious societies are three constants: holiness as the *telos*, discipline as essential means, and *ecclesiola* groups (the societies themselves) as the context in which the first two are cultivated.

---

52. Simon, *John Wesley*, 137–38. Wesley also gave direction to an existing society at Frederica (Heitzenrater, *Wesley and the People*, 68–73). Wesley reported to the SPCK about the society at Savannah: "Some time after the Evening Service [on Sunday afternoon], as many of my parishioners as desire it meet at my house (as they do likewise on Wednesday evening) and spend about an hour in prayer, singing, reading a practical book, and mutual exhortation. A smaller number (mostly those who desire to communicate the next day) meet here on Saturday evening; and a few of these come to me on the other evenings, and pass half an hour in the same employments." See Wesley, *Bicentennial Works*, 18:176. For a similar description of the Frederica society, see Wesley *Bicentennial Works*, 18:160.

53. Simon, *John Wesley*, 5.

54. Heitzenrater, *Wesley and the People*, 39. Heitzenrater mentions Thomas á Kempis, Jeremy Taylor, Robert Nelson, and William Beveridge as authors from the holy living tradition influential upon Wesley. See also Heitzenrater, *Wesley and the People*, 48 for the influence of William Law's 1729 *A Serious Call to a Devout and Holy Life*. J. D. Walsh notes others in the religious societies influenced by Law's *Serious Call* in Walsh, "Origins," 142–43.

55. Watson, *Early Methodist Class Meeting*, 44. He is specifically referring to the effect of Wesley's reading of William Law.

The Moravian Pietist Antithesis: Mutual Relational Knowledge as Means to Genuine Faith in the Bands

Standing in contrast to the emphasis on discipline as the means to holiness in the religious societies, the Moravian bands serve as an *antithesis*, positing genuine faith as the *telos* with mutual relational knowledge as the critical means. The Moravian position as antithesis in this progression is clarified in an introduction to a twenty-first-century exploration of Christian maturity by Gordon T. Smith, who writes,

> In order for us to have a complete theology of the Christian life ... we need to find substantive answers to three questions. First, what is the *beginning* of the Christian life? What do we mean by conversion and initiation into Christian faith? What does it look and feel like to come to faith in Christ? Second, what is the character of Christian *maturity*? If conversion is a beginning, comparable to infancy, what does it look like to be mature, to grow up in one's faith? Here one would consider the goal or objective—the *telos* of the journey in Christ. And third, what is the approach and means of *formation* so that we grow up in our salvation? How does a person newborn in Christ grow and mature in Christian faith? A comprehensive theology of the Christian life—of religious experience from a biblical perspective—would address all three questions: the beginning, the end or goal, and the means by which one moves toward maturity.[56]

Regarding the first of Gordon T. Smith's questions, pertaining to conversion and the beginning of the Christian life, the Moravian understanding was revolutionary for Wesley with its emphasis on assurance of salvation by faith as a gift to be received through the immediacy of the Holy Spirit's work in a person's life.[57] The depth of the shift in Wesley's understanding is epitomized in his journal entry after encountering a storm during his return voyage from America to England following two years of close relationship with the Moravians: "*I went to America to convert the Indians; but Oh! Who shall convert me?* Who, what is he that will deliver me from this evil heart of unbelief? I have a fair summer religion. I can talk well; nay, and believe myself, while no danger is near: but let death look me in the face, and my spirit is troubled. Nor can I say, 'To die is gain!'"[58]

---

56. Smith, *Called to be Saints*, 9.

57. For an overview of Wesley's development on assurance, see Outler, *John Wesley*, 197–220.

58. Wesley, *Bicentennial Works*, 18:211 (emphasis added).

Wesley's doubt of his conversion provoked by his fear of death in the face of this Atlantic storm in January 1738 is reflective of his fear of a storm during his travel to Georgia with a group of Moravians aboard the *Simmonds* two years earlier and the self-questioning it incited.[59] He recorded his January 1736 experience of attending the Moravians' evening worship aboard the ship when the storm hit:

> In the midst of the psalm wherewith their service began the sea broke over, split the mainsail in pieces, covered the ship, and poured in between the decks, as if the great deep had already swallowed us up. A terrible screaming began among the English. The Germans calmly sung on. I asked one of them afterwards, "Was you not afraid?" He answered, "I thank God, no." I asked, "But were not your women and children afraid?" He replied mildly, "No; our women and children are not afraid to die." From them I went to their crying, trembling neighbors, and pointed out to them the difference in the hour of trial between him that feareth God and him that feareth him not. . . . This was the most glorious day which I have ever hitherto seen.[60]

In the 1736 and 1738 storms, Wesley had encountered the insufficiency of the intensely disciplined Anglican spirituality as he had practiced it until those fearful experiences, and the contrast of his own fear with the calm of the Moravians in 1736 served as an impetus for his desire for close relationship with them. The storm on board the *Simmonds* solidified Wesley's sense that the Moravians "had the faith and assurance he coveted for himself."[61] Whereas the Anglican approach could devolve into a "stern, objective, moralistic piety of High Churchmanship,"[62] David

---

59. Wesley *Bicentennial Works*, 18:141–43; Heitzenrater, *Wesley and the People*, 64–65; Hammond, "Versions of Primitive Christianity, 36–41.

60. Wesley, *Bicentennial Works*, 18:143.

61. Heitzenrater, *Wesley and the People*, 66.

62. Walsh, "Origins," 142. Walsh uses the phrase in reference to William Law's early writings, noting his *Christian Perfection* and *A Serious Call to a Devout and Holy Life* (1729). Wesley read and was influenced by both works, exemplified by his description of *A Serious Call*: "A treatise which will hardly be excelled, if it be equalled, in the English tongue, either for beauty of expression, or for justness and depth of thought." See Wesley, *Works* (Jackson), 7:297. Walsh mentions the influence of Law's early writings on the Oxford Methodists and others in Anglican religious societies, and claims, "The High Church piety which produced or attracted many devout Anglicans of the age offered to some too many anxieties and too many uncertainties and led them along a wearisome path that ended on the edge of the abyss" ("Origins," 142), which is descriptive of some aspects of Wesley's experience from 1736–1739.

Lowes Watson comments that it "did little to foster an expectancy of divine initiative toward the believer," and "it was this which Wesley found so immediately compelling about the Moravians."[63]

The Anglican "little societies" in Georgia were not the only groups with whom Wesley met during his twenty-two months in America, as his close contact with the Moravians also led to his introduction to their primary *ecclesiola* structure of bands. Although Wesley may not have directly participated in the Moravian bands prior to the May 1738 organization in London of what would become the Fetter Lane Society,[64] his close association with the Moravians from the time he began learning German on the *Simmonds*[65] would have exposed him to their *ecclesiola* practice of mutual confession in bands. The Moravians organized themselves into bands aboard the ship[66] and met consistently in bands while Wesley lived and worshiped frequently with them in Savannah.[67] Colin Podmore describes the bands:

> These distinctively Moravian fellowship groups, introduced in Herrnhut in 1727, usually consisted of between three and eight people. . . . The bands were marked by total frankness on the part both of the member describing the state of his soul and of his fellow members in their criticism of him. Thus they had something of the function of the confessional and anticipated to some degree modern "group therapy." In Spangenberg's view they promoted the private absolution advocated by the Augsburg Confession. Such intimate discipleship groups were hitherto virtually unknown in the Church of England.[68]

---

63. Watson, *Early Methodist Class Meeting*, 44.

64. There is debate over the degree to which the approach of the Fetter Lane Society was predominantly Moravian or a mix of Moravian and Anglican pietism. Colin Podmore argues for its Moravian character in Podmore, *Moravian Church in England*, 39–71, while Kevin M. Watson argues that there was also significant Anglican influence (*Pursuing Social Holiness*, 34–38).

65. Wesley states that he began learning German to be able to communicate with the Moravians. See Wesley, *Bicentennial Works*, 18:137.

66. Fries, *Moravians in Georgia*, 103. Fries cites the diary entry from October 30, 1735, of Moravian bishop David Nitschmann. See also Hammond, "Versions of Primitive Christianity," 39.

67. On Moravian bands in Savannah, see Fries, *Moravians in Georgia*, 129. On the frequency of interactions between Wesley and the Moravians in Georgia, he lived in their house for most of his first year in the colony. See Nelson, "John Wesley," 28. Hammond notes that Wesley participated in their worship "about eighty percent" of his days there ("Versions of Primitive Christianity," 41).

68. Podmore, *Moravian Church in England*, 31. Omitted from this quotation is

Even while not yet participating in a band, Wesley experienced the dynamics of characteristically forthright Moravian spiritual conversation when he sought August Spangenberg the day after his arrival in Georgia. Wesley records the consequential conversation in his journal:

> I soon found what spirit he was of; and asked his advice with regard to my own conduct. He said, "My brother, I must first ask you one or two questions. Have you the witness within yourself? Does the Spirit of God bear witness with your spirit, that you are a child of God?" I was surprised, and knew not what to answer. He observed it, and asked, "Do you know Jesus Christ?" I paused, and said, "I know he is the Saviour of the world." "True," replied he; "but do you know he has saved you?" I answered, "I hope he has died to save me." He only added, "Do you know yourself?" I said, "I do." But I fear they were vain words.[69]

The context of the conversation further reveals its significance, considering that Spangenberg's questions were not posed to a newcomer to Christianity. Rather, by this point, Wesley was in his eighth year as an ordained Anglican priest, having also been an active learner of and guide in the holy living tradition for a decade. Wesley came into the conversation with ample and sincere experience in the disciplined way of Anglican pietism, yet Spangenberg's questions and their underlying Moravian pietism represented a sufficiently antithetical approach to Wesley's background that the theme of the conversation "was to be the focus of Wesley's spiritual pilgrimage" for the following two to three years.[70]

David Lowes Watson describes the intensity of Wesley's search for genuine faith upon his 1738 return to England as a *cri de coeur*, citing Wesley's journal entry from the day of his ship's arrival on February 1.[71] Wesley writes, "It is now two years and almost four months since I left my native country in order to teach the Georgian Indians the nature of

---

Podmore's comment, "In them lay members of the community trained each other up in faith and morals." This is omitted because the source he cites with the statement describes a different character for the bands, with more emphasis on mutual relational knowledge through confession than the instructional nature implied in Podmore's statement. See Hahn and Reichel, *Zinzendorf und die Herrnhuter*, 68–70.

69. Wesley, *Bicentennial Works*, 18:145–46.

70. Watson, *Early Methodist Class Meeting*, 45. He states this initial conversation with Spangenberg launched Wesley toward his famous experience on May 24, 1738, on Aldersgate Street in London, and Outler points out that although Aldersgate is "the most familiar event in Wesley's life," it "was followed by a long series of spiritual upheavals and frustration which lasted well into the spring of 1739" (*John Wesley*, 14).

71. Watson, *Early Methodist Class Meeting*, 46.

Christianity. But what have I learned myself in the meantime? Why (what I the least of all suspected), that I who went to America to convert others, was never myself converted to God."[72] Wesley then describes how he experienced the highly disciplined approach he had shared with others over the previous years as insufficient, noting how the extent of his studies, work, sacrifice, and asceticism had only resulted in a "sort of faith" that the devils also have.[73] Wesley later came to a different view of the state of his faith, but at this point, while he had "submitted himself to the spiritual tutelage of the German Pietists,"[74] the Moravian antithesis recast Wesley's understanding of the beginning of the Christian life.

Such a drastically different view of Christian beginnings could resonate with Wesley because of initial similarities *in regard to the second of Gordon T. Smith's questions, pertaining to holiness as the* telos *of the Christian life*. In the journal entry cited above following the storm during Wesley's return to England, he describes the kind of faith he desperately desired:

> The faith I want is, "a sure trust and confidence in God, that through the merits of Christ my sins are forgiven, and I reconciled to the favour of God." I want that faith which St. Paul recommends to all the world, especially in his Epistle to the Romans; that faith which enables everyone that hath it to cry out, "I live not, but Christ liveth in me; and the life which I now live, I live by faith in the Son of God, who loved me and gave himself for me." I want that faith which none can have without knowing that he hath it (though many *imagine* they have it who have it not). For whosoever hath it is "freed from sin;" "the whole body of sin is destroyed" in him. He is freed from fear, "having peace with God through Christ, and rejoicing in hope of the glory of God." And he is freed from doubt, "having the love of God shed abroad in his heart through the Holy Ghost which is given unto him," which "Spirit itself beareth witness with his spirit, that he is a child of God."[75]

Wesley is thus simultaneously describing a deep desire for genuine faith that is central to the Moravian antithesis to his Anglican background and the "real holiness" that the religious societies of that same

---

72. Wesley, *Bicentennial Works*, 18:214–15. Wesley later added a footnote at this point in the entry in the 1774 edition that read, "I am not sure of this."

73. Wesley, *Bicentennial Works*, 18:215.

74. Heitzenrater, *Wesley and the People*, 66.

75. Wesley, *Bicentennial Works*, 18:216.

Anglican background had as their stated purpose from their beginning. The effects of Wesley's desired faith in his description include assurance of forgiveness and reconciliation to God *and* freedom from sin, fear, and doubt. This kind of faith continued to be proposed to him after his return to England through his relationship with the Moravian Peter Böhler, who convinced Wesley of his lack of "'that faith whereby alone we are saved,' with the full, Christian salvation."[76] Wesley later remarked that he came to agree with all that Böhler said about the nature of faith, including "the happiness or holiness which he described as fruits of this living faith."[77]

Wesley's journal entry from May 24, 1738, likely contains the most well-known paragraph of all of his writings, recounting "the most familiar event in Wesley's life."[78] The famous fourteenth paragraph in which Wesley describes his experience at a Moravian-influenced society on Aldersgate Street of his heart being "strangely warmed,"[79] however, is preceded by a summary of Wesley's life to that point with a focus on his experience in the previous five months, including an emphasis on Böhler's conception of faith and its effects:

> When Peter Böhler, whom God prepared for me as soon as I came to London, affirmed of true faith in Christ . . . that it had those two fruits inseparably attending to it, "dominion over sin, and constant peace from a sense of forgiveness," I was quite amazed, and looked upon it as a new gospel. If this was so, it was clear I had not faith. But I was not willing to be convinced of this. . . . Nor could I therefore allow it to be the true till I found some living witnesses of it. He replied, he could show me such at any time; if I desired it, the next day. And accordingly the next day he came again with three others, all of whom testified of their own personal experience that a true, living faith in Christ is inseparable from a sense of pardon for all past, and freedom from all present sins. They added with one mouth that this faith was the gift, the free gift of God, and that he would surely bestow it upon every soul who earnestly and perseveringly sought it. I was now thoroughly convinced. And, by the grace of God, I resolved to seek it unto the end.[80]

---

76. Wesley, *Bicentennial Works*, 18:228.
77. Wesley, *Bicentennial Works*, 18:234.
78. Outler, *John Wesley*, 14.
79. Wesley, *Bicentennial Works*, 18:249–50.
80. Wesley, *Bicentennial Works*, 18:248.

Therefore, it is evident that the potential of the combination of experiential acceptance by God and power over sin sufficiently resonated with Wesley's conception of the *telos* of Christian life to firmly set his intention in the direction commended to him by Böhler and his Moravian companions. Böhler's guidance to Wesley shared the familiar *telos* of Wesley's holy living tradition but was also distinct since it was not focused on the call toward greater discipline as Wesley had zealously encountered in sources like Jeremy Taylor and William Law. Rather, "the advice of Peter Böhler" to Wesley and his latest "little society" of Anglicans was to "meet together once a week to confess their faults to one another, and pray for one another that they may be healed."[81] In other words, Böhler advised them to meet in a "Herrnhut-style band."[82]

Podmore comments on how this moved confession from the periphery to the center of the Anglican participants' experience:

> The idea of confession was not foreign to Holy Club members, but a society based on the Moravian form of pastoral care, involving group confession, was decidedly novel. Horneck, admittedly, had provided for discourse about spiritual concerns of the members of religious societies, but only if time allowed, and only as a voluntary additional activity. Here, mutual confession, followed by prayer for forgiveness and the healing of the soul, was not just a feature of the Society, but its *raison d'être*.[83]

Thus, the type of forthright individual conversation Wesley had with Spangenberg was given group structure and became the purpose of the bands of the Fetter Lane Society, whereby they later became part of the Methodist order as "the primary venue in which early Methodists sought to grow in holiness."[84] Whereas Zinzendorf created the bands to be a setting in which participants would converse "on the whole state of their hearts, and conceal nothing from each other, but . . . wholly

---

81. Wesley includes a version of the rules for the Fetter Lane Society attributed to the advice of Böhler. See *Bicentennial Works*, 18:236–37. Wesley's version in his journal includes eleven rules, while two versions from Moravian sources identically attribute the beginning of the Fetter Lane Society to Böhler's advice and include thirty and thirty-three rules. See Trousdale, "Moravian Society," 29–35. These versions are included as appendices in Watson, *Pursuing Social Holiness*, 187–92.

82. Podmore, *Moravian Church in England*, 40.

83. Podmore, *Moravian Church in England*, 41. Heitzenrater notes that Holy Club members sometimes compared diary entries "as a means of confessing their own sins" (*Mirror and Memory*, 89).

84. Watson, *Pursuing Social Holiness*, 1.

[commit] themselves to each other's care in the Lord,"[85] Wesley likewise noted that those who received the gift of genuine faith "felt a more tender affection than before to those who were partakers of like precious faith: and hence arose such a confidence in each other, that they pour'd out their souls into each other's bosom."[86] The Moravian bands provided Wesley with a "means of closer union" in which participants would "pour out their hearts without reserve, particularly with regard to the sin which did still easily beset them, and the temptations which were most apt to prevail over them."[87]

This speaking and hearing of confessions in the bands cultivated mutual relational knowledge among the group members, making the bands a critical context for the kind of genuine faith Wesley adopted from the Moravian antithesis. However, significant divergence became apparent between Wesley's conviction that there are "degrees of faith"[88] and the Moravian insistence that, rather than growing in faith and sanctification, Christians do not grow in holiness but, "from the moment one is justified, he is entirely sanctified. Thereafter till death he is neither more holy nor less holy."[89]

Therefore, Wesley needed a dialectic synthesis between the Anglican thesis he had already experienced as inadequate and the Moravian antithesis that had revolutionized his understanding of conversion while resonating with his understanding of the *telos* of Christian life because—rather than the "sanctification gap" described in later evangelicalism—the Moravian approach represented a sanctification "collapse." Heitzenrater comments,

> The English Moravians had, in Lutheran fashion, collapsed sanctification into justification and, in Pietist fashion, extended forgiveness of sins (imputed righteousness) into freedom from sin (infused righteousness). This approach resulted in the expectation of a sinless perfection (including a full measure of the

---

85. Spangenberg, *Life of Nicholas*, 86–87.
86. Wesley, *Works* (Jackson), 8:257.
87. Wesley, *Works* (Jackson), 8:257.
88. Wesley, *Bicentennial Works*, 19:132, 153–55.
89. Zinzendorf to Wesley as recorded in Wesley, *Bicentennial Works*, 19:213. The exchange was in Latin, as Wesley also recorded it. This translation is from Outler, *John Wesley*, 370.

fruits of the Spirit) as the necessary mark or evidence of salvation (genuine conversion)."[90]

Regarding Gordon T. Smith's third question of "the means by which one moves toward maturity,"[91] this sanctification "collapse" highlighted the fundamental difference between Wesley and the Moravians, who had no need for means of maturation within a soteriology that claimed "a babe-in-Christ is as pure in heart as any father-in-Christ. There is no difference."[92] This view represented a displacement of the role of discipline in Wesley's experience of Moravian pietism fundamentally opposed to his background in Anglican pietism. The shift is illustrated in the difference between Wesley's exchanges with Spangenberg in Georgia in 1737 and London in 1739. In his journal entry for July 31, 1737, Wesley records a series of questions he posed to Spangenberg along with the responses, including Wesley's question, "Ought we so to expect the Holy Ghost to convert either our own or our neighbor's soul as to neglect any outward means?"[93] Spangenberg responded, "Many things are mentioned in Scripture as helps to an entire conversion. So reading the Scripture (2 Chr. 34:14), hearing it (Acts 16:14), fasting (Joel 2:12), self-examination (Lam. 3:40), the instructions of experienced persons (Acts 2:37), fervent prayer. None therefore ought to neglect any of these, when it is in their power to use them."[94]

However, in the Fetter Lane Society two years later, Spangenberg had come to agree with James Hutton's and Philipp Heinrich Molther's view that disciplines had no role in the conversion of a Christian. Wesley's journal entries for November 4 and 7, 1739, recount,

> Sun. 4: Our society met at seven in the morning and continued silent till eight. One[95] then spoke of looking unto Jesus and exhorted us all to lie still in his hand.
>
> In the evening I met the women of our society at Fetter Lane, where some of our brethren strongly intimated that none

---

90. Heitzenrater, *Wesley and the People*, 91. For Wesley's criticism of Luther's view of sanctification, see Wesley, *Works* (Jackson), 7:204.

91. Smith, *Called to Be Saints*, 9.

92. See Zinzendorf to Wesley (September 3, 1741) in Wesley, *Bicentennial Works*, 19:214. Translation from Outler, *John Wesley*, 371.

93. Wesley, *Bicentennial Works*, 18:531.

94. Wesley, *Bicentennial Works*, 18:531.

95. The edition of Wesley's journal edited by Nehemiah Curnock inserts a bracketed identification of this person as Spangenberg. Wesley, *Journal* 2:313.

of them had any true faith, and then asserted, in plain terms: (1) that, till they had true faith, they ought to be "still"; that is (as they explained themselves), to abstain from the means of grace, as they are called—the Lord's Supper in particular; (2) that the ordinances are not means of grace, there being no other means than Christ.

Wed. 7: Being greatly desirous to understand the ground of this matter, I had a long conference with Mr. Spangenberg. I agreed with all he said of the power of faith. I agreed that "whosoever is" by faith "born of God doth not commit sin." But I could not agree either that none has any faith so long as he is liable to any doubt or fear; or, that till we have it, we ought to abstain from the Lord's Supper or the other ordinances of God.[96]

This encounter with quietism within Moravian pietism essentially negated the place of discipline in the sanctification of Christians and eventually caused Wesley to separate from the Fetter Lane Society. Wesley describes a conversation in which Molther

expressly asserted (1) that to those who have a clean heart the ordinances are not *matter of duty*. They are not *commanded* to use them; they are *free*; they *may* use them, or they *may not*. (2) That those who have not a clean heart *ought not* to use them, particularly to communicate, because God neither *commands* nor *designs* they should (commanding them to none, designing them only for believers) and because they are not "means of grace," there being no such thing as means of grace, but Christ only.[97]

Therefore, the disciplines that Wesley understood throughout his life as "means of grace," which he describes as "outward signs, words, or actions, ordained of God, and appointed for this end, to be the ordinary channels whereby he might convey to men, preventing, justifying, or sanctifying grace,"[98] were "works, and therefore inherently antithetical to faith" in the view of the Moravians.[99] Wesley could not accept the quietist

---

96. Wesley, *Bicentennial Works*, 19:119.
97. Wesley, *Bicentennial Works*, 19:147.
98. Wesley, *Bicentennial Works*, 1:381.
99. Knight, *Presence of God*, 42. See Wesley's description of this view of the Moravians in his letter to Herrnhut on September 3, 1741, included in Wesley, *Bicentennial Works*, 19:217–18.

view that "the Christian who has faith need not use them; the person without faith must not."[100]

Because of the semblance between the Moravian conception of the *telos* of Christianity and Wesley's own, he could accept their reconstruction of his understanding of conversion and their practice of confession in bands that cultivated genuinely converting faith. He was also convinced, however, that the mutual relational knowledge from people's experience in bands needed to be complemented by ongoing commitments of "doing no harm . . . doing good, [and] . . . attending upon all the ordinances of God," which he would soon establish as the "General Rules," the foundational commitments of the Methodist order.[101]

The Wesleyan Pietist Synthesis: Discipline and Mutual Relational Knowledge as Means to Sanctification in the Methodist Order

Finally, therefore, the Methodist order of United Societies, class meetings, and band meetings serves as a *synthesis*, positing sanctification as the *telos* with the twofold means of discipline and mutual relational knowledge.[102] This can be seen in Wesley's description of the societies in one of Methodism's foundational documents: "Such a society is no other than 'a company of men having the form and seeking the power of godliness, united in order to pray together, to receive the word of exhortation, and to watch over one another in love, that they may help each other to work out their salvation.'"[103] The biblical theme of the form and power of godliness is repeatedly present in Wesley's writings,[104] reflective of what he saw as the best gifts to be gleaned from the two streams of pietism he had experienced. His history with the Moravians and the mutual relational knowledge characteristic of their bands was significant in

---

100. Knight, *Presence of God*, 41.

101. "General Rules" appears in Wesley, *Bicentennial Works*, 9:69–73.

102. Wesley had other types of groups to meet specific needs of various groups of society members, but they were modifications of these three types of groups that constituted the Methodist order. For overviews of the "select societies" and "penitent bands," see Watson, *Early Methodist Class Meeting*, 120–21; Henderson, *John Wesley's Class Meeting*, 121–26.

103. Wesley, *Bicentennial Works*, 9:2:69. Wesley's usage of "men" is outdated, as women were also part of the Methodist societies, classes, and bands.

104. The theme is taken from 2 Tim 3:1–5. For examples of the theme in Wesley, see Wesley *Bicentennial Works*, 1:285; 1:498; 9:527; 19:341. See also Chilcote, *Recapturing the Wesleys' Vision*, 55–65.

cultivating the experiential "power of godliness" that his disciplined life in the religious societies had lacked, but Wesley saw danger in dispensing with the "form" of his Anglican background, leaving the "power" without the appropriate means to keep it moving toward maturity in cooperation with God's grace.

As the form and power of godliness represent the gifts of Anglican and Moravian pietism to Wesley, the potential distortions of the two are represented in his writings by the dangers of "two mutually exclusive 'heresies'"[105] with which Wesley was accused in his own day: *formalism* and *enthusiasm*.[106] Henry H. Knight III comments,

> The formalists in the Anglican church, recognizing the need for human responsibility, stressed human "religious" activity. In the process they lost a sense of God's own initiative and activity. . . . Enthusiasts, such as the Moravians at Fetter Lane, wanted to maintain a lively sense of the activity of God, but sought to do so by encouraging human passivity. . . . Neither the Anglican formalist nor the Moravian enthusiast could provide a means to the Christian life as envisioned by Wesley, because both had minimal expectations for the Christian life. . . . Neither saw the Christian life as involving change over time within an ongoing relationship with God, or as continual growth in love.[107]

Knight also comments on this in connection with Wesley's insistence on the essential place of disciplined spiritual practice of the means of grace within mutual relational groups:

> Especially important is Wesley's critique of common understandings of immediacy and mediation. The formalists stressed mediation, and thus located grace automatically within the means of grace. But this made grace available at the expense of a relationship with the living, active, sovereign God. Ironically, this routinization of grace made God seem absent or distant, rather than present or near.
>
> By denying mediation in order to emphasize immediacy, the enthusiasts sought to experience the living God. But without the means of grace, it became difficult to distinguish the experiences of God from one's own self-generated feelings and desires.

---

105. Bundy and O'Malley, "Foreword," vii.

106. The contrasts of formalism (with its underlying perfectionism) and enthusiasm (with its underlying antinomianism), with Wesley's ability to synthesize the truth hidden in either side, is central to Knight's thesis in *Presence of God*.

107. Knight, *Presence of God*, 10, 12.

It was Wesley's insight that, to faith, God is immediately present in the means of grace. To the person of faith, prayer becomes a conversation, scripture becomes the voice of God, and the Lord's Supper a meal with the risen Christ. Such faith must be nurtured in small communities in which each person is accountable to a common discipline. With this faith, immediate and mediated presence may become a single, unified experience of God.[108]

When Wesley and "eighteen or nineteen" of his early followers separated from the Fetter Lane Society in July 1740,[109] he immediately incorporated his gleanings from Anglican and Moravian pietism into "the first Wesleyan Methodist Society"[110] at the Foundery, and the movement of United Societies began. As the Moravian-influenced group of Anglicans had previously done at Fetter Lane, the new group at the Foundery involved a "two-tiered structure"[111] of a society that included confessional bands.[112]

In the Foundery Society, as in the many Methodist societies that would follow, the society itself was the largest organizational unit—"the 'umbrella' group of the organization in that all other related groups came under its jurisdiction."[113] The Methodist societies were clearly reflective of the Anglican societies with which Wesley had been connected throughout his lifetime, and it was this type among his groups that Wesley described as being "united in order to pray together, to receive the word of exhortation, and to watch over one another in love, that they may help each other to work out their salvation."[114] Wesley's United Societies gleaned from the tradition of his father at Epworth and Horneck's original design by utilizing a written set of rules, establishing

---

108. Knight, *Presence of God*, 192.
109. Wesley, *Bicentennial Works*, 19:162.
110. Watson, *Pursuing Social Holiness*, 49.
111. Henderson, *John Wesley's Class Meeting*, 68–69.

112. The Methodist bands were always voluntary for society members. Henderson notes, "By June of 1741 the Foundery Society had grown to 900 members, the Bristol/Kingswood work was growing steadily, and new societies were being established in the Mid-lands and as far north as Newcastle-on-Tyne. The bands were not increasing in number as rapidly as the societies, and Wesley was concerned about the need for better supervision," leading to the innovation of the class meetings (*John Wesley's Class Meeting*, 79).

113. Henderson, *John Wesley's Class Meeting*, 84.
114. Wesley, *Bicentennial Works*, 9:2:69.

expectations for members regarding moral conduct and practice of spiritual disciplines (including "the public worship of God; the ministry of the Word, either read or expounded; the supper of the Lord; family and private prayer, searching the scriptures; and fasting, or abstinence").[115] In contrast to later Methodism as a denomination, the early Methodist societies intentionally aligned with the distinctive characteristic of the pietists as *ecclesiolae*. The society meetings "were carefully scheduled so as not to conflict with any of the services of the Church of England" as "a calculated symbol" of Methodism's role as a renewal movement within the Anglican church.[116] David Lowes Watson comments,

> The reality of *ecclesiolae* . . . of which his societies were a self-evident manifestation, was something [Wesley] affirmed from his earliest years. . . . He grounded his societies in the Anglican tradition, the mainstream of English Protestantism; and as long as he lived, he regarded them as valid only insofar as they were firmly part of the larger church—*ecclesiola in ecclesia*. It is precisely this presupposition of Wesley . . . which is key to an understanding of the Methodist societies and classes. He never perceived them as anything other than integral to the visible Church of England.[117]

While the structure of Wesley's societies reflected influences of his father and Horneck, the societies as large-group experiences of dozens or hundreds of participants that included women as participants and leaders from the beginning[118] suggests the lasting influence of Susanna Wesley's "quasi-society" at the Epworth rectory. Far from the nature of the small study and discussion group of the "little society" of the Holy Club at Oxford, the gatherings of the *United Societies* were characterized by "lecture, preaching, public reading, hymn singing, and 'exhorting.' . . . The physical arrangement was an audience of fifty or more people, arranged in rows, usually listening to a speaker give a prepared talk. Little

---

115. Wesley, *Bicentennial Works*, 9:6:73. It is clear that Wesley intended the expectations to be known and observed by society members. The final paragraph of the "General Rules" includes, "If there be any among us who observe them not, who habitually break any one of them, let it be made known unto them who watch over that soul, as they must give an account. We will admonish him of the error of his ways. We will bear with him for a season. But if then he repent not, he hath no more place among us. We have delivered our own souls" (Wesley, *Bicentennial Works*, 9:7:73).

116. Henderson, *John Wesley's Class Meeting*, 85.

117. Watson, *Early Methodist Class Meeting*, 6.

118. Henderson, *John Wesley's Class Meeting*, 97–98.

or no provision was made in this particular mode for personal response or feedback."[119]

Provision for personal response was not necessary in the society meetings because the mutual relationships were so central in the other Methodist groups. Wesley adopted the confessional *band meetings* in the Foundery Society from its inception, with the modifications of the Moravian model being a rejection of the Moravian practice of having "monitors"[120] and that the Methodist bands were not designed with a specific leader but were intended for mutuality in relationships among the members.[121] The forthright and searching conversation characteristic of the Moravian bands is reflected in Wesley's rules for the bands, including their stated purpose ("to obey that command of God, 'confess your faults one to another, and pray one for another that ye may be healed'") and questions:

> Some of the questions proposed to every one before he is admitted amongst us may be to this effect:
>
> 1. Have you the forgiveness of your sins?
> 2. Have you peace with God, through our Lord Jesus Christ?

---

119. Henderson, *John Wesley's Class Meeting*, 84.

120. The monitors in the Herrnhut bands were to work with the band leaders and "to tell everyone what faults are observed in him, concealing his informer." See James Hutton's letter to Wesley on November 23, 1738, in Wesley, *Bicentennial Works*, 25:586. For further commentary on Wesley's rejection of the monitors, see Watson, *Pursuing Social Holiness*, 73–74, 83–84.

121. Spangenberg comments on the original Moravian bands at Herrnhut: "The Count . . . divided all the brethren and sisters . . . into these little societies. In each of them, a brother or a sister, according to their sex, was commissioned to take particular charge of the rest" (*Life of Nicholas*, 87). Similarly, the two Moravian sources for the rules of the Fetter Lane Society each include as the fifth rule (of thirty-three) that a "person in each band be desired to interrogate the rest in order, who may be called the Leader of the Band" (Trousdale, "Moravian Society," 30, 33). However, the version of the Fetter Lane rules in Wesley's journal only has eleven rules and omits this one about a leader. Wesley's "Rules of the Band Societies" includes "to desire some person among us to speak *his* own state first, and then to ask the rest in order as many and as searching questions as may be concerning their state, sins, and temptations" (Wesley, *Bicentennial Works*, 9:77–78) but does not designate the role of a leader. Kevin M. Watson describes how, even if Wesley did not include the rule because he was not in favor of Methodist bands having leaders, he did not prohibit them, and some bands had leaders, which Wesley must have known about. He concludes, regardless of Wesley's intent, "band leaders were a common fixture of band meetings." See Watson, *Pursuing Social Holiness*, 103, 118.

3. Have you the witness of God's Spirit with your spirit that you are a child of God?
4. Is the love of God shed abroad in your heart?
5. Has no sin, inward or outward, dominion over you?
6. Do you desire to be told of your faults?
7. Do you desire to be told of all your faults, and that plain and home?
8. Do you desire that every one of us should tell you from time to time whatsoever is in his heart concerning you?
9. Consider! Do you desire we should tell you whatsoever we think, whatsoever we fear, whatsoever we hear concerning you?
10. Do you desire that in doing this we should come as close as possible, that we should cut to the quick, and search your heart to the bottom?
11. Is it your desire and design to be on this and all other occasions entirely open, so as to speak everything that is in your heart, without exception, without disguise, and without reserve?

Any of the preceding questions may be asked as often as occasion offers; the five following at every meeting:

1. What known sins have you committed since our last meeting?
2. What temptations have you met with?
3. How was you delivered?
4. What have you thought, said, or done, of which you doubt whether it be sin or not?
5. Have you nothing you desire to keep secret?[122]

Whereas participation in the intensity of the band meetings was always voluntary for society members, regular participation in *class meetings* was the "basic requirement for membership in early Methodism. In other words, at the most foundational level, a Methodist was someone who attended a weekly class meeting."[123] The class meetings were the latest of these three types of Methodist groups and were original to Methodism rather than being modifications of Anglican or Moravian pietism, yet they were the type of group in which the dynamics gleaned from each are most clearly synthesized.

---

122. See the "Rules of the Band Societies" in Wesley, *Bicentennial Works*, 9:77–78.
123. Watson, *Pursuing Social Holiness*, 3.

The content of the class meetings was simple and straightforward. Kevin M. Watson summarizes, "First, it held people accountable to keeping the General Rules. Second, the class meeting was a place where Methodists were encouraged to give weekly to the relief of the poor. Third, and most central to the time spent in the weekly meeting, it was a place where every Methodist answered the question, 'How is it with your soul?'"[124] David Lowes Watson remarks, "As Wesley introduced and developed them, the classes exercised accountability for the General Rules as well as for inward spiritual growth."[125] He continues and emphasizes,

> The class meeting [was] not only the basic unit of Methodist organizational structure, but also the most effective means of spiritual nurture for the membership as a whole. All Methodists . . . had to meet once a week as members of their class to give an account of their discipleship. . . . The "path to perfection" began and continued with an accountability for the basics of Christian discipleship—the means of grace and the works of obedience—without which no genuine progress could be made in the Christian life.[126]

Wesley could not have developed this level of accountability to the kind of disciplined life stipulated in the "General Rules" within the Fetter Lane Society with its Moravian and quietist influences. This component of the class meetings, and, therefore, of early Methodism in general, was the fruit of Wesley's background in Anglican pietism. However, to understand the class meetings as essentially about discipline and accountability is incomplete since they also incorporated a high value on mutual relational knowledge as Wesley had learned from Moravian pietism. This was true both in one-on-one relationships between class members and their class leader (reminiscent of Wesley's initial conversation with Spangenberg) and in mutual relationships among the class members. Wesley highlights the importance of the class leader's knowledge of the class members: "There could be no better way to come to a sure, thorough knowledge of each person, than to divide them into classes . . . under the inspection of those in whom I could most confide."[127] Likewise, describing the close relationships that developed among class members, Henderson comments,

---

124. Watson, *Class Meeting*, 25.
125. Watson, *Early Methodist Class Meeting*, 115.
126. Watson, *Early Methodist Class Meeting*, 122.
127. Wesley, *Bicentennial Works*, 19:258. See also Watson, *Class Leaders*, 25–28.

> The members of a class often stayed together for years, cultivating the most intimate and helpful of friendships. In this circle of companionship, it was difficult to be evasive or hypocritical. Deep levels of trust and affection were engendered: an optimum environment for the cultivation of personal character. Hearty thanksgiving and praise to God accompanied and affirmed every step of progress; loving and understanding sympathy and encouragement bolstered personal failures. These Methodists were people who believed that the real joy of human life was spiritual fellowship and moral growth.[128]

The class meetings provided Wesley with an avenue for cultivating this kind of mutual relational knowledge among members through personal sharing that was at a level appropriate to require of everyone in a society rather than the "intense confessional"[129] more appropriate for those electing to participate in a band. Knight comments, "Rather than an inward inquiry, the class member gave an account of his or her discipleship during the week in accordance with the three General Rules. . . . A person could admit being beset by sin without specifying the exact nature of that sin."[130]

Henderson aptly summarizes the nature and purpose of the Methodist *ecclesiolae*:

> The design of the Wesleyan program had the goal of holiness in constant focus: the societies proclaimed and explained the doctrine, the class meeting was designed to implement the behavioral quest for holy lifestyle, and the bands facilitated the cultivation of inner purity and the purging of attitudes. It was an interlocking system, woven around a common theme.[131]

REFLECTIONS OF WESLEYAN PIETISTIC EVANGELICALISM IN THE SFM

The focus of this chapter is not only the history of Wesleyan pietistic evangelicalism as explored above, with attention given to Wesley's adaptations of the outward "form" of Anglican pietism and the inward "power" of Moravian pietism, but also considers the contribution of this

---

128. Henderson, *John Wesley's Class Meeting*, 102.
129. Watson, *Early Methodist Class Meeting*, 98.
130. Knight, *Presence of God*, 100.
131. Henderson, *John Wesley's Class Meeting*, 115.

Wesleyan tradition to the SFM. Therefore, the following two reflections are observed.

First, the widespread employment of sanctification-oriented ecclesiola groups based on discipline and mutual relational knowledge in the SFM is the movement's primary reflection of Wesleyan pietistic evangelicalism. As explored in chapter 1, the SFM arose as an attempt to address the sanctification gap in twentieth-century evangelicalism, so it is not surprising that as the SFM entered its organizational phase, it would frequently utilize a method that was central in evangelicalism's history prior to the emergence of the sanctification gap by encouraging pietistic *ecclesiola* groups in a manner similar to the Methodist order since it had been such a widespread expression of pietistic *ecclesiolae*. Therefore, the utilization of such groups in four prevalent organizations of the SFM is explored here. Crucial to this brief exploration is that each of these organizations and their groups function as *ecclesiolae*, organizations that serve to cultivate renewal of the church from within rather than separating and forming new denominations.

Asbury Theological Seminary hired professors of spiritual formation Reginald Johnson in 1978 and Steve Harper in 1980, with Mulholland hired as professor of New Testament in 1979. Harper, Mulholland, and three others met regularly in a group for spiritual formation through their mutual relationships during a period when spiritual formation groups were already in place among students.[132] Kenneth Cain Kinghorn credits Thomas A. Carruth—who had been hired by Frank Stanger in 1964 to head the predecessor of the seminary's Department of Spiritual Formation (the Department of Prayer and Spiritual Life)[133]—with the cultivation of these groups: "He trained student spiritual directors, and, by 1980, more than fifty spiritual formation groups were meeting weekly with their directors. These sessions were similar to John Wesley's class meetings."[134]

The Upper Room Academy for Spiritual Formation began its first two-year academy (with Mulholland as part of the faculty) in 1983, is currently in the midst of its forty-second two-year academy, and has had "covenant groups" as a central component of its curriculum throughout

---

132. Mulholland dedicates *Invitation to a Journey* to this group, and Harper comments that it "put into a book form what we had been talking about." Harper, email message to the author, November 11, 2019.

133. See chapter 1 of this project.

134. Kinghorn, *Story of Asbury*, 243.

its history. The covenant groups have two "essential functions": first, "to provide a setting for sharing the personal stories of faith and life within the group"; and second, "for participants to sort out, question, wrestle with, and process the learnings and meanings of the day."[135] These mutual relational groups take place within semi-annual sessions of each academy, which is described as "an experience of disciplined Christian community emphasizing holistic spirituality—nurturing mind, body, and spirit. The program is ecumenical in nature and fosters spiritual rhythms of study and prayer, silence and liturgy, solitude and relationship, rest and exercise."[136]

Renovaré was founded in 1988 following Foster's[137] 1986 sabbatical in which he believed that "God opened up a vision of a great revival, which would draw on the several streams of Christian piety, which until now had been isolated from one another."[138] Foster discussed the vision with James Bryan Smith, a United Methodist pastor who had been experimenting with adapting the early Methodist system into a model for small groups in his congregation.[139] Renovaré began from a convergence of Foster's vision with James Bryan Smith's implementation of "the Wesleyan form of small group formation."[140] This led to the publication of *A Spiritual Formation Workbook*, which sought to help "Christians meet to learn the six traditions of the Church, to do the related disciplines, to hold each other accountable, and to encourage one another."[141] This promoted Renovaré's mission as stated in the *Workbook*: "To provide

---

135. Upper Room Academy for Spiritual Formation, "Two-Year Academy," 127. Johnny Sears, director of the URA, states that this is "the current description" of covenant groups in the URA, "but should be representative of the original vision." Sears, email message to author, September 29, 2023.

136. Upper Room Academy for Spiritual Formation, "Mission."

137. Olson and Collins Winn include Foster as one of their four contemporary "exemplars" of the "pietist impulse," noting, "Foster's Renovaré movement can be seen as a revival of Pietism for American Christians.... A major emphasis of Renovaré is small-group devotion and practice of the spiritual disciplines with the aims of encouragement and accountability," and that Renovaré "contains within it a creative re-expression of Pietism's living ethos" (*Reclaiming Pietism*, 170–71).

138. Reside, "Renovaré," 89.

139. Reside, "Renovaré," 89.

140. Reside, "Renovaré," 89–90.

141. Smith, *Spiritual Formation Workbook*, 15. *A Spiritual Formation Workbook* identifies the "six traditions of the Church" as contemplative, holiness, charismatic, social justice, evangelical, and incarnational. Further elaboration on these traditions is found in Foster, *Streams of Living Water*.

individual churches and their members with a balanced, effective small-group strategy for spiritual growth."[142] Based on the introduction to historic traditions of Christianity and spiritual disciplines in *A Spiritual Formation Workbook*, Renovaré's groups guide "members through an examen, a discussion of spiritual disciplines, and toward a commitment to practicing one or more disciplines over the next week. Members return and report about their experiences, successes, and failures. . . . Because of the scale, [these] small groups encourage intimacy, providing a greater degree of support and accountability."[143]

The Transforming Center was founded by Ruth Haley Barton in 2002, and offers "retreats, resources, and relationships . . . designed to provide [Christian leaders] with a safe place to be honest about the challenges of spiritual leadership, to experience rhythms of solitude, prayer and community, and to deepen [their] understanding of leadership that flows from [their] transforming [selves]."[144] The Transforming Center's program of quarterly retreats is called a Transforming Community, which includes "substantive teaching on spiritual formation themes and practices, guided experiences with spiritual disciplines,"[145] and group spiritual direction for participants. Barton describes the group spiritual direction experience: "people . . . assist one another in being more attentive and responsive to God's presence in all of life. They meet to reflect on their spiritual journeys . . . to notice Jesus' presence and activity in each other's lives through the real presence of the Holy Spirit, and to support one another in responding faithfully to that presence."[146]

Mulholland's writings on spiritual formation are foundational in the Transforming Community curriculum, and the Transforming Center was a primary SFM organization in which he invested his energies in the last five years of his life, teaching annually on Transforming Community retreats from 2011–2015.

---

142. Smith, *Spiritual Formation Workbook*, 11.

143. Reside, "Renovaré," 76–77. Foster notes in the foreword to Smith's *A Spiritual Formation Workbook* that they "were led to study many small-group movements, such as the Benedictines in the sixth century, the Franciscans in the thirteenth century, the Methodists in the eighteenth century, and Alcoholics Anonymous in the twentieth century. We also began developing a balanced vision of Christian faith and practice and a practical strategy for spiritual growth" (*Spiritual Formation Workbook*, 9).

144. Transforming Center, "About Us."

145. Transforming Center, "Transforming Community."

146. Barton, *Life Together in Christ*, 63–64.

Therefore, although the Transforming Center began later than the other organizations highlighted here (well after the first decade of the SFM's organizational phase), it is included because it illustrates the importance of *the second concluding observation: as Wesleyan pietistic evangelicalism needed Johann Albrecht Bengel, so the SFM needed Mulholland.*

Barton, founder of the Transforming Center, describes how Mulholland's work in spiritual formation met her need for the content to be reliably grounded in biblical theology when she read *Invitation to a Journey*, even though it differed noticeably from what she had previously experienced in evangelicalism:

> Finally, I was able to understand—from a strongly biblical and theological perspective—what had been happening to me in the context of the spiritual disciplines I was practicing outside my former box. Finally, I was able to explain to those who were afraid I was falling off the Christian path that what was happening in my life was orthodox, deeply rooted in our own Christian tradition. . . . Finally, I had the confidence to begin communicating a clear and nuanced biblical rationale for why spiritual formation is central to the message of the gospel and therefore central to the message of the church.[147]

Although the contextual dynamics differ, this exegetical grounding of an emerging tradition is reflective of Wesley's encounter with the writings of Bengel, who represents a third stream of pietism (Würtemmberg pietism) not explored above but vital for Wesley and the development of Methodism. Bengel's impact on Wesley was different from that of Horneck, Spangenberg, Zinzendorf, or Böhler because it was not through a forthright conversation, religious society, nor confessional band that Bengel influenced Wesley, but through his published biblical exegesis. Bengel, referred to as "the major theologian of Würtemmberg Pietism . . . [and] the great biblical exegete of Pietism,"[148] dedicated "his last major writing to analyzing the doctrinal deficiencies and emotional immaturity of the Zinzendorf movement"[149] in which he "spoke for many when he lamented in 1751 that the Count had never achieved sufficient maturity and integrity."[150] While Bengel's criticism of Zinzendorf could have resonated with Wesley, there is no evidence that Wesley ever read

---

147. Barton, "Foreword," 10–11.
148. Wallman, "Johann Arndt," 36.
149. Yeide, *Studies in Classical Pietism*, 85–86. The work referred to is Bengel, *Abriß*.
150. Yeide, *Studies in Classical Pietism*, 83.

it.[151] Instead, it was Bengel's exegetical scholarship that sparked Wesley's admiration and also formed the basis of a significant part of Bengel's criticism of Zinzendorf. Hermann Ehmer comments,

> In contrast to Bengel who always was concerned with the coherence of the whole Bible, the Moravians—according to Bengel's view—used the Bible as a little treasure chest from which one could draw an appropriate verse for every occasion. . . . It appeared to Bengel that the Moravians esteemed the hymns of Zinzendorf more highly than Holy Scripture.[152]

F. Ernest Stoeffler states that Bengel was "the one expositor of the Bible whose authority on biblical interpretation was well-nigh universally acknowledged by Continental Pietists,"[153] and Bengel appears to have been equally as authoritative a voice in Wesley's view. In Wesley's preface to his *Explanatory Notes Upon the New Testament*, he acknowledged Bengel's pervasive influence:

> I once designed to write down barely what occurred to my own mind, consulting none but the inspired writers. But no sooner was I acquainted with that great light of the Christian world . . . [Bengel], than I entirely changed my design, being thoroughly convinced it might be of more service to the cause of religion, were I barely to translate his *Gnomon Novi Testamenti*, than to write many volumes upon it. Many of his excellent notes I have therefore translated. Many more I have abridged, omitting that part which was purely critical, and giving the substance of the rest.[154]

---

151. Yeide, *Studies in Classical Pietism*, 165.

152. Ehmer, "Johann Albrecht Bengel," 233. Ehmer notes that Bengel also rejected the Moravian self-understanding as "the eschatological community."

153. Stoeffler, *Continental Pietism*, 199.

154. Wesley, *Explanatory Notes*, iv. See Stoeffler, *Continental Pietism*, 199–201 for further clarification of the extent of Bengel's influence on Wesley's *Explanatory Notes*. Stoeffler states, "It must be remembered that Wesley was constitutionally incapable of following anyone else's opinions fully. Hence we must not expect a slavish translation of Bengel. Furthermore, Bengel wrote consciously for scholars, Wesley for his sincere but often unlettered preachers. Again, Bengel wanted to be as explicit and as intellectually convincing as possible in his explanations. Wesley, on the other hand, meant to produce a commentary which would be as brief as possible, which could be printed cheaply and distributed widely. Finally, Bengel wanted to save the credibility of the Bible for the world of critical scholarship while Wesley was interested mainly in broadcasting its message to a needy world. Under the circumstances we find that Wesley's *Notes* display a certain amount of independence of Bengel. . . . Still, there is overwhelming evidence that Bengel's *Gnomon* was Wesley's constant companion while he wrote the bulk of his

Wesley's *Explanatory Notes Upon the New Testament* was distributed widely in multiple editions during his lifetime, influencing preachers and members of the Methodist societies, and became part of the doctrinal standards of Methodism by 1763.[155] Therefore, Bengel's biblical scholarship grounded both pietism and Methodism in credible exegesis.

Mulholland occupies a similar place of importance among the "short list of the founders" of the SFM[156] since, among the names of the early SFM contributors listed in chapter 1, he alone was a scholar in biblical studies. The exegetical foundation Mulholland provided to the movement was essential for validating the SFM as thoroughly biblical for its evangelical constituency.

CONCLUSION

The inevitably relational nature of Wesleyan spirituality as explored in this chapter is clearly evident in Mulholland's emphasis on what he terms "corporate spirituality." He writes,

> Our relationships with others are . . . the places where our growth toward wholeness in Christ happens. There is a temptation to think that our spiritual growth takes place in the privacy of our personal relationship with God and then, once it is sufficiently developed, we can export it into our relationships with others and "be Christian" with them. But holistic spirituality, the process of being conformed to the image of Christ, takes place in the midst of our relationships with others, not apart from them. We learn to be Christ's for others by seeking to be yielded and obedient to God in the midst of our relationships.[157]

As established in this chapter, this conviction within Mulholland's contribution to the SFM is the legacy of the profound influence of pietism on Wesley, beginning with the influence of Anglican pietism through its tradition of religious societies and their cultivation of discipline as a means to holiness. When Wesley encountered Moravian pietism, it caused a reconstruction of his understanding of the nature of genuine

---

Notes" (*Continental Pietism*, 199).

155. Wesley's *Explanatory Notes* became doctrinal standards for Methodism through the "Model Deed." See Heitzenrater, *Wesley and the People*, 238–39.

156. Porter, "In Memoriam," 2.

157. Mulholland, *Invitation to a Journey*, 43–44. For a fuller exploration of the same theme, see also Mulholland, *Invitation to a Journey*, 143–57.

faith and convinced him of the value of confessional bands as a context in which such faith could be cultivated in mutual relationships among participants. From the time that the first of the Methodist United Societies began at the Foundery, Wesley synthesized the influences of Anglican and Moravian pietism on his personal and ministry efforts toward sanctification into the "Methodist order" of societies, classes, and bands, which emphasized the spiritual discipline characteristic of Wesley's Anglican background and the mutual relational knowledge characteristic of his connection to the Moravians. This contribution is reflected in the SFM in two ways: (1) the widespread utilization of sanctification-oriented *ecclesiola* groups that emphasize spiritual disciplines and mutual relational knowledge; and (2) the correspondence of the role that Bengel played in pietism and Methodism with that of Mulholland in the SFM.

CHAPTER 3

Mertonian Contemplative Monasticism's Contribution to the Spiritual Formation Movement

IN BLOESCH'S 1967 IDENTIFICATION of the "crisis of Piety," he points his fellow Protestants toward their pietist forebears,[1] and he clarifies in later writings that this was a distinctly different direction than toward contemplative monasteries: "The commandment we hear in Scripture is not that the people of God withdraw from the world into a hermitage or monastery but that they permeate the world with a message of healing and redemption."[2] Bloesch's pietistic evangelicalism is fundamentally opposed to the mysticism inherent in contemplative monasticism, as he writes,

> It cannot be denied that there is a fundamental incongruity between mysticism and biblical Christianity. In stark contrast to the biblical ethos, mysticism is uncompromisingly introspective. Its focus lies on the exploration of the depths of the soul, not the preaching of Christ to the masses.... Jesus mingled with people, whereas mystics elevate solitude over fellowship. This inward proclivity comes not from the Bible but from Platonism and Neoplatonism.[3]

---

1. See Bloesch, "Crisis of Piety," and chapter 2 of this project.
2. Bloesch, *Spirituality Old and New*, 92. Tom Schwanda observes that Bloesch's views in *Spirituality Old and New* were "a significant retreat from his earlier supportive affirmation of contemplation and Christian mysticism." See Schwanda, "To Gaze," 99.
3. Bloesch, *Spirituality Old and New*, 68.

As Bloesch represents this opposition among some pietistic evangelicals, it is also evident in some of their number who are Wesleyan, and the criticism can be more directly pointed at the SFM. An example is Ben Witherington III, who writes in a book he intended as a corrective to non-Wesleyan trends in the SFM of his frustration that SFM literature had "adopted and adapted certain ascetical and medieval monastic models and forms of spiritual formation, baptized them for normal Christians, and called them good. . . . Spiritual formation and practice is not necessarily all about silence, individual quiet times, and a hermitlike withdrawal from society."[4] Witherington repeatedly cites similar sentiments of fellow Wesleyan scholar William H. Willimon, who writes,

> Nowhere is Jesus' human nearness (and, in a curious way, his divine distance) more apparent than in the portrayal of Jesus as moving from one dinner party to the next. He was no ragged renunciator of the world. He was a party person. . . . There were times when Jesus went alone into the desert to pray, but we know next to nothing about what actually transpired in that solitude. More typical is for Jesus to be constantly interacting with people—mixing it up with a crowd, meeting travelers on the road, and most typical of all, eating and drinking with gusto at parties. . . . His life implies that we are fully human, not in our solitude or loneliness but only through a web of relationships and connections with others, including God . . . . God in Jesus Christ is encountered not through solitary walks in the woods, or even by reading a book (!), but rather at a mundane dinner table.[5]

This perspective from Bloesch, Witherington, and Willimon reflects views held by many earlier evangelicals, including Wesley. In the context around Wesley's often-cited comment on the indispensability of "social holiness," he writes in criticism of "Mystic Divines":

> Supposing them to have laid the foundation right, the manner of building thereon which they advise is quite opposite to that prescribed by Christ. He commands to build up one another. They advise, "To the desert! To the desert! and God will build

---

4. Witherington, *Shared Christian Life*, x–xi. Of significance for the topic of this chapter is that Witherington relates this sentiment in connection with a story of being surprised that one of Merton's fellow monks of Gethsemani began a conversation with him, including that the monk "talked a blue streak" about Merton (*Shared Christian Life*, x–xi).

5. Willimon, *Why Jesus?*, 39–40.

you up!" Numberless are the commendations that occur in all their writings, not of retirement intermixed with conversation, but of an entire seclusion from men, (perhaps for months or years,) in order to purify the soul.... Accordingly, our blessed Lord, when his disciples were in their weakest state, sent them forth, not alone, but two by two. When they were strengthened a little, not by solitude, but by abiding with him and with one another, he commanded them to "wait," not separate, but "being assembled together," for "the promise of the father" ... "Holy solitaries" is a phrase no more consistent with the gospel than holy adulterers. The gospel of Christ knows of no religion, but social; no holiness but social holiness.[6]

Bloesch, Witherington, and Willimon advocate responding to the crisis of piety of the late twentieth and early twenty-first centuries through the pietistic approaches of Wesley and others of their predecessors. Their caricatures of the "medieval monastic models," however, dismiss the context of intentional solitude *and* community from which the large majority of the writings of the Christian mystical tradition emerge with insistence that the two are interrelated and essential. As argued in this chapter, Witherington's criticism is accurate that the SFM emphasizes solitude with considerably more frequency than other expressions of pietistic evangelicalism and that it does so by Protestant adaptations of monasticism. However, Protestants who have adapted models of monasticism have done so because of their perception of solitude's value for the Christian community, as individuals become increasingly open to the work of God's grace through time alone with God, increasing their capacity to relate to God and others in love. Bonhoeffer describes his Finkenwalde experiment of designing a "church, monastic-like [school] in which the pure doctrine, the Sermon on the Mount, and worship can be taken seriously."[7] He goes on, "Those who want community without solitude ... plunge into the void of words and feelings, and those who

---

6. Wesley, *Works* (Jackson), 14:319–21. Paragraph 4 makes it clear that Wesley is criticizing quietism, which Merton also criticized. See chapter 4 of this book for an exploration of this commonality. Based on the view of solitude expressed here, it is unsurprising that Wesley did not include solitude in his categorizations of the means of grace, although it could be seen as an appropriate fit in his list of "instituted" or "particular" means of grace, which consist of prayer, searching the Scriptures, the Lord's Supper, fasting, and Christian conference. See Knight, *Presence of God*, 3–5; Wesley, *Works* (Jackson), 8:322–23.

7. These words come from a letter Bonhoeffer sent to Erwin Sutz on September 11, 1934. See Bonhoeffer, *Testament to Freedom*, 24.

seek solitude without community perish in the bottomless pit of vanity, self-infatuation, and despair. Whoever cannot be alone should beware of community. Whoever cannot stand being in community should beware of being alone."[8]

In stark contrast to Bloesch's desire to address the crisis of piety by a rejection of mysticism, Lovelace's identification of the sanctification gap came from precisely within it. Lovelace identifies the central role that reading Merton's *Seven Storey Mountain* had in his conversion: "As I read, I sensed the reality of the presence of God.... In Merton's metaphor, it seemed as though a window in the depths of my consciousness had suddenly been opened.... I felt that I was in contact with God."[9] After describing his initial attraction to becoming a Trappist, his move into Reformed Protestantism, and his perspective on Protestantism's sanctification gap and its origins, Lovelace closed the article prescriptively, including "restudy" of "the great Catholic mystical tradition" as a necessary step for Protestants to address the gap.[10] Six years later, Lovelace reiterated Merton's influence. In his preface to a compilation of his essays on "an evangelical theology of renewal," Lovelace comments that Merton was not only the major voice in his conversion to Christianity, but that he saw his own work as parallel to Merton's because the two were striving "in the same direction."[11]

Lovelace's account of Merton's instrumental role of opening a "window" toward "contact with God" was not an isolated instance of influence. Rather, as "arguably the greatest Catholic spiritual writer of the century,"[12] Merton's impact was widespread within and beyond Catholicism, as evidenced in his role in the pre-SFM relational phase described in chapter 1.[13] Lovelace's account reflects the goal to which Merton most often pointed his readers through his voluminous writings: "Christian

---

8. Bonhoeffer, *Life Together*, 82.

9. Lovelace, "Sanctification Gap," 363. David Vincent comments on the enormous sales numbers of Merton's *Seven Storey Mountain*: "There was little in the form of Merton's memoir to suggest such success. It followed the conventional structure of a devotional biography.... What made the account distinctive was Merton's overwhelming emphasis on the spiritual value of solitude, and its accompanying discipline of silence." See Vincent, *History of Solitude*, 208–9.

10. Lovelace, "Sanctification Gap," 368.

11. Lovelace, *Dynamics of Spiritual Life*, 17.

12. Holt, *Thirsty for God*, 191.

13. See chapter 1 above.

contemplation as an experiential contact with God."[14] While contemplation as a practice and the contemplative life as a path of pursuit had been described for centuries in Christianity,[15] the meaning and application of the terms were predominantly limited to monasticism until Merton's publications introduced him beyond monastic communities as "a new phenomenon: a contemplative monk extending the invitation to contemplation to everyone."[16] As William H. Shannon summarizes, "Merton's unique contribution to American spirituality was to make contemplation an 'in' subject for all who were willing to undergo the spiritual discipline it called for."[17]

Although contemplation is such a pervasive theme in Merton's writings, the term itself is "used with a wide variety of meanings,"[18] and Merton avoids offering a concise definition.[19] In his essay "What Contemplation is Not," he writes,

> The only way to get rid of misconceptions about contemplation is to experience it.... Contemplation cannot be taught. It cannot even be clearly explained. It can only be hinted at, suggested, pointed to, symbolized. The more objectively and scientifically one tries to analyze it, the more he empties it of its real content, for this experience is beyond the reach of verbalization

---

14. Merton, *Inner Experience*, 42. Shannon observes, "There is no theme more prominent in Thomas Merton's writings, no subject he wrote more about and in more detail, than contemplation." See Shannon, "Contemplation," 79.

15. For an overview of the terms and their historical usage, see Coombs and Nemeck, *Discerning Vocations*, 24–32.

16. Shannon, "Contemplation," 80.

17. Shannon, "Contemplation," 81.

18. Egan, "Contemplation," 211.

19. Shannon comments, "Merton expresses... a statement that is about as close to a 'definition' of contemplation as he would ever want to come. 'Contemplation, by which we know and love God as He is in Himself, apprehending Him in a deep and vital experience which is beyond the reach of any natural understanding, is the reason for our creation by God.'" See Shannon, "Contemplation," 80, which cites Merton, "The Gift of Understanding," in Merton, *New Seeds*, 225. Shannon also attempts his own summary of Merton's conception of contemplation: "Merton wrote so much about contemplation that it is difficult to summarize his ideas.... In a circular letter written to his friends in 1963, he wrote on the theme 'What the contemplative life means to me.' 'It means to me,' he stated, 'the search for truth and for God. It means finding the true significance of my life and my right place in God's creation.' Contemplation, then, is more than an exercise of prayer; it involves the experience of (1) seeking God, (2) coming to know one's true self, and (3) learning one's relationship to the world" ("Contemplation," 81). The letter cited is "To 'My Dear Friend' [c. 1963]," in Merton, *Thomas Merton* (2008), 8.

and rationalization. Nothing is more repellent than a pseudo-scientific definition of the contemplative experience."[20]

Numerous scholars have previously explored Merton's understanding and practice of contemplation,[21] and it is a much more expansive topic than this project engages. It remains, however, an essential component in understanding Merton and contextualizing his contribution to the SFM, and the same is true of a closely related theme in Merton's life and writings: monasticism. While Shannon observes contemplation as the most prominent theme in Merton's writings,[22] monasticism is evident as a theme of virtually equal persistence and frequency for Merton, spanning from among his earliest prose publications until the presentation he delivered hours before his death.[23] As Merton's voluminous comments on contemplation and monasticism evolved through the decades that he wrote on the topics, consistencies and inconsistencies can be observed.[24] In his journal entry for January 25, 1964, Merton writes, "My ideas are always changing, always moving around one center, and I am always seeing that center from somewhere else. Hence, I will always be accused of inconsistency."[25]

In reference to this journal entry, Shannon and Bonnie B. Thurston each separately identify monasticism as Merton's "one center." Shannon comments, "Yes, there was a center. It was . . . his monastic commitment. Despite his seeming unsettledness, that center held. Somehow everything

---

20. Merton, *New Seeds*, 6.

21. For example, the Thomas Merton Center at Bellarmine University lists more than twenty-five theses and dissertations related to Merton and contemplation. See the Thomas Merton Center, "Theses and Dissertations."

22. See this chapter above.

23. While it is far from conclusive evidence to the contrary of Shannon's claim, the centrality of monasticism in Merton's writing is highlighted in the quantity of manuscripts by Merton on the respective topics at the Thomas Merton Center, which currently lists 177 manuscripts on monasticism and 57 on contemplation. See Thomas Merton Center, "Monastic and Religious Life"; and Thomas Merton Center, "Contemplation." Merton's works on monasticism span from 1948 with *Seven Storey Mountain* to the address he gave on December 10, 1968, in Bangkok on the morning of his death titled "Marxism and Monastic Perspectives." The address is published as an appendix in Merton, *Asian Journal*, 326–43.

24. An example of this is Merton's varying views on whether contemplation was primarily applicable for monasticism or for everyone. See Shannon, *Thomas Merton's Paradise Journey*, 279–83.

25. Merton, *Vow of Conversation*, 19.

about him comes together . . . in the unity of his monastic vocation."[26] Thurston states accordingly, "If one does not understand Merton as a monk, one does not understand Merton."[27]

Merton's contribution to the SFM, however, does not lie in drawing Protestants toward lifelong monastic vows, nor does his contribution to the SFM consist in imposition upon non-monastics practices of contemplation as pursued by those who lived in the context of the radical commitments of cloistered communities. Rather, the primary contribution to the SFM of Merton's contemplative monasticism is found in a practice Merton viewed as essential to both contemplation and monasticism, identified clearly by Richard Anthony Cashen: "Merton related all aspects of monasticism to solitude, and solitude to contemplation."[28]

SOLITUDE AS ESSENTIAL IN MERTON'S CONTEMPLATIVE MONASTICISM

Merton writes in a 1950 letter to Thérèse Lentfoehr, "My heart consents to nothing but God and solitude,"[29] which aptly summarizes the centrality of solitude in Merton's spirituality. As Cashen observes, "There is scarcely any area of [Merton's] thought into which solitude does not enter. It is an essential and central theme which helps to unify Merton's thought."[30] The interrelated triangle of contemplation, monasticism, and solitude is inseparable for Merton.[31] For example, regarding the centrality of solitude in monasticism, he writes,

> The monastic community exists not merely in order that each individual may find support, exhortation, correction, and encouragement, but also and above all that all may more easily

26. Shannon, *Thomas Merton's Paradise Journey*, 278.
27. Thurston, *Shaped by the End*, xiv.
28. Cashen, *Solitude in the Thought*, 5.
29. Lentfoehr, "Spiritual Writer," 105.
30. Cashen, *Solitude in the Thought*, 3.
31. Silence could legitimately be added to this group, making it a quadrilateral. John F. Teahan comments, "Silence and solitude, though separable for purposes of analysis, are so closely interwoven in Merton's life and thought that any interpretation of either element that neglects to consider its counterpart will be inadequate." See Teahan, "Solitude," 522. His point is valid. However, this project focuses on solitude as the primary Mertonian contribution to the SFM because silence was always prevalent in the Quaker tradition that came to be highly influential on the SFM and because solitude is understood as the context for silence.

attain to their common end, which is union with God in solitude. The monks therefore help one another not only to grow grain and produce the bread of the body, but also bring one another to the spiritual ovens of solitude from which they are nourished with the hot, fresh bread of the Spirit.[32]

Merton's association of solitude and contemplation is just as close. He writes, "The attack on the contemplative life . . . becomes, naturally and logically, an attack on solitude. Consequently, the defence of the contemplative life today implies also a defence of a certain kind of solitude."[33]

In order to explore solitude as the primary contribution of Merton's contemplative monasticism to the SFM, it is necessary to understand solitude's general meaning in Merton's life and writings, the "certain kind of solitude" that he sought to defend, and similarities and differences between Mertonian solitude and its reflection in the SFM.

THE MEANING OF SOLITUDE FOR MERTON

Merton's writings on solitude contain multiple themes within them, indicative of the breadth and development of his thought on the subject. The most significant of these themes, explored below, include interior and exterior solitude as means toward love rather than an escape, the contrast between true and false solitude, and solitude as a place of healing. Cashen identifies three significant periods within the years of Merton's monasticism relative to his thought on solitude: the first beginning with his arrival at Gethsemani in 1941; the second beginning with his appointment as master of scholastics in 1951; and the third beginning in 1961, following the previous year's publication of "Notes for a Philosophy of Solitude" and the beginning of construction of the building on the monastery grounds that was first intended to provide a place for conferences with visitors and eventually became his hermitage in 1965.[34] These three periods are referred to below as Merton's early solitude, middle solitude, and late solitude, and Cashen's three time periods provide a helpful framework for exploration of the themes in Merton's writing on solitude

---

32. Merton, *Silent Life*, 36.
33. Merton, "Solitary Life," 213.
34. Cashen, *Solitude in the Thought*, 14–43. He refers to the respective periods as "the first ten years in the desert" (1941–1950), "blossoming in the desert" (1951–1960), and "the fruitful desert" (1961–1968).

by situating within them the major markers in Merton's life in relation to solitude:

1. Merton's 1941 decision to enter the monastery and his December 10 arrival at Gethsemani, which he described as "the last lap of my journey into the desert"[35]

2. His subsequent dissatisfaction with the lack of exterior solitude he found in the monastery, due in part to life in a cenobitic order and in part to an influx of new monks following World War II, which Merton described as "two hundred seventy lovers of silence and solitude . . . packed into a building that was built for seventy"[36]

3. Merton's appointment by his abbot (Dom James Fox) in June 1951 as master of scholastics,[37] on which he later reflected, "The kind of work I once feared because I thought it would interfere with 'solitude' is, in fact, the only true path to solitude"[38]

4. The September 1952 permission given to Merton to use a former toolshed, which he named St. Anne's, for solitude in the afternoons[39]

---

35. Merton, *Seven Storey Mountain*, 407.

36. Merton describes the gap between what he sees as the purpose of monasticism and his experience of it during his early years at Gethsemani: "This is the real purpose of the monastic life: a more or less habitual state of simple prayer and union with God which varies in intensity at different times of the day, which finds a particular and proper rhythm in the life of each individual, and which brings the soul of the monk at all times under the direct and intimate influence of God's love. But now, let us suppose that within four or five years, several hundred men decide that they want lives of silence, prayer, labor, penance, and constant union with God in solitude. And suppose they all decide to enter the same monastery. . . . Thus two hundred seventy lovers of silence and solitude are all packed into a building that was built for seventy. . . . Meanwhile, new buildings have to be put up, and the farm has to be completely reorganized and expanded, so that all these new arrivals may be fed and housed. Since all this work has to be done in a hurry, many machines are needed. . . . The young monk who makes his vows at Gethsemani . . . is walking into a furnace of ambivalence which nobody in the monastery can fully account for." See Merton, *Sign of Jonas*, 4–5. See also Merton, *Seven Storey Mountain*, 428, in which he describes Gethsemani as an example of how "monasteries produce very few pure contemplatives."

37. See Merton, *Sign of Jonas*, 328–29. He comments regarding his appointment to the office, "Now I know the reason why I had to resist the temptation to become a Carthusian was in order to learn how to help all the other ones who would be one way or another tempted to leave the monastery" (*Sign of Jonas*, 329).

38. Merton, *Sign of Jonas*, 333.

39. The first mention of the shed in Merton's journal is September 3, 1952, in *Search for Solitude*, 14. Merton writes five months later, "It seems to me that St. Anne's is what I have been waiting for and looking for all my life and now I have stumbled into quite

5. Merton's first written request on Christmas Day 1952 to live as a hermit[40]

6. The correspondence from September 1952 until October 1955 through which he explored the possibility of transferring to the eremitical orders of the Carthusians or Camaldolese[41]

7. The 1955 construction of a fire watchtower that Fox proposed Merton could use as a hermitage, which was approved in September, although Merton requested and received the position of novice master instead[42]

8. Merton's "frenetic year" in 1959 of strategizing to leave Gethsemani for other monastic settings, ending with the Vatican's denial of his formal request[43]

9. Merton's July 1959 request to Fox to live as a hermit at Gethsemani, to which Fox was receptive, but Merton decided to wait to pursue it further[44]

---

by accident.... In the silence of St. Anne's everything has come together in unity and the unity is not my unity but Yours, O Father of Peace." See Merton, *Search for Solitude*, 32. For an overview of Merton's experiences in St. Anne's, see Shannon, *Silent Lamp*, 154–56. Jim Forest notes that Merton wrote parts of *No Man Is an Island* and *Bread in the Wilderness* in St. Anne's. See Forest, *Living with Wisdom*, 123–24.

40. This was in the form of a letter to his abbot, Dom James Fox, but Merton did not deliver the letter because Fox became ill the same day. See Merton, *Search for Solitude*, 26–28.

41. Merton, *Search for Solitude*, 15. Although the 1955 events are not recorded in his journal, Merton reflects on them in Merton, *Search for Solitude*, 311. See also Shannon, *Silent Lamp*, 156–57.

42. Michael Mott ascribes some of Merton's decision not to live in the watchtower to his inability to drive a vehicle there from the monastery, and also says, "By that time Merton knew that the hermit who is not on good terms with himself is on the way to disaster. In 1955, Merton was not on good enough terms to live in solitude on the top of the fire tower on Vineyard Nob or anywhere else." See Mott, *Seven Mountains*, 286–88.

43. In his editorial introduction to Merton's *Search for Solitude*, Cunningham describes this time in Merton's life: "His old desire for a more retired life with its attendant temptation to look to the more eremitical Carthusians and Camaldolese comes back with a vengeance. The chance visit of a Benedictine prior who offers him a new life in a Cuernavaca (Mexico) monastery unleashes a frenetic year of correspondence, plans, poring over maps for suitable monastic sites in Latin America, canonical strategies to leave Gethsemani for other places—either in the rural areas of the West, or more likely in Central or Latin America" (*Search for Solitude*, xvii). These possibilities dominate Merton's May 7 to December 17, 1959 entries in Merton, *Search for Solitude*, 277–359.

44. See Merton, *Search for Solitude*, 289–91, 303–4.

10. The 1960 construction of the retreat house on the monastery's "Mount Olivet" that he could also use for occasional solitude[45]
11. The 1965 permission for Merton to live as a hermit at Mount Olivet, fulfilled with him becoming a full-time hermit on August 20[46]
12. His exploration of possibilities of living as a hermit of Gethsemani in other locations, including Alaska, California, New Mexico, and Asia, because of the frequency of visitors to his hermitage in Kentucky[47]

Merton's Early Solitude: Interior and Exterior Solitude as Means to the End of Love

Merton's early attraction to monasticism included a hope that the monastery would provide a place for him to flee from the world. He describes a 1941 experience of reading in an encyclopedia about the Trappists, which led him to read about the Cistercians and Carthusians:

> What I saw on those pages pierced me to the heart like a knife. What wonderful happiness there was, then, in the world! There were still men on this miserable, noisy, cruel earth, who tasted the marvelous joy of silence and solitude, who dwelt in forgotten mountain cells, in secluded monasteries, where the news and desires and appetites and conflicts of the world no longer reached them.[48]

By 1949, however, in his eighth year as a monk, he was aware that relocation to a monastery did not extract him from the world, nor vice-versa. He writes, "If you try to escape from this world merely by leaving the city and hiding yourself in solitude, you will only take the city with

---

45. Merton, *Search for Solitude*, 389; Mott, *Seven Mountains*, 337–38, 347, 350–53. Matthew Kelty, one of Gethsemani's novices under Merton, describes the slowly increasing quantity of time Merton was allowed to have in solitude at Olivet in Kelty, "Man," 30.

46. See Merton, *Vow of Conversation*, 205–6; Shannon, *Silent Lamp*, 249–52. See also Merton, *Thomas Merton* (1992), 214–22, which Merton wrote in May 1965 as a description of a day in the hermitage.

47. Cashen, *Solitude in the Thought*, 40–41; Forest, *Living with Wisdom*, 217–21. See also Hart, "Introduction," xxvii–xxix.

48. Merton, *Seven Storey Mountain*, 346.

you into solitude."⁴⁹ The opening paragraphs of "Solitude" in *Seeds of Contemplation* express the views of solitude present in multiple essays in the book that had been deepening in him through his first years in the monastery:

> Physical solitude, exterior silence and real recollection are all morally necessary for anyone who wants to lead a contemplative life: but like everything else in creation they are nothing more than means to an end, and if we do not understand the end we will make a wrong use of the means.
>
> Therefore we have to remember that we look for solitude in order to grow there in love for God and in love for other men. We do not go into the desert to escape people but in order to find them: we do not leave them in order to have nothing more to do with them, but to find out the way to do them the most good. But this is always only a secondary end.
>
> The one end that includes all others is the love of God.
>
> The truest solitude is not something outside you, not an absence of men or of sound around you: it is an abyss opening up in the center of your own soul.⁵⁰

This section of *Seeds of Contemplation* demonstrates themes that were present in Merton's early writing on solitude and remained persistent in later works on the topic. First, from Merton's earliest monastic writings, solitude is emphasized as a means of loving God and other people rather than escaping them. He writes in the *Seeds of Contemplation* essay "We Are One Man":

> Some men have perhaps become hermits with the thought that sanctity involved some kind of escape from other men. But the only justification for a life of deliberate solitude is the conviction that it will help you to love not only God but also other men. Otherwise, if you go into the desert merely to get away from crowds of people you dislike, you will not find peace or solitude either: you will only isolate yourself with a tribe of devils. Go into the desert not to escape other men but to find them in God.⁵¹

The paradoxical theme of solitude as a means toward the end of love rather than as means of withdrawal or avoidance never lessened in

---

49. Merton, *Seeds of Contemplation*, 57.
50. Merton, *Seeds of Contemplation*, 58–59.
51. Merton, *Seeds of Contemplation*, 42.

Merton's writings on solitude, but only strengthened as his experience of solitude matured.[52] In his reflection on perhaps the most well-known event of his life, while on an errand into the city, he writes, "In Louisville, at the corner of Fourth and Walnut, in the center of the shopping district, I was suddenly overwhelmed with the realization that I loved all those people, that they were mine and I theirs, that we could not be alien to one another even though we were total strangers."[53] He continues, "the whole illusion of a separate, holy existence is a dream. . . . The conception of 'separation from the world' that we have in the monastery too easily presents itself as a complete illusion."[54] Merton's reflection makes explicit the inextricable connection for him between his solitude and this epiphanic experience of divine love for others while surrounded by an urban crowd:

> This changes nothing in the sense and value of my solitude, for it is in fact the function of solitude to make one realize such things with a clarity that would be impossible to anyone completely immersed in other cares. . . . My solitude . . . is not my own, for I see now how much it belongs to them—and that I have a responsibility for it in their regard, not just in my own. It is because I am one with them that I owe it to them to be alone, and when I am alone they are not "they" but my own self. There are no strangers![55]

Merton expresses this conviction concisely and clearly more than a decade after the publication of *Seeds of Contemplation*, in what Shannon refers to as "one of the best, most insightful articles Merton ever wrote" and "his best sustained writing on the topic"[56] when, in his "Notes for a Philosophy of Solitude," he comments, "True solitude is not mere separateness. It tends only to *unity*."[57]

Equally as persistent as the theme of solitude's cultivation of the Christian's capacity to love were Merton's experiences and descriptions

---

52. For example, see Merton's 1966 "Love and Solitude" in *Love and Living*, 15–24. The essay was written in 1966 as a preface for the Japanese translation of *Thoughts in Solitude*.

53. Merton, *Conjectures*, 153.

54. Merton, *Conjectures*, 154.

55. Merton, *Conjectures*, 155.

56. Shannon, *Silent Lamp*, 159; See also Shannon, "Solitude," 444. The article referred to is "Notes for a Philosophy" in Merton, *Disputed Questions*, 177–207. Cashen refers to Merton's "Notes for a Philosophy" as "crucial" and "his most developed thoughts on solitude to that date" (*Solitude in the Thought*, 29).

57. Merton, *Disputed Questions*, 186.

of the relationship between interior and exterior solitude.[58] Similar to the passage cited above from "Solitude" in *Seeds of Contemplation*, he writes in other essays in the book, "There is no true solitude except interior solitude,"[59] and "The solitude that is important to a contemplative is, above all, an interior and spiritual thing. . . . It is possible to live in deep and peaceful interior solitude, even in the midst of the world and its confusion."[60] Cashen summarizes Merton's concept of interior solitude:

> The more important, absolutely essential "interior solitude" or solitude of the heart . . . becomes the domain of man's spiritual life, the inner atmosphere in which the quest for God takes place, the inner sanctuary where one meets God. It includes the purifying process of the interior desert in which false ideas, illusions, and delusions are burned away that a man may discover his true self, his true identity as a son of God. In the solitude of the inner sanctuary one also meets the solitude of God, and in His solitude, the solitudes of all other men. Interior solitude is essential to true personhood, that basic foundation of compassion and mature love.[61]

Merton's desire for solitude played a large role in his decision to enter the monastery, and that desire shaped the trajectory of his continual search for greater solitude from his arrival at Gethsemani until his death twenty-seven years later.[62] While he agreed that interior solitude was paramount, his quest for exterior solitude, which he saw as "morally necessary for anyone who wants to lead a contemplative life,"[63] is one of the most prominent characteristics of his biography.

Thus, while interior solitude was the goal, the orientation of Merton's entire life as a monk was toward the exterior solitude that he saw as most conducive to it. As he writes in 1960, "Without the efficacious desire

---

58. Teahan credits "two of the greatest Cistercians, St. Bernard and William of St. Thierry," with influence on Merton's distinction between interior and exterior solitude. See Teahan, "Solitude," 524.

59. Merton, *Seeds of Contemplation*, 42.

60. Merton, *Seeds of Contemplation* (1960), 53.

61. Cashen, *Solitude in the Thought*, 2–3.

62. For a brief overview of this trajectory, see Teahan, "Solitude," 522–38, and a detailed survey in Cashen, *Solitude in the Thought*, 7–49. See also O'Connell, "Hermitage," 197–200, in which he traces Merton's dream of living as a hermit from 1949 until his 1968 death.

63. Merton, *Seeds of Contemplation*, 57–58. As in this passage, Merton also sometimes refers to exterior solitude as "physical solitude" and elsewhere as "concrete" solitude, as in Merton, *Search for Solitude*, 29.

of exterior solitude, interior solitude will always remain a fantasy or an illusion."[64]

Merton's Middle Solitude: True and False Solitudes

Cashen notes that, after Merton's first decade in the monastery, "as he let more people into his life, both through the bundles of mail he received after the success of *The Seven Storey Mountain* and through his assignment as Master of Scholastics in 1951, he eased his rigidity, his tight categories, and opened his perspective."[65] Shannon concurs, noting that in Merton's 1955 *No Man Is an Island*, "We discover a very different Merton from the man who wrote *The Seven Storey Mountain*: a Merton who has learned that faith generates questions as well as answers."[66] This opening of perspective is evident in the expansion of Merton's descriptors of solitude that began to acknowledge more subtle interior motivations. He probes his own motivation for solitude in a 1949 journal entry:

> I am thinking of the possibilities of, say, spiritual narcissism in our life.... I wonder how much of that there is in my enthusiasm for solitude! Perhaps quite a lot.... Narcissistic solitude as a substitute for the responsibility of living with people. Yet at the other pole is the crass activism that delights in company and noise and movement and escapes the responsibility of living at peace with God. Our whole life must be a dialectic between community and solitude. Both are tremendously important, and our contemplative life subsists in the fruitful antagonism between these two terms.[67]

---

64. See the essay "Renaissance Hermit" in Merton, *Disputed Questions*, 166. The degree to which exterior solitude was essential for interior solitude was a source of conflict between Merton and the censors of his order, particularly regarding his "Notes for a Philosophy." See Shannon, "Reflections," 84–88 and Lentfoehr, "Solitary," 70–74. In his rewrite of *Seeds of Contemplation*'s "Solitude" into "Learn to Be Alone" in *New Seeds*, Merton adds a paragraph that reads, "How can people act and speak as if solitude were a matter of no importance in the interior life? Only those who have never experienced real solitude can glibly declare that it 'makes no difference' and that only solitude of the heart really matters! One solitude must lead to the other!" (*New Seeds*, 80; compare to Merton, *Seeds of Contemplation*, 58–59).

65. Cashen, *Solitude in the Thought*, 20.

66. Shannon, *Silent Lamp*, 22.

67. See the entry for December 29, 1949, in Merton, *Entering the Silence*, 389.

Merton develops questions such as this about motivation for solitude and introduces his concepts of true and false solitudes in the second half of a 1955 essay titled "The Inward Solitude" in *No Man Is an Island* with the statement, "Solitude is so necessary for both society and for the individual that when society fails to develop the inner life of the persons who compose it, they rebel and seek false solitudes."[68] In 1960, he explored the concepts further in his landmark "Notes for a Philosophy of Solitude." Both articles explore true and false solitudes from a variety of overlapping and repetitious angles, and Shannon summarizes, "False solitaries want at all costs to be noticed by society, through admiration and approval or even, if need be, through opposition."[69] He also comments, "Whether it be opposition or approval, the important thing is that they are being noticed. This sham solitariness calls attention to itself."[70] In "Notes for a Philosophy of Solitude," Merton connects false solitude with characteristics he labels as the "individualist" and true solitude with the "person."[71] Merton comments, "Only the false solitary sees no danger in solitude. But his solitude is imaginary, that is to say built around an image."[72]

"The true solitary," in contrast, is humble, selfless, and

> does not renounce anything that is basic and human about his relationship to other men. He is deeply united to them—all the more deeply because he is no longer entranced by marginal concerns. What he renounces is the superficial imagery and the trite symbolism that pretend to make the relationship more genuine and more fruitful. . . . He renounces vain pretenses of solidarity that tend to substitute themselves for real solidarity, while masking an inner spirit of irresponsibility and selfishness.[73]

---

68. See "Inward Solitude" in Merton, *No Man*, 185. Paragraphs 7–10 of the essay explore true and false solitudes.

69. Shannon, *Thomas Merton's Paradise Journey*, 104.

70. Shannon speculates that Merton's concept of false solitude emerged from autobiographical reflection upon a painful encounter with Gregory Zilboorg, a psychiatrist he met at a 1956 conference in Minnesota ("Reflections," 94). Zilboorg claimed Merton's obsession with living in ever-increasing solitude was pathological, telling Merton (in the presence of Fox), "You want a hermitage in Times Square with a large sign over it saying 'HERMIT'" (Mott, *Seven Mountains*, 297).

71. Merton, *Disputed Questions*, 178, 184–85, 205.

72. Merton, *Disputed Questions*, 185.

73. Merton, *Disputed Questions*, 186.

Merton also comments, "Pure interior solitude does not shrink from the good things of life or from the company of other men because it no longer seeks to possess them for their own sake. No longer desiring them, it no longer fears to love them. Free from fear, it is free of bitterness. Purified of bitterness, the soul can safely remain alone."[74]

Merton's Late Solitude: Solitude as a Place of Healing

The concepts developed during the period of Merton's middle solitude continued into his late solitude, as he includes a section on true and false solitudes in his 1961 rewrite of *Seeds of Contemplation*'s "We Are One Man," published in *New Seeds* as "Solitude Is Not Separation." In the rewrite, he inserts a new section above his previous statement: "There is no true solitude except interior solitude."[75] The insertion focuses on society's relationship to the false solitude of the "individualist" and the true solitude of the "person":

> True solitude is the home of the person, false solitude the refuge of the individualist. The person is constituted by a uniquely subsisting capacity to love—by a radical ability to care for all beings made by God and loved by Him. Such a capacity is destroyed by the loss of perspective. Without a certain element of solitude there can be no compassion because when a man is lost in the wheels of a social machine he is no longer aware of human needs as a matter of personal responsibility. One can escape from men by plunging into the midst of a crowd! Go into the desert not to escape other men but to find them in God.[76]

This passage represents a paradoxical characteristic of Merton's life, as it was during the years that he had increasing time in exterior solitude at "Mount Olivet" that he began to write extensively on social issues such as war, racism, and nonviolence.[77] Shannon observes that from 1961 through the rest of his life, a central question for Merton was,

---

74. Merton, *No Man*, 188.

75. Merton, *Seeds of Contemplation*, 42.

76. Merton, *New Seeds*, 53. "Go into the desert" was part of the original essay (Merton, *Seeds of Contemplation*, 42).

77. Significant among these writings are Merton's *Seeds of Destruction*, *Faith and Violence* and *Peace in the Post-Christian Era*. For an overview of the relationship between Merton's solitude and his writing on racism, see Harris, "Thomas Merton's Spiritual Formation," 184–204.

"Should I, as a monk of Gethsemani, vowed to silence and solitude, speak out against the terrible violence of war that threatens the very life of the planet, or should I keep a discreet silence as the appropriate stance for a monk?"[78] Shannon continues, "By 1961 quite a lot had happened to Thomas Merton and he was quite certain that what he had said about spirituality had a great deal to do with the social problems of the day and especially with the issue of war. What had happened to him was that his solitude had issued into what all true solitude must eventually become: compassion."[79]

Merton's life with increasing solitude at Mount Olivet in the 1960s presents this counterintuitive notion of a monk offering prolific commentary on the social problems of the world outside his monastery. He believed that extensive solitude was necessary for him to cultivate the perception of societal dynamics required to comment on them. As he writes in 1962,

> Even contemplative and cloistered religious, perhaps especially these, need to be attuned to the deepest problems of the contemporary world. This does not mean that they must leave their solitude and engage in the struggle and confusion in which they can only be less useful than they would be in their cloister. They must preserve their unique perspective, which solitude alone can give them, and from their vantage point they must understand the world's anguish and share in it in their own way.[80]

Merton also writes similarly in 1966, "Someone has to try to keep his head clear of static and preserve the interior solitude and silence that are essential for independent thought."[81] Merton saw the great social problems of the globe and the interior conflicts of individuals as inextricably linked with one another.[82] In the introduction to his edited collection of Mahatma Gandhi's teachings on nonviolence, Merton writes, "The first thing of all and the most important of all was the inner unity, the overcoming and healing of inner division, the consequent spiritual and

---

78. Shannon, "Introduction," 2.
79. Shannon, "Introduction," 2.
80. Merton, *Faith and Violence*, 68.
81. Merton, *Faith and Violence*, 150.
82. Elena Malits comments on this period of Merton's life, "As he more and more agonized over the world's wounds, he was convinced that solitude invited him to discover how he might let the healing process take place in himself." See Malits, *Solitary Explorer*, 58.

personal freedom, of which national autonomy and liberty would only be consequences."[83] Accordingly, not only did Merton's solitude provide the context for perception of social crises, but it also provided temporal and geographical space "where the deep wounds of his life could surface and be confronted."[84] On the second of six days of solitude that he was permitted to spend at the hermitage from June 3–8, 1963, he writes, "Solitude—when you get saturated with silence and landscape, then you need an interior work, psalms, scripture, meditation. But first the saturation. How much of this is simply a restoration of one's normal human balance? Like waking up, like convalescence after an illness."[85]

The more complete his exterior solitude was, the more opportunity he had for deep places in him that needed healing to come to the surface. Christine M. Bochen comments, "In the solitude of the hermitage, he was able to see himself more clearly, to realize how muddled and distracted he was, to admit how he was not free."[86] This dynamic is evident in a journal entry from Merton's sixth month of life as a hermit at Mount Olivet:

> A basic conviction grows more and more clear to me. That I am called into solitude by God's will in order to be *healed* and purified. That there are deep wounds in me which would cause me despair if I saw them all at once—but I see them gradually and retrospectively. . . . Hence I cannot play with this vocation. I must gradually learn to hear and obey Him directly in everything.[87]

In an article published one year later, he comments on a distinction between contemporary eremitical life and the lives of the early Christian monks in the Egyptian and Syrian deserts, including the "apparent inhumanity" in the collections of their sayings:

> The first function of a modern hermitage would seem to be quite the opposite: to relax and to heal and to smooth out one's distortions and inhumanities. . . . Hence the mission of the solitary is first the full recovery of man's human and natural measure. . . . The Christian solitary life today should bear witness to the

---

83. Merton, *Gandhi on Non-Violence*, 6.

84. Burton-Christie, "Work of Loneliness," 40. He adds, "Whether or not Merton ever resolved these questions or saw these wounds healed seems less important than his having learned to face himself honestly" ("Work of Loneliness," 40–41).

85. Merton, *Turning Toward the World*, 327.

86. Bochen, "Introduction," xv.

87. Merton, *Learning to Love*, 358.

fact that certain basic claims about solitude and peace are in fact true. And in doing this, it will restore people's confidence, first in their own humanity and beyond that in the grace of God.[88]

Merton's wounds, his humanity, and the search for love of God and of others in exterior and interior solitude to which they drove him became unexpectedly and powerfully evident in March through October of 1966 when he fell in love with a student nurse (referred to in the edited version of his journals as "M.") who cared for him during recovery from surgery in Louisville.[89] Whether the relationship was ultimately positive in Merton's life is debated, but it signified a lessening of his deep obstacles to giving and receiving love.[90] During the months when his dilemma between his monastic vows and his love for M. was most intense, he writes about their love, "I feel I must fully surrender to it because it will change and heal my life in a way that I fear, but I think is necessary—in a way that will force me first of all to *receive an enormous amount of love* (which to tell the truth I have often feared)."[91] Although Merton wrestled with the possibility of leaving the hermitage and monastery for a life with M., he did not do so, acknowledging "my need for love, my loneliness, my inner division [as] the struggle in which solitude is at once a problem and a 'solution.'"[92]

Merton writes in 1966 that true solitude makes one "wide open to heaven and earth and closed to no one,"[93] and his relationship with M. in

---

88. The quotation is taken from Merton, *Contemplation*, 254–55. The article was originally published as Merton, "Christian Solitude."

89. For accounts and perspectives on the relationship, see Mott, *Seven Mountains*, 435–54, 461–62; Griffin, *Follow the Ecstasy*, 77–130; Forest, *Living with Wisdom*, 193–203; Bochen, "Introduction," xvi–xxiv; Burton-Christie, "Rediscovering Love's World," 64–82; Bourgeault, "Merton in Love," 20–25; Lane, "Merton's Hermitage," 123–50.

90. See Bourgeault, "Merton in Love," 21, which acknowledges the variety of opinions on the relationship. Burton-Christie comments, "Clearly the experience had a powerful impact on Merton's evolving sense of himself and God, opening up within him a capacity for intimacy and relatedness that had long eluded him. However, it seems also to have revealed and even exacerbated patterns of immaturity and self-absorption in Merton's character that hindered him from coming to grips with the meaning of love in his life" ("Work of Loneliness," 40). James R. Lauridson characterizes Merton's relationships with women into his young adulthood as "immature and incomplete." See Lauridson, "Merton and the Feminine," 3. For the trajectory toward health of Merton's relationships with other women, see Thurston, "I Never Had a Sister," 4–8.

91. Merton, *Learning to Love*, 77.

92. Merton, *Learning to Love*, 234.

93. Merton, *Love and Living*, 17.

the same year was evidence that his life in the hermitage had contributed to such an openness rather than reinforcing false solitude's pattern of isolation. Michael Mott comments on the effect of the relationship: "He loved greatly and was greatly loved. He was overwhelmed by the experience and it changed him forever. While this brought a sense of humiliation no exercise of Rancé could have achieved, Thomas Merton never again talked of his inability to love, or to be loved."[94] James R. Lauridson concurs and argues that the relationship with M. "was the last of a series of encounters with the feminine that allowed Merton to develop a healthy human and monastic understanding of himself and the feminine."[95]

This intensely relational progression cannot be extracted from Merton's quest for and experiences in solitude. The development of his conception of solitude as a place of healing during his years in the hermitage is illustrated in two of his writings on the desert fathers. In a 1967 article, Merton includes his translation of a saying from the early Christian monastics:

> At Scete a hermit was suffering in absolute isolation with no one to console or help him in any way. He got his things together in order to leave the desert. "Then divine grace appeared to him in the form of a virgin who encouraged him and said: Do not go away *but stay here with me*, for none of the evils you have imagined has ever happened to you. *He obeyed and stayed there*, and at this moment his heart was healed."[96]

The connection to Merton's relational and eremitical life is evident in that, although Merton had previously published two books as collections of sayings of the desert fathers in 1959 and 1960, he did not include this story in those publications.[97] Although speculative, it is credible to connect the story's 1967 inclusion with his life as a hermit, his temptation to leave eremitical life, and the healing by God's grace that he believed was uniquely available to him there.

Even though Merton had lobbied so long for hermits to be allowed in the Trappist order and for sanction from his superiors for him to live as

---

94. Mott, *Seven Mountains*, 438. "Rancé" refers to Armand Jean le Bouthillier de Rancé, who founded the Trappists.

95. Lauridson, "Merton and the Feminine," 3.

96. Merton, *Contemplation*, 271. The article was originally published as Merton, "Cell." The saying is included in a different translation in Ward, *Desert Fathers*, 76.

97. Merton expanded his limited edition *What Ought I to Do?* into *Wisdom of the Desert*.

one, his life after he lived in solitude at Mount Olivet was far less than the eremitical ideal he had described and sought for decades. In addition to visitors, writing projects, and the voluminous correspondence he maintained, his status as a world-renowned writer brought other unwanted distractions. For example, he writes in a March 1968 journal entry of a "disturbing and curious incident":

> Some woman had come unannounced from California claiming she *had* to see me. Against my better judgment I consented to do so. An attractive, poised person, in some way intriguing, with guarded statements about time cycles, the apocalypse, or coming crisis, a mission. . . . She intends to stay here (not at the monastery, the Abbot refused her) in the neighborhood and continue "her work" in which I am supposed to play some mysterious part. . . . I am afraid of the whole business—a great mess of false mysticism involving me, the Abbey, etc. . . . How to deal with it? I'm trying to keep out of her way and she has not (as far as I know) tried to see me since Friday.[98]

Several weeks later, Merton received a telegram from someone cryptically asking him to meet where they met before, and he perceived that it must have been "the woman from California with the apocalyptic mission. Very embarrassing! A sort of clandestine meeting is suggested."[99] Merton left a note for her at the monastery entrance to explain that a meeting was impossible, and then he comments in his journal,

> All of which brings up the problem of real solitude: I don't have it here. I am not really living as a hermit. I see too many people, have too much active work to do, the place is too noisy, too accessible. People are always coming up here, and I have been too slack about granting visits, interviews, etc., going to town too often, socializing, drinking, and all that. All I have is a certain privacy, but real solitude is less and less possible here. Everyone now knows where the hermitage is.[100]

The accessibility of the hermitage prompted Merton to explore possibilities of relocating as a hermit of Gethsemani to other sites, including New Mexico, California, Alaska, and Asia, for increased solitude, but the topic of Merton's eventual influence on the SFM is informed by two benefits that shaped the SFM through Merton's paradoxical status as an

---

98. Merton, *Other Side*, 61.
99. Merton, *Other Side*, 82.
100. Merton, *Other Side*, 82.

accessible hermit. The first benefit has been described above in chapter 1 as part of the pre-SFM relational phase, particularly through the friendships Merton developed with Protestant seminary professors Hinson and Shipps during their visits to the abbey, which also resulted in Merton's visits to each of their seminary campuses. Those relationships, and the influence on the SFM that followed, could not have developed as they did if Merton's life at Mount Olivet had been fully eremitical and inaccessible to visitors, nor would they have developed in the same way if Merton had lived with the high accessibility of a parish priest rather than as a monk.

The second benefit concerns the model of Merton's solitude. If his monastic life had been as fully eremitical as he often stated was his wish, and even if that fully eremitical life had still included his writing efforts, then his works on contemplation and solitude may still have been influential on the SFM, but inevitably to a lesser degree. Because eremitical life in Protestantism has never been a common phenomenon, the life of a hermit living in complete solitude would not have resonated with evangelical Protestants to the same extent as Merton's semi-eremitism.[101] Since engaged activism is as essential a part of the foundation of evangelicalism as complete solitude is for eremitism,[102] Merton's semi-eremitical accessibility made his teachings on and example of solitude adaptable for others whose circumstances would always be dissimilar to his.

Merton's relationship with Catherine de Hueck Doherty provides a lens through which the semi-eremitism of Merton's influence on the SFM is clarified.[103] Before entering the monastery, Merton volunteered with Doherty at Friendship House in Harlem, and he deliberated over whether to join her work of providing social services and racial advocacy for the poor full time or become a Trappist at Gethsemani.[104] They continued to correspond through the subsequent years, and she writes

---

101. While Protestant hermits are not completely without precedent, there have never been many, and—although it is perhaps impossible to quantify—the fundamental concepts of eremitism and evangelicalism are too incongruous to make the rare existence of evangelical hermits anything but anomalies. However, anomalies do exist. Merton mentions a German Protestant hermit in *Waters of Siloe*, 114.

102. For activism as one of Bebbington's four evangelical priorities, see chapter 1 above.

103. For an overview of Merton's relationship with Doherty, see Merton and Doherty, *Compassionate Fire*, ix–xiv, 96–104; Mott, *Seven Mountains*, 186–98, 201–2, 309–11; Harris, "Thomas Merton's Spiritual Formation," 187–89.

104. For Merton's account of this period, see chapter 3, "Sleeping Volcano," of part three in *Seven Storey Mountain*, 369–408. For a fuller account of Doherty's work, see Rademacher, "Allow Me to Disappear," 71–100.

to him in a 1961 letter, "One thing I want to tell you about is that I have returned to the ways of my people.... I decided to go back to the '*poustinia*' of my people."[105]

Doherty introduces the concept of the *poustinia* from her upbringing in Christian tradition in Russia and explains the term: "The word to the Russian means much more than a geographical place. It means a quiet, lonely place that people wish to enter, to find the God who dwells within them."[106] She describes a *poustinik* as "a person dwelling with God in a *poustinia*" and notes that, while the concept of a *poustinia* had similarities to the Western concept of a hermitage, a *poustinik* was "more available" with a "gracious hospitality" to visitors and needs in the surrounding community:[107] "For a Russian hermit has no lock or latch on his door except against the wind. Anyone at any time of day or night can knock at his door. Remember, he is in the *poustinia* not for himself but for others."[108] She comments to Merton that the distinction in Western monasticism between cenobitic and eremitical monasticism, which had occupied much of Merton's attention for decades, had always been strange to her, as the two "always went together in the old days" in Russia.[109]

Doherty applied the *poustinia* model, first as a place of weekly solitude for herself, and then made more such places available for others who served with her in the Madonna House or who came for retreats. Lorine Hanley Duquin comments, "The *poustinia* contained only a hard bed, a desk and chair, a Bible, a large cross without a corpus, drinking water, and loaf of bread. Staff workers went into the *poustinia* to fast and pray in silence for a day or two.... As guests and volunteers expressed an interest, Madonna House built small cabins in the woods for use as *poustinias*."[110]

Doherty offered guidance to people who came to visit Madonna House for retreats but were anxious about being in solitude in a *poustinia*, writing,

> Relax! You have heard the word *poustinia* and it sounds like a mysterious Russian deal of some sort. There's nothing mysterious about it! A *poustinia* is just an ordinary log cabin with a

---

105. See Doherty's letter to Merton (March 17, 1961) in Merton and Doherty, *Compassionate Fire*, 57.
106. Doherty, *Poustinia*, 30.
107. Doherty, *Poustinia*, 31.
108. Doherty, *Poustinia*, 44.
109. Merton and Doherty, *Compassionate Fire*, 65.
110. Duquin, *They Called Her*, 269.

wood stove, a table and chair, and a bed. You will find there a bible, and a little outline I wrote which tells you what to do more or less—because I can't really tell you want to do. . . . You are about to have a rendezvous, a date with Christ. For 24 hours you are going to be alone with God and the only book that you are going to read is the bible. Don't take any others! If you want to sleep, sleep. If you want to walk, walk. It's up to you. Once you enter the *poustinia* you do what the Spirit tells you to do.[111]

Retreatants were limited to twenty-four hours in a *poustinia* unless a spiritual director had given them permission to stay longer.[112] Doherty advised retreatants to have monthly solitude in the *poustinia* to move from initial excitement into the "great spiritual travail" of the desert.[113] Experiences in the *poustinias* varied widely according to the person's background and included the monthly solitude for visitors described above, a shared rotation of solitude among Madonna House staff members, a scholar, and priests who each spent three days each week in solitude and the remainder teaching in the community, and hundreds of priests who came for retreats.[114]

After Doherty's early description of the *poustinia*, Merton responded, "I was deeply moved by the *Poustinia*. . . . That is ideal. It is just right. It will be a wonderful contribution. It is the kind of thing that is most needed."[115]

111. Doherty, *Poustinia*, 71–72.
112. Doherty, *Poustinia*, 54.
113. Doherty, *Poustinia*, 54.

114. Doherty, *Poustinia*, 57–58. Doherty describes to Merton her surprise at the widespread interest in the *poustinia* in a letter from November 15, 1964: "What do you make of the sudden influx, contacts, lunges that the old contemplative orders have suddenly (or is it?) developed toward the lay apostolate, and very specially to Madonna House, and strangely to me. For behold, living amongst us is Fr. Hilarion, a Trappist of Spencer, with full permission of his abbot. Fr. Walter, I think of your Abbey, passed 2–3 days here?! The Carmelites (men) bought 350 acres near us! 2 Carmelite nuns who left their order came here, seeking answers. Benedictines, even Camaldolese, have been inquiring, not to mention a tremendous influx of priests (order and secular). 634 have passed thru our doors since 1964. But it is the contemplatives that seem to come seeking something I know not what, from Madonna House and me. Never has my utter poverty been so apparent to me. They seem to want to establish a hermetical [sic] life on the periphery [of Madonna House] yet also in depth in some way with us. I am reminded of Russia where this was often done" (Merton and Doherty, *Compassionate Fire*, 80).

115. See Merton's letter from November 12, 1962, to Doherty in Merton and Doherty, *Compassionate Fire*, 72. While Merton's statement that the *poustinia* "will be a wonderful contribution" indicates that he had some knowledge of Doherty's

Merton's combination of solitude and accessibility in the Mount Olivet hermitage, with its integration in the Gethsemani community and some degree of accessibility to visitors, is therefore more reflective of Doherty's semi-eremitical *poustinia* model than it is of the "single-minded insistence on silence and solitude" of the eremitical orders that Merton admired for so long.[116] Had it not been so, Mertonian contemplative monasticism's primary contribution to the SFM of emphasis on solitude would inevitably have been reduced, thereby leaving the SFM less distinguishable from earlier forms of Wesleyan pietistic evangelicalism.

MERTON'S SEMI-EREMITICAL "HERMITAGE"/*POUSTINIA* AS LINK TO SOLITUDE IN THE SFM

Upon learning of Merton's death, Doherty characterized his life at Mount Olivet as living in a *poustinia*.[117] Because of the spectrum of involvement in Doherty's *poustinias*, from twenty-four-hour retreats to full-time semi-hermits, Merton's life at Mount Olivet represents relational connection to Doherty and practical connection to the *poustinia* model of solitude from one end of that spectrum. A connection at the other end had no relational connection to Doherty, but did have significant resemblance to her practice and also directly influenced the emphasis on solitude in the SFM.

In 1947, D. Elton Trueblood authored *Alternative to Futility*, which proposes "the formation of a redemptive society,"[118] and eventually devel-

---

implementation of the Russian concept, it is unclear which part of the development of that implementation he would have been referring to in 1962. The only specific reference in her letters to him by that point is the letter cited above that mentions her solitude on Fridays.

116. Merton, *Silent Life*, 134. The eremitical orders Merton describes in the book are the Carthusians and Camaldolese, and the phrase cited here is in reference to Carthusians. He notes that the Camaldolese allow for still greater solitude than that of the hermits in these orders because "Camaldolese hermits may even receive permission to become a recluse. After five years of solemn profession, a hermit who is well qualified and tested may receive permission to live absolutely alone and undisturbed in his cell, never coming out to join the others in the Church or in their common gatherings except three times in a year.... The singular advantage of such a life is that it makes it possible for a pure contemplative life of real solitude and simplicity" (Merton, *Silent Life*, 152–53, emphasis added).

117. Doherty states, "You know that he was seeking a *poustinia*. Finally his superior allowed him to live in one." See Merton and Doherty, *Compassionate Fire*, 95.

118. Trueblood, *Alternative to Futility*, 29. His usage of "society" is consistent with that of Anglican pietism as explored in chapter 2. Throughout the book, Trueblood

oped into the Yokefellow movement, designed by Trueblood as a system of small renewal groups akin to an ecumenical order with no distinctions between clergy and laity.[119] In the book, Trueblood proposes a "minimum discipline" for participants of worship, solitude, silence, humanity, and austerity.[120] In the text's explanation of these disciplines, Trueblood describes solitude in terms more reflective of evangelicalism's "quiet time"[121] than the examples of Merton's solitude or Doherty's *poustinia*: "Solitude. Each person . . . must agree to spend some part of each day alone, in private prayer or other devotional exercises. These may include the devout reading of classic prayers, the use of devotional literature, silent meditation and the reading of the Holy Scriptures."[122]

This is not the extent of Trueblood's view of solitude, but it is indicative of the manner in which solitude was often considered in pietistic evangelicalism. A concurrent movement with Trueblood's Yokefellow groups, also based on emphases on spiritual practice and small group meetings, was an expression of Wesleyan pietistic evangelicalism called the Disciplined Order of Christ, founded in 1945 by Methodist pastor Albert Edward Day.[123] As Trueblood's *Alternative to Futility* was a foun-

repeatedly refers to the proposed groups as a "redemptive society."

119. Trueblood, *While It Is Day*, 104–24.

120. Trueblood, *Alternative to Futility*, 100–103. Although this was the "minimum discipline" proposed in the book, Trueblood recalls that the first group he participated in with students at Earlham College printed commitment cards that "included only five disciplines: Daily Prayer, Daily Scripture, Weekly Worship, Proportionate Giving, and Study" (*While It Is Day*, 111). He also proposes five minimum conditions of membership: "commitment, witness, fellowship, vocation, and discipline." See Trueblood, *Alternative to Futility*, 61. He expands on commitment, witness, vocation, and fellowship (*Alternative to Futility*, 61–81), and then dedicates a chapter to discipline (*Alternative to Futility*, 82–103). See also Newby, *Elton Trueblood*, 88–92. Trueblood later expresses a similar list: "The future of the Yoke we cannot know, but we are at least convinced that certain features are of enduring value. . . . The essentials are *commitment, discipline, ministry*, and *fellowship*" (*While It Is Day*, 122).

121. For "quiet time" as an evangelical spiritual discipline, see Schwanda, "Evangelical Spiritual Disciplines," 234; Johnson, "From Morning Watch."

122. Trueblood, *Alternative to Futility*, 100–101.

123. Interestingly, accounts of the beginnings of both organizations are directly connected to the spiritual aftermath of World War II. For this in respect to the Yokefellow movement, see Newby, *Elton Trueblood*, 88; respective to the Disciplined Order of Christ (originally named the New Life Movement), see McKinley, *History of the Disciplined*, 7–50. Foster identifies the organizations as two of three similar groups preceding the founding of Renovaré. See Foster, "Place to Stand." The remaining group referenced by Foster is the Evangelical Order of the Burning Heart, founded by Carl H. Lundquist, and it also shared similar emphases. It is not explored in this chapter,

dational text for the Yokefellow movement, Day's *Discipline and Discovery* became "the handbook of the Disciplined Order of Christ,"[124] and its content explored the disciplines on which membership in the order was based. E. H. McKinley summarizes the commitments of members:

> There were five vows: first, to seek the highest New Testament standard of Christian experience, which meant reading the Bible and "the best literature of devotion," prayer, participation in the corporate worship of the church, the eight personal disciplines [obedience, simplicity, humility, frugality, generosity, truthfulness, purity and charity], practice of the universal brotherhood of man, unlimited by race, class or creed, devotion of the sacredness of the individual and unselfish support for causes which have these values as their primary concern; second, to seek to promote the highest New Testament standard of Christian experience among others, by prayer, witness and loving fellowship; third, to seek first the Kingdom of God in the life of the world; fourth, to acknowledge that any praying and witnessing church was part of the Body of Christ; fifth, to recognize the testimony of the ages that said there was great value in setting aside a regular period for prayer, at least a half-hour per day, for "an earnest disciplined quest of the soul."[125]

As solitude is not explicitly part of these commitments, neither is it mentioned in *Discipline and Discovery*. As with Trueblood's description

---

however, because it was founded in 1982, early in the SFM's organizational phase.

124. McKinley, *History of the Disciplined*, 47. Day's *Discipline and Discovery* remained in print for decades, through multiple editions, from the first (1947) through a workbook edition adapted by Morris published more than forty years later (1990). Later statements of the commitments varied, but were similar in content. The 1988 edition of *Discipline and Discovery* states, "A unique feature of the D.O.C. is the practice of these seven spiritual disciplines with an annual renewal and accountability: 1. Setting aside a daily time for private prayer, meditation, serious study of the Bible and other great religious literature. 2. Personal commitment to a lifestyle which emphasizes obedience, simplicity, humility, frugality, generosity, truthfulness, purity, and charity. 3. Participation in a small group fellowship for the sharing of insights, problems, joys, and for prayer and social action. 4. Active involvement in the ministry of an organized church. 5. Witnessing to their faith to others and sharing the good news of the Kingdom of God. 6. Recognition of God's gracious gifts of body, mind, spirit, and all material things, and of their obligation to use these gifts in service to others. 7. The discipline of ecumenical fellowship recognizing that all persons are worthy of Christian love." See Day, *Discipline and Discovery*, 183.

125. McKinley, *History of the Disciplined*, 47–48.

of solitude above, this approach is characteristic of pre-SFM expressions of pietistic evangelicalism.[126]

However, elsewhere in *Alternative to Futility*, Trueblood describes solitude in terms corresponding to the desert motif that was central for Merton and Doherty but strongly resisted by Wesley[127] and which is not characteristic of the pre-SFM writings of Trueblood's contemporaries in pietistic evangelicalism:

> We need aloneness as much as we need togetherness, and . . . the good life anywhere will include some of both. For many, it is only in aloneness, when they learn not to be afraid of facing themselves without the protective chatter of the radio or anything else, that they are able to reset their compasses. Here we have the divine example of our Lord, who periodically "went apart," as well as the experience of all who have gone into the desert.[128]

---

126. Other exemplars of Wesleyan pietistic evangelicalism earlier than the SFM include A. W. Tozer and E. Stanley Jones. While they write substantively of solitude, their writings reflect this characteristic more closely related to evangelicalism's quiet time than Mertonian conceptions of solitude. See Tozer, *Best of*, 149–52. E. Stanley Jones often writes of "quiet time" and equates it with solitude in his *Abundant Living*, 239. His Christian Ashram movement is something of an exception to this generalization, as participants had one day of silence. See Mathews-Younes, *History of the Christian*, 86. Other twentieth-century Protestants wrote about solitude prior to the SFM, and while some of the writings were influential on the SFM, this project considers them as influences on the SFM rather than exceptions to this tendency in pre-SFM pietistic evangelicalism because they were in contexts other than North American evangelicalism that developed into the SFM as explored in chapter 1. Perhaps the most influential of these writings is Bonhoeffer's *Life Together* as described in this book's introduction. See also Murray, *Inner Chamber*, 17–20, 154–58; Underhill, *Study in the Nature*, 210–11.

127. See this chapter above and also Wesley's sermon "Wilderness State" in *Works* (Jackson), 6:77–91. Despite his strong opposition, however, Wesley is inconsistent, as he also states, "Not that we can in any wise condemn the intermixing solitude or retirement with society. This is not only allowable but expedient; nay, it is necessary, as daily experience shows, for everyone that either already is or desires to be a real Christian. It can hardly be that we should spend one entire day in a continued intercourse with men without suffering loss in our soul, and in some measure grieving the Holy Spirit of God. We have need daily to retire from the world, at least morning and evening, to converse with God, to commune more freely with our Father which is in secret. Nor indeed can a man of experience condemn even longer seasons of religious retirement, so they do not imply any neglect of the worldly employ wherein the providence of God has placed us." See Wesley, *Bicentennial Works*, 1:534.

128. Trueblood, *Alternative to Futility*, 98.

While there is no evidence of familiarity between Trueblood and Doherty, he later writes of solitude in terms that foreshadowed her guidance to *poustinia* retreatants of monthly solitude:

> One rare but powerful item of discipline is that requirement... [to] undertake a personal experience of solitude at least once a month. This is patterned consciously on the experience of Christ who periodically went alone, even at the price of temporary separation from the needs of his fellows. The justification of aloneness is not that of refined self-indulgence, but rather a consequent enrichment of one's subsequent contribution. A person who is always available is not worth enough when he *is* available. Everyone engaged in public life will realize the extreme difficulty of getting away each month for a period of five or six hours, but the difficulty is not a good reason for rejecting the discipline. It is the men and women who find it hardest to get away who need the redemptive solitude most sorely. They need to be where they are free from the compulsion of chit-chat, from the slavery of the telephone, and even from the newspaper. A Christianity which understands itself will make ample provision for retreat houses in which such solitude is expected and protected.[129]

Trueblood's perspective on solitude was rare in evangelicalism prior to the SFM, but it was not absolutely unique. Steere, who had become a friend of Merton and was also Trueblood's fellow Quaker and colleague in philosophy at Haverford College, wrote for participants of the EIOS about solitude as "the climate for the life of prayer" during the same years that some participants in his EIOS were working to form the URA.[130] Although Trueblood and Steere were major influences on the component of the tradition of pietistic evangelicalism that developed into the SFM, their understanding of and writing on solitude is not frequently referenced in SFM literature. Therefore, they represent a significant exception to the pre-SFM resistance to immersive solitude as a critical spiritual discipline, viewing it, like Merton and Doherty, as essential regardless of one's religious status. Although their words on solitude are not among

---

129. Trueblood, *Company of the Committed*, 43–44. A more recent advocate of a day per month in solitude is Barton, *Sacred Rhythms*, 156–57 and her *Strengthening the Soul*, 133.

130. Steere, *Together in Solitude*, ix, in reference to his "Solitude and Prayer," in *Together in Solitude*, 89–104. Steere mentions that the article was written for participants of the EIOS in 1980.

those most critical to the development of the SFM, their relationships ended up as key catalysts for the beginning of the movement. For Steere, this was the case through the network of relationships of his EIOS as discussed in chapter 1. Trueblood was a key catalyst for the movement through his relationship with Foster and his role in the publication of *Celebration of Discipline*.

James Bryan Smith reflects on the beginning of the SFM, noting, "It began, in its modern form, in 1978 when Richard Foster wrote what has become the perennially standard text on the spiritual disciplines, *Celebration of Discipline*. Within a few years of its publication, Christians who had never heard of solitude, silence, or meditation were now practicing these disciplines."[131] Trueblood encouraged Foster to write the book, helped to make it possible by commending it to his publisher, and wrote the foreword.[132] Foster devotes a chapter of *Celebration of Discipline* to guidance on the practice of solitude as one of twelve spiritual disciplines he describes as "*central* to experiential Christianity,"[133] and his chapter on solitude includes references to Trueblood, Doherty, and Merton.[134]

As the SFM developed from its transitional phase in the 1970s to its organizational phase in the 1980s and afterward, solitude became a standard emphasis in its publications.[135] In one of the movement's earliest publications after Foster's *Celebration of Discipline* to give a chapter-length treatment to solitude, Dunnam reflects the Mertonian influence on the SFM, not rejecting solitude because it was monastic as many other evangelicals had done, but expanding the dynamics of monastic solitude to all:

> Most of what has been written about solitude has been written from a Roman Catholic perspective. More narrow than that, it

131. Smith, "Techniques without Transformation," 42–48.

132. Foster, *Celebration of Discipline* (1998), x–xi, xvii–xx.

133. Foster, *Celebration of Discipline*, (1998), 1. For Foster's chapter on solitude, see Foster, *Celebration of Discipline*, (1998), 96–109.

134. Foster, *Celebration of Discipline*, (1998), 98, 102, 108, 109.

135. As examples from earlier than 2000, ordered chronologically, see Job, *Journey Toward Solitude*; Dunnam, *Workbook on Spiritual Disciplines*, 113–35; Muto, *Pathways to Spiritual Living*; Willard, *Spirit of the Disciplines*, 160–62; Peterson, *Contemplative Pastor*, 21–23; Whitney, *Spiritual Disciplines*, 173–94; Mulholland, *Invitation to a Journey*, 138–40; Blaising, "Spiritual Formation," 32–34; Westerhoff, *Spiritual Life*, 33–35; Willard, "Spirit is Willing," 230–31; Thompson, *Soul Feast*, 49–50, 80; Thomas, *Sacred Pathways*, 99–119; Ortberg, *Life You've Always Wanted*, 89–96; Tan and Gregg, *Disciplines*, 41–51; Hinson, *Spiritual Preparation*, 149–61.

> has been written from the perspective of the monastic life or the intentional religious community. The common image is that of the austere monk spending most of his time alone in his cell; or more extreme, the religious hermit who has chosen to live completely alone, away from interaction with other persons, outside the physical presence of other people. What such persons do with their solitude may interest us and provide some helpful insights, but it is hardly the model most Christians would even consider pursuing.
>
> Solitude is not only an essential discipline for those of religious orders who take vows of solitude, not only essential for those who live in community, it is a discipline for spiritual growth for all who wish to pursue the Christian life seriously.[136]

Later, Dallas Willard's writings elevated solitude from one among a list of historical disciplines for Christians to practice to being one of "the specific practices that are of most use in the development of disciples,"[137] thereby solidifying solitude's "primacy and priority among the disciplines"[138] and as an emphasis of the SFM. Willard writes,

> We need not be concerned about a complete list of such practices, and indeed there really is no such thing anyway.... What is clear and ... essential is that a small number of them are absolutely central to spiritual growth. They must form a part of the foundation of our whole-life plan for growth as apprentices of Jesus. These are, on the side of abstinence, solitude and silence, and, on the side of positive engagement, study and worship.[139]

CONCLUSION

Gillian Simpson writes in a 2022 article, "The role of solitude in the West has, in the last five decades, been of increasing interest and significance,"[140] which coincides precisely with the development of the SFM as explored in chapter 1. Simpson also comments, "The most influential of recent

---

136. Dunnam, *Workbook on Spiritual Disciplines*, 113–14. Dunnam cites Merton in the chapter on solitude (122–23).

137. Willard, *Divine Conspiracy*, 357.

138. Willard, *Spirit of the Disciplines*, 160.

139. Willard, *Divine Conspiracy*, 357. See his description of the concept of disciplines of abstinence and engagement in Willard, *Spirit of the Disciplines*, 158. See also Willard, "Foreword," 9–11.

140. Simpson, "Solitude and Religion," 121.

Christian advocates of the power of solitude is Thomas Merton ... often regarded as *the* great Christian solitary of our time."[141] As explored in the following chapters, while Merton's influence on Mulholland is much broader than only in reference to solitude, Mulholland's writing on solitude reflects significant learning from Merton, as Mulholland describes solitude not only as "fasting from fellowship with others to be alone with God,"[142] but as an "inner dynamic" and "a deep inner posture of being" one can bring to any discipline.[143] In words that sound like a summary of Merton's lifetime of pursuit of solitude, Mulholland writes,

> Solitude is, in the silence of release, beginning to face the deep inner dynamics of our being that make us that grasping, controlling, manipulative person; beginning to face our brokenness, our distortion, our darkness; and beginning to offer ourselves to God at those points. Solitude is not simply drawing away from others and being alone with God. This is part of solitude. But more than this, it is being who we are with God and acknowledging who we are to ourselves and to God.[144]

Whereas many earlier pietistic evangelicals rejected the approaches to solitude commended in monasteries, solitude is evident as an essential emphasis in the SFM because of Merton's persistent pursuit of true interior and exterior solitude that provided space for his own deep healing and thereby cultivated his capacity for love of God and others. If, as argued in chapter 2, the primary reflection of Wesley's influence in the SFM is the insistence on gathering people into specific kinds of groups, it is ironic that the primary reflection of Merton's work in the movement is the insistence on people spending significant periods of time alone.[145] Yet, as the SFM represents, the two insistences are complementary rather than mutually exclusive, and the next chapter prepares for that consideration by exploring points of synthesis between Merton and Wesley.

141. Simpson, "Solitude and Religion," 126.
142. Mulholland, *Invitation to a Journey*, 136.
143. Mulholland, *Invitation to a Journey*, 136.
144. Mulholland, *Invitation to a Journey*, 138.
145. As highlighted in the comments on Bonhoeffer and Finkenwalde in this project's introduction and on Trueblood and Steere in this chapter, Mulholland and the others who made foundational contributions to the SFM were hardly the first to accept the paradox of these two perspectives. However, juxtaposition of them is especially evident through Wesley and Merton as their respective representatives, and the combination of their influence on the SFM through Mulholland highlights the interrelatedness of both dynamics.

CHAPTER 4

Points of Synthesis Between Wesley and Merton in Spirituality and Theology

THE ARGUMENTS OF THE previous two chapters result in a paradox. Chapter 2 presented Wesleyan pietistic evangelicalism's primary reflection in the SFM as its emphasis on meeting in groups as an essential practice for sanctification, followed by chapter 3's claim that the SFM reflects solitude as essential for holiness due to the influence of Mertonian contemplative monasticism. While the arguments are not strictly incompatible, the antithetical emphases of Wesleyan groups and Mertonian solitude highlight the inherent tensions between Wesley, Merton, and their respective traditions.

Although this project argues that Mulholland and the SFM represent a synthesis of Wesleyan pietistic evangelicalism and Mertonian contemplative monasticism, the comments from Witherington and Willimon in the previous chapter illustrate that the *possible* congruence between the traditions is not a *necessary* congruence. For example, while the Wesleyan path of Shipps and Mulholland led them toward Merton, the trajectories of others within Wesleyan pietistic evangelicalism ardently keeps away from the monastery. The non-monastic, or even anti-monastic, path within Wesleyanism is compatible not only with Wesley's comments about monastic desert spirituality cited in chapter 3 but with most of his writings on Roman Catholicism.[1] Students of Wesley do not have to look far into his writings to encounter his attempts at indictment of Catholicism,

---

1. For a detailed overview of Wesley's writings on Roman Catholicism, see Yates, *Limits*. Several primary sources from Wesley on Roman Catholicism are grouped together in Wesley, *Works* (Jackson), 10:80–177.

such as his identification of "the Romish Papacy" as the beast in the book of Revelation,[2] strategy for the conversion of all Roman Catholics in Ireland,[3] or published denunciations of Roman Catholics including, "I fear many of their principles have a natural tendency to undermine holiness; greatly to hinder, if not utterly to destroy, the essential branches of it,—to destroy the love of God, and the love of our neighbour, with all justice, and mercy, and truth."[4] The quantity and force of such statements in Wesley are sufficient to cause Kelly Diehl Yates to synopsize her thesis on Wesley and Catholicism as "Wesley held a negative view of Catholicism all his life."[5]

Similarly, from the other direction, many readers of Merton quickly encounter evidence that the figurative road from Merton's monastery toward Protestant churches is often equally unamicable. *The Seven Storey Mountain* brought Merton to fame as a writer,[6] and it consistently reflects a scornful attitude toward Protestants, such as his memories of the "practically useless" lessons his father arranged for him to receive from "a little fat Protestant minister"[7] or his backhanded description of a Professor Hering as "one of the few Protestants I ever met who struck one as being at all holy."[8]

Despite this obvious dissociation between Wesley and Merton as individuals representative of the divide between their Protestant and Catholic traditions, this project's thesis is founded on the claim that both of the men had significant influence on the SFM. Therefore, after the

---

2. See Wesley's note on Rev 13:1 in Wesley, *Explanatory Notes*, 728–33.

3. See his "Short Method of Converting" in Wesley, *Works* (Jackson), 10:129–33.

4. See his "Popery Calmly Considered" in Wesley, *Works* (Jackson), 10:155.

5. Yates, *Limits*, 10. Although Wesley's "Catholic Spirit" (*Works* [Jackson], 5:492–504) and "Letter to a Roman Catholic" (*Works* [Jackson], 10:80–85) are viewed as ecumenically inspiring, Yates argues, "'Letter to a Roman Catholic,' due to its irenic nature, is indeed an exception in Wesley's writings on Catholicism" (Yates, *Limits*, 10). She explains, "His pragmatism convinced him of the need to write a document that would hopefully create space for the Methodists to preach in Ireland, but Wesley never accepted that Catholicism was 'true religion'" (Yates, *Limits*, 198). She also argues, "Wesley did not intend the message of *Catholic Spirit* to apply to Catholics," but to fellow Protestants (Yates, *Limits*, 84).

6. Paul M. Pearson notes that the initial planned print run for *Seven Storey Mountain* was five thousand copies, which would have allowed the publisher to break even on the book, but it sold more than six hundred thousand hardback copies in its first year in print. See Pearson, "Extraordinary Success."

7. Merton, *Seven Storey Mountain*, 58.

8. Merton, *Seven Storey Mountain*, 92.

arguments of the previous two chapters highlighting the SFM's juxtaposed reflections of Wesley's pietistic groups and Merton's monastic solitude, this chapter identifies points of synthesis beyond the paradox of their relationship. One piece of evidence that such points exist is, contrary to their opinions of each other's traditions cited above, both men came to be associated with the development of ecumenism in Christianity although neither was committed to ecumenicity as a primary goal.[9] Therefore, the Wesleyan and Mertonian synthesis in the SFM is not a result of direct ecumenical pursuits as if the SFM represents a meeting point halfway on a road between a Methodist society and a Trappist monastery. Instead, it is more accurate to see Wesley and Merton as each advancing the streams of their respective Christian traditions with confluence between some of those streams' subsequent tributaries. The SFM is a significant result of such confluence.

This chapter explores the major points of synthesis between Wesley and Merton in spirituality and theology, considered within the framework of Wesley's often-repeated references to 2 Tim 3:5, indicating his ongoing concern for an approach to Christianity that has both the *form* and *power* of godliness.[10] First, significant synthesis in spirituality is evident between Wesley and Merton regarding the form, as Wesley's Methodism and Merton's monasticism can both be seen as examples of the spirituality of religious orders. Second, this synthesis in spirituality's form is based on parallel synthesis in theology, as Wesley and Merton utilize varying language to offer corresponding descriptions of holiness empowered by God's sanctifying grace. Finally, the points of synthesis are applied in an analysis of Wesley's and Merton's mutual rejection of the theology and spirituality of quietism.

---

9. Hinson writes, "Thomas Merton cannot be classified as an ecumenist in any of the customary senses of the word." See Hinson, "Expansive Catholicism," 290. There are numerous examples characterizing Wesley as an ecumenist; for two from Wesleyan scholars that are of interest because of their relationship with Merton, see Shipps, "Post-Reformation Trends," 8–14; Stanger, "Methodism's Ecumenical Perspective," 21–48. On Merton and the ecumenical movement, see Hinson, "Expansive Catholicism," 290–304; Paulsell, *Merton and the Protestant*; Paulsell, "Ecumenical Dimension," 176–84.

10. For examples, see chapter 2.

SYNTHESIS IN SPIRITUALITY: THE FORM OF RELIGIOUS ORDERS

Although the previous chapter emphasized Merton's insistence on and pursuit of solitude, one of his primary frustrations with his life as a monk was the highly regimented communal nature of life in cenobitic monasticism.[11] As a member of the Order of the Cistercians of the Strict Observance, Merton's Trappist context is a direct descendant of Benedictine monasticism, and while the *Rule of St. Benedict* prescribes solitude for each member of the community, it does so as "a practical guide . . . for living the gospel and for cultivating Christian virtues in the daily life of the monastic community."[12] Benedict's *Rule* is "the most influential document in the entire history of Western monasticism,"[13] but the Benedictines and their descendants are not the only examples of monastic communities whose efforts toward sanctification were ordered around a shared rule of life.[14]

Although W. Paul Jones does not directly address points of synthesis between Wesley and Merton, his work is a unique reference because of his background as a scholar who became a Trappist monk after more than forty years as a United Methodist pastor "because he found in Trappist spirituality a powerful parallel to the Wesleyan movement."[15] He identifies three types of discipline he claims are foundational to all religious orders and equally as descriptive of Methodists, Trappists, and other traditional orders: spiritual direction, rule of life, and canon law.[16]

Spiritual Direction

Regarding spiritual direction, W. Paul Jones describes a variety of definitions and types and summarizes, "Spiritual direction is the key method

---

11. See chapter 3.
12. Okholm, "Rule of St. Benedict," 723–24.
13. Fry, *RB 1980*, 65.
14. The rules of Basil, Augustine, and Benedict became the common standards in monasticism. For a detailed survey, see Fry, *RB 1980*, 3–83.
15. Jones, *Art of Spiritual Direction*, 299; Ruffle, "Going Deeper."
16. Jones, *Art of Spiritual Direction*, 79–81. He uses "rules" rather than "rule of life," but this project uses the latter for internal consistency of terminology and because this is the form of the term that became prevalent in SFM literature.

for providing supportive accountability for growth in grace."[17] Merton roots spiritual direction in the history of monasticism, and his definition of spiritual direction aligns with Wesley's description of the purpose of the Methodist societies in his prefacing comments to Methodism's "General Rules." Merton writes that spiritual direction is "a continuous process of formation and guidance, in which a Christian is led and encouraged *in his special vocation*, so that by faithful correspondence to the graces of the Holy Spirit he may attain to the particular end of his vocation and to union with God."[18] Merton's conception of spiritual direction evidences a shared aim with Wesley's description of the structure and purpose of his societies and classes:

> A society is no other than "a company of men having the form and seeking the power of godliness, united in order to pray together, to receive the word of exhortation, and to watch over one another in love, that they may help each other work out their salvation." That it may be more easily discerned, whether they are indeed working out their own salvation, each society is divided into smaller companies, called *classes*, according to their respective places of abode.[19]

Wesley then clarifies that each class was to have one leader, whose primary responsibility was "to see each person in his class once a week at least, in order ... to inquire how their souls prosper."[20] Although Wesley never characterized this dynamic of early Methodism with the term spiritual direction,[21] due to the significant alignment between Wesley's aims

---

17. Jones, *Art of Spiritual Direction*, 78. See *Art of Spiritual Direction*, 7–24 for his overview of types and definitions of spiritual direction. His conception of spiritual direction is broader than that of many other texts on the topic. For example, a standard text is Barry and Connolly, *Practice of Spiritual Direction*, which defines spiritual direction as "help given by one Christian to another which enables that person to pay attention to God's personal communication to him or her, to respond to this personally communicating God, to grow in intimacy with this God, and to live out the consequences of this relationship" (*Practice of Spiritual Direction*, 8).

18. Merton, *Spiritual Direction and Meditation*, 13. Elsewhere, Merton offers a similar definition: "Spiritual direction is the art of guiding Christians to their proper interior and exterior perfection according to their particular vocation as manifested by their gifts, capabilities, ideals, duties of state and above all, by their place in God's plan for his church." See Merton, "Spiritual Direction," 6.

19. Wesley, *Bicentennial Works*, 9:69–70.

20. Wesley, *Bicentennial Works*, 9:70.

21. What Wesley D. Tracy states of holiness churches in the Wesleyan tradition is reflective of Wesley's terminology: "The holiness churches vigorously seek the goals of spiritual direction, but spiritual direction per se is not a common part of their

and those of spiritual direction in monastic communities, W. Paul Jones concludes, "The essence of the Wesleyan movement was disciplined care of souls. And, characteristic of an order, every member was supposed to be under spiritual direction. So essential was this that Wesley forbade his preachers to preach anywhere that communal spiritual direction would not be available when they left."[22]

Rule of Life

Regarding the rule of life, W. Paul Jones writes that it "functions as the group's reason for being, to which spiritual direction is to hold each person accountable."[23] He clarifies that in Trappist life, "several documents . . . serve compositely as the rule." These are: "The *Rule of Saint Benedict*, the Charter of Charity (inaugurating the founding), the Constitutions and Statutes of the order, and the House Rules of the particular monastery."[24] Because the Trappists were founded on a goal of "strict observance" of the *Rule of St. Benedict*, the *Rule* was the foundation of Merton's spirituality and the context in which his personal growth and his efforts at monastic renewal took place. The *Rule* is so central to Merton's Trappist life that he writes, "It is in the *Rule* and in the person of Benedict that we find the spirit, the 'form' without which no monk can truly call himself a Benedictine."[25] Merton also emphasizes the role of Benedict's *Rule* in ordering monastic life toward its intended end: "St. Benedict in his *Rule* makes it quite clear that the whole aim of the Benedictine life is to form Christ in us."[26]

Likewise, Kevin M. Watson states that Wesley's "General Rules" was "a practical guide to holiness" and "the crucial document that defined what was expected of every Methodist."[27] As explored in chapter 2, Wesley

---

vocabulary." See Tracy, "Spiritual Direction," 115.

22. Jones, *Art of Spiritual Direction*, 79.
23. Jones, *Art of Spiritual Direction*, 79.
24. Jones, *Art of Spiritual Direction*, 80–81. Emphasis added.
25. Merton, *Silent Life*, 36. Emphasis added.
26. Merton, *Basic Principles*, 67. Emphasis added.
27. Watson, *Pursuing Social Holiness*, 41. As W. Paul Jones indicates that other documents in addition to Benedict's *Rule* constitute the rule of life of Trappists, so also with Methodists. The "General Rules" is the primary document, with others supplementing it. Jones identifies the Articles of Religion, Wesley's *Explanatory Notes*, *A Collection of Hymns for the Use of the People Called Methodist*, and the "Large Minutes" (*Art of Spiritual Direction*, 81). Wesley's "Rules of the Band" (Wesley, *Bicentennial Works*, 9:77–78)

inherited from the previous tradition of pietist *ecclesiolae* the approach of adherence to a common rule of life, and in the case of earlier pietists and Wesley, their adaptations are best seen as modifications for their contexts of the adherence of monastic orders to their respective rules.[28] In Wesley's design, it was no more possible for one of his early Methodists to choose to disregard the "General Rules" and remain a Methodist than it would be for Merton to remain a monk while dispensing himself from Benedict's *Rule*.

As Benedictine communities have inherent accountability to the *Rule* through the authority of the abbots, Wesley's class meetings functioned similarly for the early Methodists. David Lowes Watson describes, "As Wesley introduced and developed them, the classes exercised accountability for the *General Rules* as well as for inward spiritual growth."[29]

Canon Law

Finally, W. Paul Jones notes that religious orders function under canon law (as would renewal movements) rather than apart from it (as would separating denominations).[30] Trappist life in general and Merton's biography within it are obvious examples of monastic orders functioning

---

and "Directions Given" (Wesley, *Bicentennial Works*, 9:79) should also be considered.

28. This relationship is evident in one of the most influential criticisms of pietism, which is in Ritschl, *Die Geschichte des Pietismus*. Olson and Collins Winn note, "Ritschl's complaint against Pietism was summed up in the second volume, where he described it as 'non-Lutheran in character, more precisely expressed, an attempt to resurrect medieval monasticism outside the cloisters.' Ritschl's main accusation was that Pietism was more Catholic than Protestant in character." See Olson and Collins Winn, *Reclaiming Pietism*, 13. They cite and translate Ritschl, *Die Geschichte des Pietismus*, 2:417. Yeide also notes that Ritschl was opposed to "certain organizational similarities between pietism and earlier monasticism" (*Studies in Classical Pietism*, 32). Further, while Moravian pietism at Herrnhut can be seen as a monastic experiment adapted to a Protestant context, Wesley's societies, classes, and bands refined the adaptation as "materially he left his followers in their original situations," allowing for accountability and mutual personal knowledge without relocating them into a new physical location. See Schmidt, *John Wesley*, 99; Watson, *Early Methodist Class Meeting*, 86. Schmidt notes that this "ensured that his movement not only had the possibility of developing within the regular structure of the national Church, but he saved it from many of the weaknesses which necessarily resulted from the improvised and essentially experimental character" of Moravian pietism (Schmidt, *John Wesley*, 99).

29. Watson, *Early Methodist Class Meeting*, 115–16. He adds, "It is a serious, though common, error to assume that they were intended primarily for fellowship. Nothing could be further from the truth."

30. Jones, *Art of Spiritual Direction*, 81.

under the canons of Roman Catholicism. Merton's journals are replete with examples of his obedience (sometimes with willingness and other times with great disagreement) to his superiors within and beyond his Trappist order.[31]

Early Methodism, however, is less distinctly characterized as functioning under the canons of the Church of England.[32] Nevertheless, the general principle of functioning for renewal within a church rather than in rebellion against it or separation from it is visible in pietism's distinguishing characteristic adopted by Wesley of *ecclesiola in ecclesia* explored in chapter 2.[33] Somewhat against his fundamental wishes, however, Wesley eventually agreed for the Methodists in America to separate from the Church of England. Thus, the Anglican canons were no longer authoritative, and the Methodists needed their own ecclesial regulations, which became known as the *Book of Discipline*. W. Paul Jones comments,

> It is possible to map the movement of Methodism from being an order within a church to functioning as a church by observing the degree to which the *regula* [the *Discipline* as a rule of life] became of "historic interest" and *The Book of Discipline* became almost totally a book of canon law. This shift has entailed a loss of Methodism's originating genius as rooted in a firm systemic base for spiritual formation through corporate and personal spiritual direction. Taking its place is Methodism's present genius for polity, the primary rule tending to be legal regulations for institutional ordering. This identifies the dilemma of most modern churches as well—what has been lost is a basic discipline for daily, personal spiritual life, nurtured by

---

31. Apel, "'Who Stands,'" 3–10.

32. For most of his life, Wesley was careful to have his societies, classes, and bands function as *ecclesiolae* rather than separating from the Church of England, but it is an overstatement to claim that early Methodism operated under the Anglican canons. See Campbell, "Are United Methodists Reaping." This may also be true of other pietist *ecclesiolae* which functioned with commitments to renew their existing churches but may not have been officially endorsed nor desired by those churches. Nevertheless, W. Paul Jones's point is valuable because his emphasis is not the extent to which Wesley did or did not abide by canon law, but how Methodism's *Book of Discipline* is indicative of contemporary United Methodism's existence as a denomination and differs fundamentally from its beginning as an *ecclesiola in ecclesia*.

33. Accordingly, see Yeide, *Studies in Classical Pietism*, 32–34, in which he explores similarities between monasticism and pietist *ecclesiolae*. He concludes, "Quite a few of the monastic orders that antedate pietism might profitably be examined as ecclesiolae."

spiritual direction within a structure that provides supportive accountability."³⁴

The Common Form: Early Methodism as a Religious Order

W. Paul Jones's observations on the disciplines of spiritual direction, rule of life, and canon law are not intended as an exhaustive analysis of the characteristics of religious orders, yet as a summary, they provide a substantive perspective from which to consider similarities in spirituality between Methodists and Trappists in general, and spirituality inclusive of the same disciplines as a major point of synthesis between Wesley and Merton. In addition to the congruencies experienced between his Methodist background and his current Trappist order, Jones finds a particularly close comparison between Franciscans and the early Methodists.³⁵ Drawing on Ernst Troelstch's identification of the "church-type" and "sect-type,"³⁶ he notes,

> The genius of the Wesleyan movement is that it forged a way by which the sect-type can function creatively within a church-type context. The renewal of Christianity today is likely to depend on our ability to do precisely this. The way in which the Wesleyan movement was able to accomplish this was by becoming an evangelical order within a Catholic (Anglican) context.... An example of a religious order comparable to the Wesleyan movement is the Franciscans. Here there is a "first order" (monks), a "second order" (nuns), and a "third order" (laypersons living a spiritually disciplined way within ordinary societal life). This Franciscan "third order" ... functions in a manner comparable to how Methodism desired to function within Anglicanism.... The Wesleyan "third order" was a creative conduit for monastic spirituality.³⁷

---

34. Jones, *Art of Spiritual Direction*, 81. His bracketed section in his statement implies that the Methodist *Book of Discipline* originally served as a rule of life for Methodists, which is not true. American Methodists first created a "Form of Discipline" when they became an independent church, succeeding the previous British *Minutes* (Heitzenrater, *Wesley and the People*, 324). Nevertheless, his general point about the development from *regula* to canon law is valid. For further perspectives of this critical development in Methodism's history, see Jones, *Art of Spiritual Direction*, 77–78; Watson, *Early Methodist Class Meeting*, 134–37; Harris, "Peculiar Difficulty."

35. Jones, *Art of Spiritual Direction*, 75–81.

36. See Troelstch, *Social Teaching*, 1:331–43.

37. Jones, *Art of Spiritual Direction*, 76–77. Although the characterization of early

Without any need to force a synthesis by overidentifying Wesleyan and Mertonian spiritualities, the fruits of Wesley's draw from monastic tradition and that of the openness Merton developed toward the world from within his monastery result in remarkable congruities. The common "form of godliness" commended by Wesley to his early Methodists and inherited by Merton from his tradition in Benedictine monasticism is summarized as spirituality centered on a rule of life consisting of disciplines cultivating sanctification of members in high-commitment community, and the historic impacts of both men can be interpreted from this perspective: Wesley's impact was largely a result of his ability to draw this spirituality out from monastic tradition to the public, and Merton's impact resulted from his ability to extend this monastic spirituality to the public from within the abbey.

SYNTHESIS IN THEOLOGY: THE POWER OF PERFECTING GRACE

Wesley is regarded by some as "the father of a robust doctrine of sanctification,"[38] and he is therefore closely associated with related terms such as holiness and Christian perfection in the development of historical theology.[39] Rex D. Matthews summarizes, "The single most consistent

---

Methodism as a religious order is not widespread among scholars, Jones is not alone. See also Heath and Kisker, *Longing for Spring*, 32–37, 41; Outler, *John Wesley*, 307; Nelson, "John Wesley," 19–20. Watson, *Early Methodist Class Meeting*, 135–36.

38. Rieger, "Sanctification," 459. Thomas C. Oden provides context for the perceived prevalence of sanctification as a theme in Wesley: "Since the teaching of sanctification is found abundantly in the ancient church tradition, it is viewed as a unique Wesleyan distinctive only by those inattentive to the patristic writers. It is also found persistently in all the classic Reformers—Luther, Calvin, and the Anglican formularies as well as the Puritan and Pietistic writers. Emphasis on this doctrine became a leading feature of the Wesleyan legacy in the evangelical revival. . . . One does an injustice to Wesley by viewing all his teaching in the light of this single point, yet those who disregard it miss something crucial in Wesley." See Oden, *John Wesley's Teachings*, 2:237. This is reflective of Wesley's description of the place of holiness in his doctrine in relation to repentance and faith: "Our main doctrines, which include all the rest, are three,—that of repentance, of faith, and of holiness. The first of these we account, as it were, the porch of religion; the next, the door; the third, religion itself." See Wesley, *Works* (Jackson), 8:472.

39. While technical distinctions can be made between sanctification and its synonyms, Wesley and Merton used various synonyms interchangeably, and this chapter also does so for brevity and consistency with the authors. Such terms include "sanctification," "sanctity," "saint," "holiness," "perfection," "Christian perfection," "spiritual perfection," "entire sanctification," "full salvation," and "perfect love." Merton's most frequently-used, related term, which is explored below and is echoed often in the SFM

theme in John Wesley's thought over the entire span of his life and ministry was 'holiness of heart and life' (or more simply, 'holy living')."[40]

Conversely, even though sanctification is an overarching theme of Merton's life and writings and inclusive of all of the others that he directly and frequently addresses (such as contemplation, solitude, monasticism, and social conflicts), sanctification is not a subject often directly examined in Merton's works by others. For example, whereas there are dozens of theses and dissertations on Wesley and sanctification, there are none to date on Merton and sanctification even though holiness can be seen as the core around which his corpus is built. This is evidenced in the centrality of his desire for sanctity as his foundational motive to become and remain a monk. In *Seven Storey Mountain*, Merton recalls a pivotal conversation with Robert Lax prior to his decision to enter monastic life:

> One of those times that turned out to be historical, as far as my own soul is concerned, was when Lax and I were walking down Sixth Avenue, one night in the spring. . . . I forget what we were arguing about, but in the end Lax suddenly turned around and asked me the question:
> "What do you want to be, anyway?"
> I could not say, "I want to be Thomas Merton the well-known writer of all those book reviews in the back pages of the *Times Book Review*," or "Thomas Merton the assistant instructor of Freshman-English at the New Life Social Institute for Progress and Culture," so I put the thing on the spiritual plane, where I knew it belonged and said:
> "I don't know; I guess what I want is to be a good Catholic."
> "What do you mean, you want to be a good Catholic?"
> The explanation I gave was lame enough, and expressed my confusion, and betrayed how little I had really thought about it at all.
> Lax did not accept it.
> "What you should say"—he told me—"what you should say is that you want to be a saint."
> A saint! The thought struck me as a little weird. I said:
> "How do you expect me to become a saint?"
> "By wanting to," said Lax, simply.
> "I can't be a saint," I said, "I can't be a saint." And my mind darkened with a confusion of realities and unrealities: the

---

literature of Mulholland and others, is "true self." On the variety of synonymous terms in Wesley, see Lindström, *Wesley and Sanctification*, 127.

40. Matthews, "John Wesley's Idea," 30.

> knowledge of my own sins, and the false humility which makes men say that they cannot do the things that they *must* do, cannot reach the level that they *must* reach: the cowardice that says: "I am satisfied to save my soul, to keep out of mortal sin," but which means, by those words: "I do not want to give up my sins and my attachments."
>
> But Lax said: "No. All that is necessary to be a saint is to want to be one. Don't you believe that God will make you what He created you to be, if you will consent to let Him do it? All you have to do is desire it."
>
> A long time ago, St. Thomas Aquinas had said the same thing—and it is something that is obvious to everybody who ever understood the Gospels. After Lax was gone, I thought about it, and it became obvious to me.[41]

Ten years later, in his seventh year at Gethsemani, Merton continues to describe his life and vocation as a pursuit of sanctification:

> Writing, far from being an obstacle to spiritual perfection in my own life, has become one of the conditions on which my perfection will depend. If I am to be a saint—and there is nothing else that I can think of desiring to be—it seems that I must get there by writing books in a Trappist monastery. If I am to be a saint, I have not only to be a monk, which is what all monks must do to become saints, but I must also put down on paper what I have become. It may sound simple, but it is not an easy vocation. To be as good a monk as I can, and to remain myself, and to write about it . . . this is very hard, because I am all mixed up in illusions and attachments.[42]

In Merton's classes for monastic novices, he identifies "the sanctification of monks" as Benedict's "distinct mission,"[43] reflecting the common aim with Wesley's societies, classes, and bands as explored in chapter 2. However, even though it is clear that sanctification is the common goal of Wesley's Methodism and Merton's monasticism, they wrote of sanctification in response to different issues and using distinctive language. Therefore, consideration of sanctification as a theological point of synthesis between them requires further examination of their commentary.

---

41. Merton, *Seven Storey Mountain*, 260–61. According to the sequence of events in *Seven Storey Mountain*, the conversation with Lax would have been in 1939.

42. Merton, *Entering the Silence*, 365.

43. Merton, *Rule of Saint Benedict*, 9.

Merton's writings that directly address sanctification repeatedly cite Thomas Aquinas, whose perspective provides a helpful additional reference point.[44] Edgardo A. Colón-Emeric examines understandings of Christian perfection in the writings of Aquinas and Wesley. Among the shared "central aspects of their doctrines,"[45] he includes "first perfection and the image of God," "the universal call to Christian (second) perfection," "perfection in love," and "freedom from sin."[46] Evidence of these aspects provides a sufficient framework for viewing sanctification as a major point of theological synthesis between Wesley and Merton. It is considered below in sections focusing on holiness as, first, intended for everyone, second, centered on love, and, third, fulfillment of purpose. For brevity, rather than attempting to survey the authors on the breadth of sanctification, the focus here is primarily on the "cognate goal" of holy living, Christian perfection.[47]

Holiness Intended for "All"

Wesley states his belief that God brought the Methodists into being "not to form any new sect; but to reform the nation, particularly the Church, and to spread scriptural holiness over the land."[48] This is reflective of his conviction that full sanctification is available to everyone, emphasized in the "paradigm expression" of the Wesleyan understanding of Christian

---

44. For example, see Merton, *Life and Holiness*, 111–12, 115; Merton, "Perfection, Christian," 8:331; Merton, *New Man*, 75.

45. Colón-Emeric, *Wesley, Aquinas*, 150. Relating to the general centrality of perfection in the two, he comments, "The perfection of the human provides Aquinas with the organizing principle for the structure of the *Summa Theologiae* and Wesley with his missiological imperative. Thus, to study Wesley and Aquinas through this doctrine is to go to the heart of their respective theologies" (Colón-Emeric, *Wesley, Aquinas*, 4).

46. Colón-Emeric, *Wesley, Aquinas*, 151–62. His heading for the first of these is "The Universal Call to Christian (Second) Perfection," noting, "When applied to human beings in this life, Aquinas' *perfectio secunda* and Wesley's Christian perfection are basically synonymous expressions" (*Wesley, Aquinas*, 151). His full list consists of six themes and three "central aspects of their doctrines": first, image of God, which he divides into two, "first perfection and the image of God" and "the universal call to Christian (Second) Perfection; second, love; and, third, sin. Then he also considers three "supporting elements": the life of the virtues, assurance, and merit (*Wesley, Aquinas*, 150–81).

47. Matthews, "John Wesley's Idea," 30.

48. Wesley, *Works* (Jackson), 8:299.

perfection in the renowned hymn Wesley published by his brother, Charles:[49]

> Love divine, all loves excelling, / Joy of heaven to earth come down
> Fix in us thy humble dwelling, / All thy faithful mercies crown!
> Jesus, thou art all compassion: / Pure unbounded love thou art;
> Visit us with thy salvation; / Enter every trembling heart.
>
> Breathe, O breathe thy loving Spirit, / Into every troubled breast;
> Let us all in thee inherit, / Let us find that Second Rest:
> Take away our bent to sinning, / Alpha and Omega be,
> End of faith, as its beginning, / Set our hearts at liberty.
>
> Come, Almighty to deliver, / Let us all thy grace receive:
> Suddenly return, and never, / Never more thy temples leave:
> Thee we would be always blessing: / Serve thee as thy hosts above:
> Pray, and praise thee without ceasing, / Glory in thy perfect love.
>
> Finish, then, thy new creation, / Pure and spotless let us be;
> Let us see thy great salvation, / Perfectly restor'd in thee.
> Chang'd from glory into glory, / Till in heaven we take our place:
> Till we cast our crowns before thee, / Lost in wonder, love, and praise![50]

Each of the four verses is a prayer that God's work in human hearts would be realized fully rather than partially (including the lines "all thy faithful mercies crown," "let us all in thee inherit," "let us all thy grace receive," and "finish, then, thy new creation"). The hymn's five uses of the word "all" highlight the plea for the full extent of God's work to be realized. Additionally, three of the uses of "all," when paired with the two uses of "every," indicate a double meaning of "all," revealing the hymn as not only a prayer that God's work would be fully complete, but that it would be so in everyone.[51] For example, the double meaning could expand "let

49. Ogden, "Love Divine," 237.

50. This is the text as edited and published by Wesley in 1779. See Wesley, *Collection of Hymns*, 368–69. For the original lyrics as written by Charles, compare Wesley, *Hymns for Those*, 13–14. For analysis of the edits, see Ogden, "Love Divine," 237–38. Two edits are particularly significant: rather than John's "take away our bent to sinning," Charles originally had, "take away our power of sinning," and rather than "pure and spotless let us be," the original said, "pure and sinless let us be." These edits are indicative both of the agreement between the Wesley brothers that Christian perfection meant freedom from sin and disagreement between them over the meaning of that freedom. For more on John's and Charles's varying views of perfection, see Matthews, "John Wesley's Idea," 32–37.

51. This insight is indebted to Victor P. Hamilton, who notes the frequency of "all"

us all in thee inherit" less poetically into "let every one of us inherit all that you intend."

Merton concurs that holiness is intended for all. He writes, "Every man has a special and even perilous vocation to complete the supreme work of art which is his sanctification."[52] Implicit in Merton's extension of solitude and contemplation beyond the monastic life is that the holiness to which the practices are conducive is not intended for monks only, but for everyone. Merton writes, "If we are called by God to holiness of life, and if holiness is beyond our natural power to achieve (which it certainly is) then it follows that God himself must give us the light, the strength, and the courage to fulfill the task he requires of us. He will certainly give us the grace we need. If we do not become saints it is because we do not avail ourselves of his gift."[53]

Indicative of this agreement, Wesley and Merton both see full sanctification of the Christian as standard rather than extraordinary. Colón-Emeric observes of Wesley, "He is convinced that at the conclusion of the life of grace, saints are the norm and the 'average Christian' is the exception."[54] Merton states the same principle unequivocally: "The fact that real holiness is uncommon does not mean that it is abnormal. Sanctity is the only normal development of the Christian's baptismal vocation. It can be said, in fact, that the Christian who is not a saint is abnormal, because he is not what he is intended to be."[55]

Perfection in Love

Mildred Bangs Wynkoop observes,

> Wesley's thought is like a great rotunda with archway entrances all around it. No matter which one is entered, it always leads to the central Hall of Love, where, looking upward toward the dome, one gazes into the endless, inviting sky. There is no ceiling to love. The return flow of love back through each doctrine

---

in Wesleyan hymns. He comments, "In almost all of Charles' hymns, he uses that word repeatedly. I think that is partly due to his separating himself from the strict Calvinism of his day that limited Christ's saving atonement to the elect" (Hamilton, email message to author, January 7, 2013). See also Oden, *John Wesley's Teachings*, 2:238.

52. Merton, *Spiritual Direction and Meditation*, 16.
53. Merton, *Life and Holiness*, 17.
54. Colón-Emeric, *Wesley, Aquinas*, 55.
55. Merton, "Perfection, Christian," 8:328.

in preaching and life serves to link every doctrine together into one dynamic architectonic and to show the theological stature and integrity of John Wesley.[56]

In none of Wesley's doctrines is this more immediately evident than in his descriptions of Christian perfection, epitomized by his statement, "This is the sum of Christian perfection: it is all comprised in that one word, Love."[57] In *A Plain Account of Christian Perfection*, Wesley describes a "ground of . . . a thousand mistakes" as

> the not considering deeply, that love is the highest gift of God; humble, gentle, patient love; that all visions, revelations, manifestations whatever, are little things compared to love; and that all the gifts above-mentioned are either the same with, or infinitely inferior to, it. It were well you should be thoroughly sensible of this,—"the heaven of heavens is love." There is nothing higher in religion; there is, in effect, nothing else; if you look for anything but more love, you are looking wide of the mark, you are getting out of the royal way. And when you are asking others, "Have you received this or that blessing?" if you mean anything but more love, you mean wrong; you are leading them out of the way, and putting them upon a false scent. Settle it then in your heart, that from the moment God has saved you from all sin, you are to aim at nothing more, but more of that love described in the thirteenth of the Corinthians."[58]

Merton's emphasis on love is just as grand. He writes, "The perfection of life is spiritual love. And Christianity believes so firmly in the power of love, in the Holy Spirit, that it asserts divine love can even overcome death. And it risks death in order to experience the fulness of life."[59] Chapter 3 explored the paradox of love as a central motive in Merton's desire for solitude, and his comments on love and sanctification (for both of which he saw solitude as essential) are strikingly communal in emphasis, contrary to the caricature of an isolated monk. He writes, "Love is our

---

56. Wynkoop, *Theology of Love*, 22.
57. Wesley, *Works* (Jackson), 6:413.
58. Wesley, *Works* (Jackson), 11:430.
59. Merton, *New Man*, 13. O'Connell notes that Merton read and was impacted by Bernard of Clairvaux's *On Loving God* during his first visit to Gethsemani, and "his own reflections on love, as rich and varied as they are throughout his life, are deeply grounded in his Cistercian heritage." See O'Connell, "Love," 268.

true destiny. We do not find the meaning of life by ourselves alone—we find it with another."[60]

As in the quotation just cited, although Merton is paradigmatic among twentieth-century writers for the desert spirituality and pursuit of solitude that Wesley attacks in his preface to *Sacred Hymns and Poems*, Merton's view of love and sanctification exemplifies Wesley's ultimate emphasis in that preface: "The gospel of Christ knows of no religion, but social; no holiness but social holiness."[61] Merton's perspective is parallel with Wesley's, but stated with terminology from Merton's Catholicism:

> Attention must be drawn to the error of individualism which neglects the truth that Christian perfection is a participation in the life of the Mystical Body of Christ, His Church. Sanctity is never a purely individual affair in which a Christian, working and striving in isolation from the Church, arrives at heroic virtue and attains a reward which is for himself alone. The fulfillment of the law is love of one's brother in Christ (Romans 13:10). The saint lives not for himself but for Christ and for his brother in Christ. His life and love are not oriented to his own perfection alone but to the perfection of the whole Christ, that is, the Church (Ephesians 4:15,16). Furthermore the holiness of the Christian is not the result of his own efforts alone, but primarily of grace and love which are communicated to him in and through the Church.[62]

Wesley and Merton also concur that this dynamic perfection in love,[63] rather than an absolute perfectionism that neither advocates, is the ultimate sense of holiness. Wesley's conviction, "Christian perfection . . . does not imply . . . an exemption either from ignorance or mistake, or infirmities or temptations,"[64] is reflected in Merton: "In Christian sanctity, a certain human weakness and imperfection are altogether compatible with the perfect love of God, as long as one acquires humility from the experience of his own wretchedness and thus learns to place an ever more total and perfect trust in the grace of God."[65]

60. Merton, *Love and Living*, 27.
61. Wesley, *Works* (Jackson), 14:319–21. See chapter 3 above.
62. Merton, "Perfection, Christian," 8:332.
63. For dynamic versus static views of perfection, see Colón-Emeric, *Wesley, Aquinas*, 1–3, 78–80, 98.
64. Wesley, *Works* (Jackson), 6:5.
65. Merton, *Life and Holiness*, 112. See chapter 5 for Mulholland's interpretation of Wesley's doctrine of Christian perfection and its relation to Merton as a flawed but

Understanding the Wesleyan and Mertonian emphasis on love as the sum of Christian perfection is key to understanding how both authors see flaws in the lives of saints as fully compatible with the biblical injunction to be perfect. Matthews comments, "This seems to be a very *imperfect* sort of 'perfection.' The paradox is that 'perfection' as Wesley understood it could co-exist with 'imperfections' or infirmities of various kinds, since its essence is an unbroken relationship of love of God and neighbor."[66]

For Wesley, this results in emphasis on the centrality of the will as the locus of sanctification.[67] In this view, holiness is a consistency of choice of love of God and neighbor. John R. Tyson notes,

> John Wesley persistently defined Christian Perfection in terms of loving God with all one's heart, mind, and strength, and loving one's neighbor as oneself (Matt. 22:37–39). This purity of intention is a consistent Christian maturity ("perfection, or "wholeness"), which fulfills God's law through love and does not willfully violate a known law of God. Intentional sin ceases to dominate and determine our lives as we are being filled and transformed by God's love.[68]

Therefore, sin for Wesley is an intentional choice of something other than love of God and love of others,[69] and while humans never outgrow

---

loving human.

66. Matthews, "John Wesley's Idea," 34.

67. See Wesley, *Bicentennial Works*, 1:398–414.

68. Tyson, *Way of the Wesleys*, 103.

69. Wesley describes his understanding of the relation of the human need for atonement, to sin, the will, and love: "The best of men still need Christ in his priestly office, to atone for their omissions, their short-comings, (as some not improperly speak,) their mistakes in judgment and practice, and their defects of various kinds. For these are all deviations from the perfect law, and consequently need an atonement. Yet that they are not properly sins, we apprehend may appear from the words of St. Paul, 'He that liveth hath fulfilled the law; for love is the fulfilling of the law.' (Rom. xiii. 10.) Now, mistakes, and whatever infirmities necessarily flow from the corruptible state of the body, are noway contrary to love; nor therefore, in the Scripture sense, sin. To explain myself a little farther on this head: 1. Not only sin, properly so called, (that is, a voluntary transgression of a known law,) but sin, improperly so called, (that is, an involuntary transgression of a divine law, known or unknown,) needs the atoning blood. 2. I believe there is no such perfection in this life as excludes these involuntary transgressions which I apprehend to be naturally consequent on the ignorance and mistakes inseparable from mortality. 3. Therefore *sinless perfection* is a phrase I never use, lest I should seem to contradict myself. 4. I believe, a person filled with the love of God is still liable to these involuntary transgressions. 5. Such transgressions you may call sins, if you please: I do

their capacity for making errors in judgment, God's grace consistently works in everyone to bring them to the point of "the humble, gentle, patient love of God and man ruling all the tempers, words, actions" of a person.[70] Likewise for Merton: "Sin is the will to do what God does not will, to know what He does not know, to love what He does not love."[71]

This emphasis on relational love as the guiding center of a holy life coinciding with the human capacity for mistakes is captured in a prayer written by Merton after fifteen years in the monastery:

> My Lord God, I have no idea where I am going. I do not see the road ahead of me. I cannot know for certain where it will end. Nor do I really know myself, and the fact that I think I am following your will does not mean that I am actually doing so. But I believe that the desire to please you does in fact please you. And I hope I have that desire in all that I am doing. I hope that I will never do anything apart from that desire. And I know that if I do this you will lead me by the right road, though I may know nothing about it. Therefore I will trust you always though I may seem to be lost and in the shadow of death. I will not fear, for you are ever with me, and you will never leave me to face my perils alone.[72]

Perfect Love as Fulfillment of Creation

While Merton's belief that "the desire to please [God] does in fact please [God]"[73] is reflective of the Wesleyan concept of perfection in love centered in the will, this does not limit Christian perfection to a matter of good intention. Rather, holy love of God and others is the path to women and men being what they were created to be. Wynkoop concludes *A Theology of Love* by stating, "God wants us, in this life, to live fully, creatively. Being good is not simply *not doing things*, but living out the dynamic

---

not, for the reasons above-mentioned." See Wesley, *Works* (Jackson), 11:396.

70. Wesley, *Letters*, 5:38–39.

71. Merton, *No Man*, 75. Wynkoop also understands a Wesleyan view of sin as misdirected love. She writes, "It is Wesley's emphasis on love that becomes the key not only to the meaning of holiness but also to the meaning of sin. Sin is love, but love gone astray. . . . Sin is love locked into a false center, the self. . . . Sin is the distortion of love. . . . Holiness is love locked into the True Center, Jesus Christ our Lord" (*Theology of Love*, 165).

72. Merton, *Thoughts in Solitude*, 79.

73. Merton, *Thoughts in Solitude*, 79.

of God's purpose."⁷⁴ The two characteristics of Christian perfection explored above (first, as a universal call, and, second, centered on love of God and one another) locate this doctrine in a theology of God as loving creator and humans as beloved creations with love at the center of the purpose of their creation.

Gordon T. Smith grounds the doctrine of perfection in this sense of fulfillment of purpose:

> To be complete in Christ, to be "perfect," is quite simply to be what one has been created to be. To say "simply," though, is to miss the force and beauty of perfection. When an engine runs exquisitely, when a pen writes effortlessly, when a bridge spans a river with a flawless combination of beauty and structural integrity, or when a coat fits us comfortably in a style and color that suit us and is just right for the day's weather, we rightly use the word *perfect*. Something works; something fits; something is true to its intent. We can apply the same concept to the human person. When we meet a saint, we encounter beauty, integrity and congruence. The call to perfection is the invitation to be that for which we were created.⁷⁵

This is reminiscent of what is perhaps Merton's most widely-read writing on sanctification in an essay titled "Things in Their Identity," in which he avoids technical theological terminology and describes sanctity by comparison of the purpose of humans and the purposes of other parts of creation.⁷⁶ He begins the essay,

> A tree gives glory to God by being a tree. For in being what God means it to be it is obeying Him. It "consents," so to speak, to His creative love. It is expressing an idea which is in God and which is not distinct from the essence of God, and therefore a tree imitates God by being a tree. The more a tree is like itself, the more it is like Him. If it tried to be like something else which it was never intended to be, it would be less like God and therefore it would give Him less glory. No two created beings are exactly alike. And their individuality is no imperfection. On the contrary, the perfection of each created thing is not merely

---

74. Wynkoop, *Theology of Love*, 385.
75. Smith, *Called to be Saints*, 19.
76. Merton, *New Seeds*, 29–36. The essay was originally included in *Seeds of Contemplation*, 24–30 and later included in *New Seeds* with only minor revisions. For the specific revisions of the essay from Merton's first typescript of *Seeds of Contemplation* to the publication of *New Seeds*, see Grayston, *Thomas Merton's Rewritings*, 47–61.

in its conformity to an abstract type but in its own individual identity within itself. This particular tree will give glory to God by spreading out its roots in the earth and raising its branches into the air and the light in a way that no other tree before or after it ever did or will do.[77]

He connects this to holiness as he writes, "The forms and individual characters of living and growing things, of inanimate beings, of animals and flowers and all nature, constitute their holiness in the sight of God. Their inscape is their sanctity. It is the imprint of His wisdom and His reality in them."[78] After describing this conception of the holiness of animals, flowers, fish, and lakes, he comments on "the great, gashed, half-naked mountain" as "another of God's saints. There is no other like him. He is alone in his own character, nothing else in the world ever did or ever will imitate God in quite the same way. That is his sanctity."[79] Merton then returns the focus to humans:

> But what about you? What about me?
> Unlike the animals and the trees ... if we are never anything but ... people, we will not be saints and we will not be able to offer to God the worship of our imitation, which is sanctity.
> It is true to say that for me sanctity consists in being myself and for you sanctity consists in being *your* self and that, in the last analysis, your sanctity will never be mine and mine will never be yours, except in the communism of charity and grace.
> For me to be a saint means to be myself. Therefore the problem of sanctity and salvation is in fact the problem of finding out who I am and of discovering my true self.
> Trees and animals have no problem. God makes them what they are without consulting them, and they are perfectly satisfied.
> With us it is different. God leaves us free to be whatever we like. We can be ourselves or not, as we please. We are at liberty to be real, or to be unreal. We may be true or false, the choice is ours.[80]

While Merton's language in this passage varies significantly from anything in Wesley that might be considered his description of "the problem of sanctity and salvation," predecessors of Merton's concepts of the

77. Merton, *New Seeds*, 29.
78. Merton, *New Seeds*, 30.
79. Merton, *New Seeds*, 31.
80. Merton, *New Seeds*, 31–32.

true and false self are evident in Wesley. For example, his response to a despairing critic who was nearing death fits Wesleyan characteristics of sanctified people and Merton's concept of the true self. Wesley writes,

> "Sir," said that unhappy man, at my first interview with him, "I scorn to deceive you or any man. You must not tell me of your Bible; for I do not believe one word of it. I know there is a God; and believe he is all in all, the *Anima mundi* [the soul of the world], the *Total mens agitans molem, et magno se corpore miscens* [the all-informing soul, which spreads through the vast mass, and moves the whole]. But farther than this I believe not: All is dark; my thought is lost. But I hear," added he, "you preach to a great number of people every night and morning. Pray, what would you do with them? Whither would you lead them? What religion do you preach? What is it good for?"
>
> I replied, "I do preach to as many as desire to hear, every night and morning. You ask, what I would do with them: I would make them virtuous and happy, easy in themselves, and useful to others. Whither would I lead them? To heaven; to God the Judge, the lover of all, and to Jesus the Mediator of the new covenant. What religion do I preach? The religion of love; the law of kindness brought to light by the gospel. What is this good for? To make all who receive it enjoy God and themselves: To make them like God; lovers of all; contented in their lives; and crying out at their death, in calm assurance, 'O grave, where is thy victory! Thanks be unto God, who giveth me the victory, through my Lord Jesus Christ.'"[81]

What, for Wesley, is "the religion of love" that makes people "enjoy God and themselves . . . like God; lovers of all" is an apt description of fulfillment of the purpose for which one is created and is highly compatible with Merton's concept of the true self, which came to be reflected often in the SFM through the work of Mulholland and others.[82]

APPLICATION OF THE SYNTHESES: DIRECT OPPOSITION TO QUIETISM

This chapter's points of synthesis in Wesleyan and Mertonian spirituality and theology are evident in their shared opposition to quietism based on

---

81. Wesley, *Works* (Jackson), 8:8. Paragraph break added.

82. See chapter 5 for Mulholland's development from within his Wesleyan tradition of Merton's concepts of the true and false self.

mutual insistence on human cooperation with God's grace as essential in sanctification.[83] Wesley's encounter with quietism through the Moravians is a major part of his biography from 1736–1740 and resulted in significant writings from him.[84] Merton's encounter came through his study of the mystical tradition he embraced, but of which he considered quietism a false branch.[85] Despite the varying circumstances and traditions from which the two encountered and rejected quietism, their refutations of it are remarkably congruent and are reflected in the SFM.

Knight comments that the quietism Wesley encountered in "the Moravian doctrine of 'stillness' . . . was directly opposed to Wesley's active waiting on God's grace by way of using the means of grace. The controversy over the means of grace became so severe, and the stakes for the Christian life so high" that Wesley left the Fetter Lane society and took others with him, marking the Foundery society's beginning.[86] Knight summarizes,

> While the controversy centered on how one becomes a Christian, the implications of it strongly affect the importance of means of grace for the Christian life. The theological preunderstandings which were brought to the conflict center around four basic issues: (1) whether there are degrees of faith, (2) the relation of immediate and mediated presence, (3) the relation of Christ to means of grace, and (4) the role of human activity in salvation.[87]

---

83. For an overview of quietism, see Gannon and Traub, *Desert and the City*, 231–32, 236–41; Chan, "Quietism." For Wesley's response, see Knight, *Presence of God*, 36–49; Tuttle, *Mysticism*, 36–41; Hammond, "Restoring Primitive Christianity," 222–24. For Merton's response, see Bailey, *Thomas Merton on Mysticism*, 68–69, 93–97, 174, 202–3.

84. See Smith, "Eighteenth Century Encounters," 141–56.

85. See the chapter "False Mysticism," in Merton, *Ascent to Truth*, 66. Bailey sees the Quakerism of Merton's mother, and his few early experiences therein, as underlying his "almost violent . . . refutation of Quietism." See Bailey, *Thomas Merton on Mysticism*, 93. While Merton does consider quietism a dangerous error, he also notes, "On the other hand, a greater danger in our day is the hectic *activism* which measures perfection by exterior results and by the quantity of work done." See Merton, "Perfection, Christian," 8:332.

86. Knight, *Presence of God*, 36.

87. Knight, *Presence of God*, 38. See Knight, *Presence of God*, 36–49 for his exploration of each issue. In summary: (1) Wesley believed there are degrees of faith, whereas the Moravians taught that one either had faith fully or none at all; (2) Wesley believed in both the immediate presence and action of the Holy Spirit in a person's life and God's work mediated through the means of grace, whereas the Moravians denied the latter; (3) the Moravians believed that Christ was the only means of grace and all practices were "works," which those without faith must not use in order to avoid attempts at

Merton's resistance to quietism did not spring from a particular conflict like Wesley's with the Moravians nor yield the quantity of related writing that Wesley's did. However, Merton's immersion in Christian mysticism as both a participant and a teacher in the Benedictine tradition caused him to comment on quietism in contexts of writing and teaching on the mystical tradition in Christianity. In the first chapter of *The Ascent to Truth*, Merton writes,

> There are . . . two extremes to be avoided. On the one hand, false mysticism ascribes to human nature the power and the right to acquire supernatural illuminations by the effort of our own intelligence. On the other hand, false mysticism darkens the intelligence altogether in a formal rejection of truth in order to seek Divine Union in an ecstasy of blind love which takes no account of the intelligence, which accepts deification as *a gift so pure that no effort is required on the part of the one who receives it*.[88]

Later, in a chapter dedicated to "false mysticism," he writes, "The errors of Quietism with respect to the knowledge of God consist in a formal rejection of theology, a depreciation of God's revelation of Himself to man in Christ the incarnate Word, in the complete rejection of formal prayer and meditation, and in the belief that supernatural contemplation can be 'acquired' by the mere cessation of mental activity."[89] He also adds, in a comment particularly resonant with Wesley's view, that a common characteristic of much false mysticism is that "it claims to arrive at special supernatural knowledge by means other than those normally ordained by God."[90]

There is irony in the substantial similarities of these criticisms of quietism from Wesley and Merton. Merton, in part, wrote *Ascent to Truth* from his desire to explore the apophatic theology of St. John of the Cross as true mysticism in contrast to false mysticisms such as quietism. As evident in Wesley's preface to *Hymns and Sacred Poems* and his sermon "The Wilderness State," after Wesley's exploration of mystical theology during his years in Georgia, he came to have "repugnance" toward apophatic

---

earning salvation and those with faith need not use, whereas Wesley denied their distinction and insisted that Christ works by the Holy Spirit through the means of grace; and (4) because of the third point just mentioned, Wesley believed Christians must use the means of grace and can do so while only trusting in Christ.

88. Merton, *Ascent to Truth*, 16. Emphasis added.
89. Merton, *Ascent to Truth*, 66.
90. Merton, *Ascent to Truth*, 67.

theology and John of the Cross's concept of the dark night of the soul.[91] Therefore, Merton writes of his opposition to quietism as a defense from within apophatic mysticism, while Wesley's opposition to quietism was directly connected to his intention to avoid "the rock on which [he] had the nearest made shipwreck of the faith . . . the writings of the mystics,"[92] generally the same tradition of writings Merton was seeking to defend.[93]

Wesley follows his description of his near-shipwreck of Christianity on the writings of the mystics in a letter to his older brother with an explanation of whom he means by "mystics: under which term I comprehend all, and only those, who slight any of the means of grace."[94] Colón-Emeric observes, "One could define mysticism in this way but then one would have to refrain from applying the term mystic to persons like St. John of the Cross and Pseudo-Dyonisius whose theology and practice were strongly sacramental."[95] Indeed, Wesley's inconsistency is that his language expands his opposition to a principle of quietism to include all of mysticism.[96] Hammond clarifies that Wesley "by no means rejected the entire mystical tradition, as strict practices of self-denial often associated with mysticism continued. What he fundamentally objected to was the quietism of some mystics which he believed had the effect of degrading Scripture, reason, and the means of grace."[97]

---

91. Heath, *Naked Faith*, 78.

92. Wesley, *Letters* (Jackson), 1:207.

93. See Hammond, "Restoring Primitive Christianity," 222–26 for mystics Wesley read in Georgia.

94. Wesley, *Letters* (Jackson), 1:207. Wesley's and Merton's theological view of the means of grace are inclusive of sacraments.

95. Colón-Emeric, *Wesley, Aquinas*, 257. Likewise, if Wesley had known of Merton, he could not have considered him a mystic by this standard.

96. Tuttle concedes that Wesley did not thoroughly reject mysticism, but Tuttle still understands the rejection too broadly: "Wesley was no longer drawn to mysticism as such; but he continued to admire the individual mystics. . . . In fact, that which appealed to Wesley most about the mystics was that which was most incompatible with mysticism as a whole" (*Mysticism*, 127). See Colón-Emeric's evaluation of Tuttle's thesis, including, "Tuttle advances some solid textual evidence in support of his thesis but flounders upon an objectionable definition of mysticism which regards the mystical as fundamentally separate from genuine Christian experience" (*Wesley, Aquinas*, 257).

97. Hammond, "Restoring Primitive Christianity," 224–25.

The Common Core: Grace that Leads to Union and Requires Cooperation

Wesley's and Merton's shared opposition to quietism highlights a common core of not only their rejection of quietism but also of their theology and spirituality. *First, Wesleyan and Mertonian theology and spirituality are each founded on similar understandings of grace.*[98] Oden summarizes Wesley's understanding of grace: "It sees God's favor at work throughout the whole narrative of salvation. (1) Common grace is present in the whole of nature and history, preceding all acts of human decision. (2) Saving grace is given in Jesus Christ and received by faith alone. (3) Completing grace is given through the Holy Spirit to nurture the life of faith toward holy living."[99]

Likewise, Merton succinctly describes grace across the span of a Christian's experience: "Grace: the power and the light of God in us, purifying our hearts, transforming us in Christ, making us true sons of God, enabling us to act in the world as his instruments for the good of all men and for his glory."[100] One cannot understand the theology nor spirituality of Wesley, Merton, nor much of Christian tradition without understanding grace in this sense common to them.[101] Merton expounds his understanding of grace:

> Our concept of grace may be hazy and unreal. In fact, the more the notion of grace is treated by us in a semimaterialistic, objectified way, the more unreal it will be. In practice, we tend to think of grace as a kind of mysterious substance, a "thing," a

---

98. For an overview of Wesley on grace, see Oden, *John Wesley's Teachings*, 2:137–56. Merton has not been examined with similar theological categories. For a brief mention of the same Augustinian and Thomistic influences as Oden mentions for Wesley, see Carr, *Search for Wisdom*, 14–15.

99. Oden, *John Wesley's Teachings*, 2:137. Oden sees this as "in most ways Augustinian." Collins disagrees in his *Theology of John Wesley*, 73. Collins does see Wesley's understanding of grace as a synthesis of Catholic and Protestant emphases. He states, "Not only did Wesley embrace both Protestant (free) and Catholic (co-operant, responsible) conceptions of grace, but also he was remarkably diverse in his understanding of holiness, a holy love that was informed not simply by Catholic resources, by eastern and western fathers for example, but also by Protestant ones, especially Anglicans and German Pietists" (*Theology of John Wesley*, 16; see also *Theology of John Wesley*, 180). For an accessible overview of Wesley on grace according to his conception of the *ordo salutis*, see Harper, *Way to Heaven*.

100. Merton, *Life and Holiness*, 7.

101. Other traditions, such as some strands of Reformed theology, understand grace differently. For example, see Horton, *Putting Amazing Back*, xiii–xiv; Horton, *Rediscovering the Holy Spirit*, 18, 215.

commodity which is furnished us by God—something like fuel for a supernatural engine. We regard it as a kind of spiritual gasoline which we find necessary in order to make our journey to God. Of course, grace is a great mystery, and can only be spoken of in analogies and metaphors which tend to be misleading. But certainly this metaphor is so misleading as to be altogether false. Grace is not "something with which" we perform good works and attain to God. It is not a "thing" or a "substance" entirely apart from God. It is God's very presence and action within us. Therefore, clearly it is not a commodity we "need to get" from him in order to go to him. For all practical purposes we might as well say that grace is the quality of our being that results from the sanctifying energy of God acting dynamically in our life. That is why in primitive Christian literature, and especially in the New Testament, we read not so much of receiving grace as of receiving the Holy Spirit—God himself.[102]

Second, Wesleyan and Mertonian theology and spirituality view union as God's gracious purpose. In his introduction to Merton's teaching to monastic novices on mysticism, Michael M. McGregor summarizes, "When stripped of the history and tradition that Merton takes such pains to trace, mysticism, in his mind, is simply union with God, and the path to it is opened primarily by grace and prayer."[103] Merton's life can be seen as a pursuit of this union and cultivation of it in others. Wesley also states the centrality: "One happiness shall ye propose to your souls, even an union with Him that made them; the having 'fellowship with the Father and the Son;' the being joined to the Lord in one Spirit."[104] Such language of union with God is infrequent in Wesley because of his aversion to mysticism,[105] but as Stephen Martyn argues, "this theme of union with God can be seen permeating his sermons, letters, tracts, journal entries, and conversations. It was the thread that held together the whole and the fuel that flames the fires of holy zeal in a remarkable life. Wesley had various names for this goal, the most common being 'Christian perfection.'"[106]

---

102. Merton, *Life and Holiness*, 30.
103. McGregor, "Foreword," vii.
104. Wesley, *Bicentennial Works*, 1:408.
105. Although infrequent, Kenneth Milton Loyer observes the increased frequency of Wesley's eschatological emphasis on union with God in Wesley's sermon, "New Creation." See Loyer, "To Crown All," 109–25.
106. Martyn, "Journey to God," 142.

Martyn's insight regarding the Wesleyan theme combined with McGregor's identification of mysticism as "simply union with God" highlights the legitimacy of characterizing Wesley's theology and spirituality as mystical despite his repudiation of the term.[107] Elaine A. Heath argues that "Christian mysticism in the Wesleyan tradition has been suppressed and marginalized, even though it is the fountainhead for the original missional ecclesiology in that tradition."[108] She describes a mystic in terms appropriate to Wesley and his hopes for his early Methodists: "One for whom the immediate presence of God and the drawing of God toward union, is a lived, fundamental reality. God's presence is both immanent and transcendent, transforming the mystic inwardly while compelling him or her to an outward life of increasing love and compassion."[109]

Third, Wesleyan and Mertonian theology and spirituality view human cooperation with God's grace as essential for growth in love. This commonality is central to their opposition to quietism considered above. As Merton writes—"Quietism is [an] error; it underestimates the need to practice virtue by overstressing passivity"[110]—so Wesley admonishes in a sermon on Paul's injunction to "work out your own salvation with fear and trembling; for it is God who is at work in you, enabling you both to will and to work for his good pleasure."[111] Wesley writes, "You can do something, through Christ strengthening you. Stir up the spark of grace which is now in you, and he will give you more grace."[112]

CONCLUSION

Chapter 1 historically contextualized the SFM as an expression of inherently non-fundamentalist evangelicalism. After surveying Wesley and Merton in some detail in chapters 2 and 3 and exploring points of synthesis between them in this chapter, an additional descriptor can now be added: *the SFM is an inherently non-fundamentalist pietistic evangelical expression of non-quietist contemplative mysticism.* A brief recap here will expound on the parts of the description in preparation for the final

---

107. Underhill describes "union between God and the soul" as "the one essential of mysticism." See Underhill, *Essentials of Mysticism*, 6.

108. Heath, "Ecstasy," 1.

109. Heath, "Ecstasy," 5.

110. Merton, "Perfection, Christian," 8:332.

111. Phil 2:12b–13.

112. Wesley, *Works* (Jackson), 6:513.

chapter's focus on Mulholland's contribution as the SFM's foundational confluence of Wesleyan and Mertonian influences.

The SFM is inherently *non-fundamentalist* and *evangelical* because it arose from traditions within American Protestantism that developed from the "classical evangelicalism" of the Protestant Reformation of the sixteenth century and the "pietistic evangelicalism" of the eighteenth century and first half of the nineteenth century, but was distinct from, and occasionally a reaction to, the "fundamentalist evangelicalism" of the late nineteenth century to the present.[113] As explored in chapter 2, the SFM's widespread utilization of pietistic *ecclesiola* groups oriented toward the sanctification of participants is a direct reflection of Wesleyan societies, classes, and bands. Chapter 3 established the direct relation between Merton's contemplative monasticism and the increase in writing on solitude from pietistic evangelicals in the years following his death. The present chapter's exploration of points of synthesis between Wesley and Merton in the spirituality of religious orders and theology of perfecting grace was applied to their mutual refutation of quietism combined with the sense in which both men can be understood with the tradition of Christian mysticism.

The SFM's identification as an inherently non-fundamentalist, pietistic evangelical expression of non-quietist contemplative mysticism contextualizes it as a confluence of Wesleyan and Mertonian influences without being solely either. Just as Wesley's works are unlikely to lead readers toward contemplative monasticism, Merton's books have likely not produced many new pietistic evangelicals.[114] Nevertheless, Wesleyan and Mertonian influences are both evident in the SFM, and this project can now proceed to explore Mulholland as the primary person through whom those influences were established.

---

113. See chapter 1 of this project. As indicated there, the terms for the three periods of evangelicalism are from Dorrien, *Remaking of Evangelical Theology*, 2–3.

114. Because of the context offered in this chapter, Wesley is most accurately understood as mystical (because of his emphasis on union with God), but not as contemplative (because of his aversion to apophatic theology and spirituality). Chapter 5 explores this further.

CHAPTER 5

Mulholland's Contribution to the Spiritual Formation Movement as a Confluence of His Wesleyan and Mertonian Influences

MULHOLLAND'S SPAN OF THIRTY-TWO years of teaching in the SFM (from his 1983 Place of Scripture lectures in the URA to his 2015 For the Sake of Others teaching at the Transforming Center) is pervasively and uniquely Wesleyan and Mertonian. Evidence of this is considered throughout the remainder of this chapter, and it is epitomized in the 1983 URA Place of Scripture lectures and the resulting 1985 publication of *Shaped by the Word*. The lectures and the first edition of the book are replete with references to Wesley (thirty-eight times in the text) and Merton (twenty-eight times in the text).[1] While *Shaped by the Word* epitomizes the confluence, it is also evident in a survey of the citations in Mulholland's works on spiritual formation.[2] Analysis of references in the full body of Mulholland's published works on spiritual formation is indicative of Wesley and Merton as his two, central, extrabiblical sources, with 148 references to Wesley, seventy-two to Merton, and the next most frequent being Kenneth Leech with seventeen.[3] The Wesleyan and Mertonian synthesis continued through Mulholland's four sessions of his

---

1. The frequencies of these citations are much higher than for any other source in *Shaped by the Word*, with the next most frequent being five citations of Aelred Squire.

2. Mulholland's published works that cite both Wesley and Merton are *Shaped by the Word*, *Invitation to a Journey*, *Way of Scripture*, "Word Became Text," "Spirituality and Transformation," "Wesleyan Doctrine of Scripture," and "Invitation to an Academic Journey."

3. The majority (twelve) of Mulholland's references to Kenneth Leech are in *Invitation to a Journey*, mostly to Leech, *Experiencing God*.

final teaching in 2015 at the Transforming Center, citing Merton in each of the first three sessions and Wesley in the fourth.[4]

While this analysis of frequency of citations of sources in Mulholland's works is indicative of the prevalence of Wesleyan and Mertonian influence, the remainder of this chapter explores deeper evidence by surveying Mulholland through the framework of the characteristics of the SFM proposed in previous chapters and exploration of Wesleyan and Mertonian themes in Mulholland's major spiritual formation works, *Shaped by the Word*, *Invitation to a Journey*, and *The Deeper Journey*, and then concludes with an exploration of the Wesleyan and Mertonian influences in Mulholland's major biblical studies work, his commentaries on the book of Revelation.

REFLECTIONS OF MULHOLLAND'S WESLEYAN AND MERTONIAN CONFLUENCE IN THE SFM

The SFM is described in previous chapters as an essentially non-fundamentalist, pietistic, evangelical expression of non-quietist contemplative mysticism, and the two halves of the description provide a framework for exploring Mulholland's Wesleyan-Mertonian confluence. Mulholland's essentially non-fundamentalist, pietistic evangelical characteristics are explored below as his "Wesleyan accent," and the non-quietist, contemplative mystical characteristics as his "Mertonian accent."[5]

Mulholland's Wesleyan Accent in the SFM: Non-Fundamentalist, Pietistic, Evangelical

Among the most significant reasons Mulholland's teaching resonated with the emphases of the SFM from the time of its early organizational

---

4. Mulholland, "Sake of Others."

5. The term "accent" is chosen here to emphasize that the respective distinctions are significant but not mutually exclusive in respect to Wesley or Merton. For example, the Wesleyan accent is non-fundamentalist, but neither is Merton a fundamentalist. Mulholland's non-fundamentalism is a Wesleyan accent, however, because Mulholland is within the evangelical tradition with Wesley, and fundamentalism developed from within evangelicalism. Similarly, although neither Wesley nor Merton were quietists, quietism is part of the Mertonian accent since it primarily originated within Roman Catholic mystical tradition.

phase and onward was that he promoted a "high view"[6] of Scripture compatible with the biblicism of evangelicalism while also being consistently *non-fundamentalist* and remaining substantively *evangelical*.[7] Mulholland delineates an evangelical understanding of the relation of the Holy Spirit to the Christian Scriptures consistent with the fundamentally pneumatological emphasis of spiritual formation. He writes,

> Today there tends to be a polarity in the understanding of inspiration. More conservative Christians tend to think of the Bible as the inspired Word of God, with all inspiration relating to its writing. Less conservative Christians tend to think of inspiration as something that happens to the individual reader. . . . However, there is a unique conjoining of both halves of the inspirational dynamic. God's inspiration of the writer and God's inspiration of the reader are two halves of a whole, and to lose either half is to filter out of our hearing of the scripture a tremendous amount of the living, penetrating, transforming Word of God. We might end up doing one of two things: slavishly worshiping the Bible or standing back and critically assessing and picking from among the biblical tidbits those that seem to "inspire" us. Either extreme is deadly and deadening to spiritual wholeness. There needs to be the vital conjoining of both halves of the inspirational equation. . . . The Spirit of God at work in our lives brings us into companionship with the text in such a way that the Word of God begins to shape the word that God speaks us forth to be in the world. When we begin to open the scripture in this perspective, there is an openness for us to be addressed by the Word incarnated in what we call the scripture.[8]

6. The origin of this phrase should be further explored. It is present in debates about fundamentalism and inerrancy. Craig D. Allert comments, "The problem is not that evangelicals have a high view of Scripture but rather that a high view of Scripture has been usurped by verbal plenary theorists—the determination of what is high and what is low comes from them." See Allert, *High View*, 11. Michael R. Licona generalizes the differences between "high" and "low" views of Scripture: "If I truly have a high view of Scripture, I will embrace it as God has given it to us rather than insist it conforms to a model shaped by how I think he should have given it. If I refuse to do this, I may sincerely believe that I hold a high view of Scripture when I actually hold a high view of my view of Scripture. . . . A 'high view' of Scripture regards it as being divinely inspired and authoritative. In contrast, a 'low view' of Scripture views it as being entirely of human origin. According to a low view, while Scripture provides some teachings that are beneficial for living successfully and for treating others in a manner that promotes peace, it should not be an authoritative guide for how we should live." See Licona, *Jesus, Contradicted*, 191.

7. See the descriptions of "evangelicalism" and "fundamentalism" in chapter 1.

8. Mulholland, *Shaped by the Word* (2000), 44.

Mulholland's 2012 article, "The Wesleyan Doctrine of Scripture (as Contrasted with Fundamentalism)," addresses fundamentalism more directly than his earlier writings and clearly reflects the Wesleyan and Mertonian influences evident from his earliest spiritual formation works.[9] Mulholland sees fundamentalism as an expression of a propositional understanding of truth contrasting with his relational understanding of truth, which he sees as consistent with Wesley and Merton.[10] He establishes his claim, "The Wesleyan doctrine of Scripture moves in a direction quite different from that of fundamentalism"[11] with both a summary statement of Wesley and a citation of Merton:

> When understood as a collection of propositional truths, God's revelation becomes "information." By contrast, in the words of Thomas Merton, "God manifests himself not in information but in life-giving power." The living and transforming God himself, not information about him is the *content* of revelation. Similarly, John Wesley believed Scripture to be the vehicle of a transforming encounter with God, resulting in regeneration of the inner being and the consequent reordering of one's life.[12]

Later in the article, Mulholland cites and expounds on Wesley's guidelines for reading Scripture, which had been a consistent principal source for Mulholland's teaching on formational reading since his 1983 URA lectures,[13] and Merton is cited in Mulholland's interpretation of Wesley's guidelines:

9. Mulholland, "Wesleyan Doctrine of Scripture."

10. These views are prevalent throughout Mulholland's "Wesleyan Doctrine of Scripture" article, including the following statements: "Wesley and most of his descendants developed a doctrine of Scripture that focused on its role in transforming the believer's inner being as the ground for reordering behavior. Fundamentalism, on the other hand, developed a doctrine of Scripture that tended to focus on reordering of behavior in obedience to a body of propositional truths" ("Wesleyan Doctrine of Scripture," 27). "For the Wesley brothers the role of Scripture was not the appropriation of propositional truths but the actualization of a relationship of loving union with God for the sake of the world" ("Wesleyan Doctrine of Scripture," 37). Mulholland also introduces his 2012 course on spiritual formation with this propositional versus relational distinction, stating, "The basic watershed in dealing with the question of truth is whether truth is propositional or relational. . . . I base my understanding of Scripture on the understanding that truth is relational—that propositions are what we construct around those relational realities." See Mulholland "Spiritual Formation," 19:08–21:17.

11. Mulholland, "Wesleyan Doctrine of Scripture," 31.

12. Mulholland, "Wesleyan Doctrine of Scripture," 30–31. The citation is of Merton, *Opening the Bible*, 20.

13. Mulholland, "Wesleyan Doctrine of Scripture," 31–35; Mulholland, "Place of

> What it means for Scripture to be "inspired" is lifeless apart from the inner and outer "transformation" of the whole person. This transformative dimension is seen in [Wesley's] injunction, "frequently to pause, and examine ourselves by what we read, both with regard to our hearts and lives." Thomas Merton echoes Wesley: "The basic claim made by the Bible for the Word of God is not so much that it is to be blindly accepted because of God's authority, but that it is recognized by its transforming and liberating power."[14]

Mulholland states that both Wesleyans and fundamentalists have a "high view of Scripture," but he does not define the often-used yet somewhat ambiguous and variously-employed phrase.[15] However, since he offers what he elsewhere refers to as his "definition of . . . the nature of scripture"[16] as a "summary" of Wesley's understanding, it follows that Mulholland considered himself to hold a high view of Scripture distinct from that of fundamentalists, as he writes, "A summary of Wesley's doctrine is the Word that became flesh in Jesus of Nazareth also became 'text,' providing a vehicle for a transforming encounter with God, so that he who is the Word might through the Holy Spirit become flesh in us."[17]

This summary was the last of several variations of this statement that Mulholland taught and published from at least as early as 2002 through the rest of his life.[18] The earliest is, "The Word becomes text in order to

---

Scripture," lecture 5. Wesley's guidelines are the subject of a chapter and included as an appendix in all three editions of *Shaped by the Word*. The guidelines still formed part of his teaching twenty-nine years after the first URA in Mulholland, "Spiritual Formation," lecture 7. The guidelines are found in Wesley, *Works* (Jackson), 14:252–53.

14. Mulholland, "Wesleyan Doctrine of Scripture," 35, citing Wesley, *Works* (Jackson), 14:253 and Merton, *Opening the Bible*, 18.

15. Mulholland, "Wesleyan Doctrine of Scripture," 27–28.

16. Mulholland and Barton, "Spiritual Transformation," 30:57–31:26. He states, "Since [*Shaped by the Word*] was . . . thirty . . . years ago, I have continued to work with the definition of what the nature of Scripture is. And at this point, I have come to this: that the Word, the Word that was God, the Word that was with God, the Word that was God, the Word that became flesh, that the Word also became text to provide a place of transforming encounter with God so that the Word might become flesh in us for the sake of the world."

17. Mulholland, "Wesleyan Doctrine of Scripture," 36.

18. No variation of the statement is in the 2000 revised edition of *Shaped by the Word*, and Mulholland uses it in a URA session in 2002 indicating that he likely developed it during the intervening time. See Mulholland, "Spirituality," session 1, 15:10–15:45. In his Fall 2004 syllabus for NT 520: New Testament Introduction at ATS and repetitions of the course thereafter, Mulholland presents the course in three parts, introducing the New Testament as a historical document, a literary document, and a

provide a place of transforming encounter with God so that the Word might become flesh in us in our world."[19] Whatever criticisms fundamentalists or others might have of Mulholland's view,[20] for evangelicals who instinctively require a high view of Scripture but are open to alternatives to the fundamentalist understandings of the nature of the Bible, Mulholland's Merton-informed Wesleyan accent provides a substantive option exemplified in his conclusion to "The Wesleyan Doctrine of Scripture":

> It would be a grave error to imply that fundamentalists are any less interested in Christian discipleship than are Wesleyans. Like Wesleyans, fundamentalists are carefully attentive to the redeeming work of Jesus Christ, to the importance of being born anew by the Spirit of God, and to a life of Christian discipleship. But when it comes to the primary nature and role of the Bible, there are . . . major differences. For fundamentalism, the Bible itself, with its comprehensive and rationally accessible inerrant divine truths or propositions, is the depository and residence of inspiration. The Bible and its truths are the primary objects of attention. For John Wesley, for whom the Scriptures are truly the Word of God, the primary role of Scripture resides not in the text as divine information but in the Holy Spirit's use of it for a transforming encounter with the risen Christ, the true Word of God. Christ as the encountered Redeemer, not the Bible, is of primary interest and importance. The Bible is the means the Holy Spirit uses for inner regeneration and the sanctified life.[21]

In addition to these non-fundamentalist and evangelical characteristics, Mulholland's Wesleyan accent in the SFM is also noticeably *pietistic*. Mulholland's investment in SFM-related organizations with sanctification-oriented *ecclesiola* groups is explored in chapter 2, and beyond that foremost mark of pietism, Mulholland's work also displays each of Olson's and Collins Winn's ten hallmarks of the movement.[22] Rather than a full analysis of the ten hallmarks in Mulholland, it is most helpful

---

spiritual document. The topic listed to introduce the third part of the course is "The Word Became Text," indicating that the concept became central in his teaching by that time. See Mulholland, "NT 520." Published variations of the statement begin in 2004. See Mulholland, "Biblical Spirituality," 209; "Word Became Text," 85–92; *Way of Scripture*, 16–27; "Invitation to an Academic," 134.

19. Mulholland, "Biblical Spirituality," 209.

20. For a Reformed critique of *Shaped by the Word*, see Williams, "Role of Scripture," 50–59.

21. Mulholland, "Wesleyan Doctrine of Scripture," 38.

22. See chapter 2; Olson and Collins Winn, *Reclaiming Pietism*, 84–85.

to highlight Olson's and Collins Winn's seventh and eighth hallmarks ("Christian life lived in community" and "world transformation toward the kingdom of God"), as they are directly contrary to a particular criticism—of the SFM in general, and therefore, implicitly, of Mulholland as one of the SFM's central and foundational contributors—of the movement as overly individualistic and promotional of spiritual narcissism.[23]

Witherington's critique typifies this view of the SFM. He claims that Wesley's approach

> stands at odds with some of the models of spiritual formation we hear so much about in our era—models that promote extreme introspection, individual isolation and individualistic seeking, spiritual athleticism of various kinds, and even spiritual navel-gazing of a sort. Sometimes when reading some of this literature, it seems almost as if ordinary Christians are being told "get thee to a nunnery" if you want to be truly spiritually formed. What has happened in the age of narcissism and "me first" is that spiritual formation exercises and inventories have all too often taken on the character and ethos of our age, including the radical individualism of the culture. When you take a spiritual inventory that keeps asking questions about your *feelings* about God or how close you personally *feel* to God, there is a good reason to become uneasy. The language and praxis of psychology and psychological counseling have crept into the discussions of spiritual formation as if emotions were some sort of good guide or gauge to the state of someone's soul or his or her relationship with God.[24]

Yeide notes virtually the same criticisms as Witherington offered of the SFM as being predominant regarding pietism, and he attributes the focus of his doctoral research to the desire to correct the historical distortions. He writes,

---

23. See Porter, "Sanctification," 147–48, in which he includes this criticism of the SFM as the last of the eight that he refutes.

24. Witherington, *Shared Christian Life*, vii–viii. Witherington uses these generalizations, but does not reference any specific authors or "models." The connection of the criticism to Mulholland is stronger than a possible inference, however. Prior to reading *Shared Christian Life*, this project's author contacted Witherington since he and Mulholland were long-time colleagues within the same department of the faculty at ATS and mentioned the development of this book on Mulholland's contribution to the SFM. Witherington's response did not mention Mulholland but said, "You should have a look at my book on Wesleyan and Biblical Spiritual Formation called *A Shared Christian Life*." Witherington, email message to the author, October 6, 2021.

> Those movements in Christian history that had given the most acute attention to disciplined Christian life were often presented in negative, and not wholly accurate terms. Pietism seemed especially maligned in this regard, being portrayed as an individualistic, introverted, emotion-dominated movement. My Ph.D. dissertation was a consequence of these needs and suspicions; it was an analysis of the works of F. C. Oetinger, an [eighteenth]-century pietist, in which it was easily demonstrated that he had developed an eschatologically oriented social ethic that was anything but individualistic, introverted, and emotional.[25]

Although Witherington is critiquing the SFM rather than pietism, and Yeide is defending pietism rather than the SFM, because of the high degree of influence of pietism on the SFM, the overlap in criticisms of the two movements is indicative of the high degree of their shared emphases. While Yeide's focus in *Studies in Classical Pietism* is on the *ecclesiolae* as the distinguishing characteristic of the pietists, his analysis of Francke, Zinzendorf, Bengel, Oetinger, and Johann Jakob Moser is replete with the pietists' corporate and social emphases.[26] Olson and Collins Winn concur with the non-individualistic nature of pietism, stating, "One of the most common false views of Pietism is that it promotes spiritual individualism.... [But] Pietists valued highly both the church and the Christian community outside the church."[27] They continue, "People who label Pietism otherworldly and withdrawn from social endeavors ... have clearly not studied Pietism. Unfortunately, the unjustified image ... persists. But nothing could be further from the truth."[28] They admit that some on the fringes of the tradition have tended toward withdrawal, but this is atypical of the movement and its founders. They conclude, "To be sure, not all Pietists have been socially active in terms of world transformation.... However ... at its best, Pietism always includes an impulse toward social transformation 'for God's glory and neighbor's good.'"[29]

If there are fringe voices within the SFM of whom Witherington's charge of "radical individualism" is accurate, those voices are inconsistent with Mulholland's foundational contribution to the movement,

---

25. Yeide, *Studies in Classical Pietism*, 11.

26. Yeide devotes a chapter to each of these individuals in *Studies in Classical Pietism*.

27. Olson and Collins Winn, *Reclaiming Pietism*, 99.

28. Olson and Collins Winn, *Reclaiming Pietism*, 100.

29. Olson and Collins Winn, *Reclaiming Pietism*, 103.

as Mulholland's focus is often on the spiritual journey as "a cruciform path from a pervasively self-referenced life into a thoroughly Christ-referenced life, a life of cruciform love in the world, a Christlike life for others."[30] He identifies the movement from self-referenced life to life referenced toward God and others as the central dynamic in Christian spiritual formation:

> In our pervasively privatized and individualistic Western culture, we almost automatically think of spirituality and transformation to wholeness in the image of Christ as something between an individual and God. Christlikeness, however, is a life of loving union with God poured out for the sake of others. Christlikeness is characterized by compassion, kindness, lowliness, meekness, and longsuffering in its relationships with others (Col. 3:12). It is a life radically other-referenced for the well-being of the other (Phil. 2:3–4). Genuine spirituality and transformation unite our relationship with God and our relationships with others in a symbiotic reality. The nature of our relationship with God manifests itself in the nature of our relationships with others (cf. Matt. 25:31–46, where Jesus is unmistakably clear that the way we treat others reveals our relationship with God). This is why Jesus reduces the entire Torah to a single, two-sided mode of being: totally other-referenced love (*agape*) for God and completely other-referenced love for others. In this tripartite conjunction between us, God, and the other, we discover our true identity as a self that we can love (*agape*) in a totally un-self-referenced way. This is the goal of genuine spirituality and transformation.[31]

He then summarizes, "Transformation in the spiritual life is the process of growth from a false identity as a pervasively self-referenced being to the true identity of a pervasively God-referenced being."[32]

The development of Mulholland's frequently-referenced definition of spiritual formation indicates how essential he understood the growth out of self-referenced living to be in Christian maturation. His definition's original form in the 1985 edition of *Shaped by the Word* is "Christian spiritual formation is the process of being conformed to the image of

30. Mulholland, *Deeper Journey*, 163. The terms "self-referenced" and "Christ-referenced" occur more than eighty times in *Deeper Journey*. He elsewhere also uses "other-referenced" or "God-referenced" as contrasts with "self-referenced." See also Mulholland, "Spirituality and Transformation," 218–21.

31. Mulholland, "Spirituality and Transformation," 220.

32. Mulholland, "Spirituality and Transformation," 221.

Christ."[33] However, by the publication of *Invitation to a Journey* in 1993, he had expanded the definition to "a process of being conformed to the image of Christ for the sake of others."[34] The additional phrase, "for the sake of others," thereafter became a hallmark of Mulholland's contribution to the SFM, was consistently emphasized in each of his works, and he saw it as the element of his definition to which he most hoped his readers would always be attentive. He writes, "The fourth element in our definition of spiritual formation, *for the sake of others*, is the one we must never forget. . . . All of God's work to conform us to the image of Christ has as its sole purpose that we might become what God created us to be *in relationship with God and others*."[35] Mulholland expounds on this in "Part IV: Companions on the Way: Corporate and Social Spirituality" in *Invitation to a Journey*.[36] His statements—such as, "If spiritual formation is, indeed, being conformed to the image of Christ for the sake of others, *the ultimate test of our spirituality lies in the nature of our life in the world with others*"[37] and "corporate spirituality is the only context within which we can grow toward wholeness in the image of Christ"[38]—are simultane-

33. Mulholland, *Shaped by the Word*, 27.

34. Mulholland, *Invitation to a Journey*, 15. He does not state his reason for adding the phrase, and "for the sake of others" can be seen as implicit to "the image of Christ" in his original version of the definition. However, he implies a possible reason for the addition in a conversation with Barton in response to her question of how he came to the definition, as he indicates that he had been invited to teach four sessions on spiritual formation to a group of clergy. See Mulholland and Barton, "Spiritual Transformation," 1:30–4:30. This indicates that the cause of the change was initially very practical, as adding it to the previous three components as in the first edition of *Shaped by the Word* served the retreat's need for a fourth session. This does not mean that the addition was only pragmatic. He previously used the phrase to describe the manner in which the lifestyles of God's people as citizens of New Jerusalem would be confrontational with the values of the world in *Revelation: Holy Living*, 348, which is congruent with subsequent usages. All subsequent published instances of the definition include the addition. Another less substantial change to his definition is published in the 2016 edition of *Invitation to a Journey*: "A process of being *formed in* the image of Christ for the sake of others" (*Invitation to a Journey*, expanded ed., 19; emphasis added). Mulholland requested a few months before his death that his editor, Al Hsu, make the change in the forthcoming edition. Hsu indicates that Mulholland did not indicate the reason for the edit, but speculates that "formed in" is less strict and more inviting (Hsu, email message to the author, June 24, 2022).

35. Mulholland, *Invitation to a Journey*, 40.

36. Mulholland, *Invitation to a Journey*, 141–68.

37. Mulholland, *Invitation to a Journey*, 142.

38. Mulholland, *Invitation to a Journey*, 157.

ously highly reflective of Mulholland's Wesleyan pietistic tradition and difficult to identify with Witherington's criticism of the SFM.

Mulholland's Mertonian Accent in the SFM: Non-Quietist, Contemplative, Mystical

There is no emphasis in the SFM more central than its *non-quietist* focus on spiritual disciplines.[39] While Mulholland did not originate this emphasis, he nurtured it from an early point in the SFM, first, with his ability to address a non-fundamentalist yet evangelical discipline of reading Scripture through The Place of Scripture in Spiritual Formation sessions and *Shaped by the Word*, and, later, though addressing the general role of disciplines in spiritual formation in *Invitation to a Journey*.[40] Each of these contributions was expounded on in his subsequent teaching and publications.

---

39. As explored in the introduction, the prevalence of emphasis on spiritual disciplines in SFM literature has led some to equate Christian spiritual formation with practice of disciplines, leading to an underappreciation of its primarily theological nature. As an example, Howard describes spiritual formation as "the means by which growth is fostered in Christian life." See Howard, *Brazos Introduction*, 23–24.

40. In Mulholland, *Invitation to a Journey*, 103–19, he identifies the "classical spiritual disciplines" as prayer, spiritual reading, and liturgy (under which he adds to prayer and spiritual reading, worship, daily office, study, fasting, and retreat). He distinguishes between these classical disciplines and "personal" disciplines: "The classical disciplines . . . form the 'roadbed' on which we move through the stages of the journey . . . [and are] the larger matrix within which other very specific and personal disciplines are to be offered to God as an exercise of faith and a means of grace. [The classical disciplines] can be viewed as the scaffolding within which the reconstruction of our life toward wholeness takes place. The classical disciplines of the spiritual pilgrimage are the practices that the church has come to realize are essential for deepening one's relationship with God, enriching one's life with others and nurturing one toward wholeness in Christ. While the classical disciplines . . . have both personal and corporate dimensions, the personal disciplines are acts of loving obedience by which we offer our brokenness and bondage to God for liberation. Such disciplines are uniquely shaped to the form of our personal unlikeness to Christ; an example of a personal discipline would be the commitment to abstain from indulging in something that had been destroying us. Without the classical disciplines, personal disciplines can quickly become privatized and even pathological—privatized in the sense of keeping our relationship with God firmly under our control and permitting us to adjust the call to discipleship to fit our agenda, our likes and dislikes, our wants and wishes; pathological in the sense of a spirituality that binds us to inadequate or destructive responses to life. Without personal disciplines, on the other hand, the classical disciplines can quickly become a debilitating façade that covers one's deep needs for transformation" (*Invitation to a Journey*, 76).

Mulholland's understanding of disciplines is nuanced, avoiding the errors of quietism on one side and Pelagianism on the other. In direct contrast to quietism, Mulholland sounds very Wesleyan and Benedictine in his call for Christians to travel the "long and rigorous path of disciplines."[41] Whereas quietism views engagement in spiritual disciplines as problematic over-reliance upon the will,[42] Mulholland views spiritual disciplines as essential in the process of Christian spiritual formation. He comments forthrightly, "The Christian's journey toward wholeness in the image of Christ for the sake of others progresses by means of spiritual disciplines,"[43] which he describes as "[acts] of releasing ourselves in a consistent manner to God, opening [our lives] in a regular way to allow God's transforming work."[44]

Mulholland sees discipline as curative for a culture that habitually pursues instant gratification, yet, despite his view of the necessity of rigorous practice of spiritual disciplines, he is aware that increased discipline is far from universally helpful spiritual guidance. He writes,

> While the avoidance of discipline characterizes much of our culture, the acceptance of disciplines can also be symptomatic of brokenness. There are those for whom disciplines become a rigid structure of life that allows no room for divine serendipities or graced interruptions of the disciplines. There are those for whom disciplines become such a fixed order of being and doing that the possibility of changes in the pattern becomes unthinkable. There are those for whom the disciplines become the total content of their relationship with God, and works righteousness the shape of their spirituality. Somewhere between the extremes of avoidance of discipline and the imprisonment of discipline is the holistic practice of balanced spiritual disciplines which become a means of God's grace to shape us in the image of Christ for others.[45]

---

41. Mulholland, *Invitation to a Journey*, 102–3; "Holiness Emphasis Lectures," 26:59–28:20.

42. See Chan, "Quietism." See also Chan, *Spiritual Theology*, 23, in which Chan quotes Michael Molinos: "To will to operate actively is to offend God because He wishes to be the sole agent. Therefore one must relinquish one's whole self to him and thereafter remain as dead. . . . By doing nothing the soul annihilates itself and returns to its beginning and its origin, the essence of God." For the quotation, Chan cites de Guibert, *Theology*, 148. De Guibert does not provide a reference for the citation.

43. Mulholland, *Invitation to a Journey*, 75.

44. Mulholland, *Invitation to a Journey*, 38.

45. Mulholland, *Invitation to a Journey*, 103.

Accordingly, Mulholland not only guides readers and students away from undisciplined quietist spirituality, but also from the Pelagian-influenced misuse of spiritual disciplines as means of human control of the process of spiritual formation because of the tendency "to turn [transformation] into a self-help project, a do-it-yourself operation."[46] Because of this, for Mulholland, disciplines are simultaneously essential yet not the key factor in human agency in spiritual formation.[47] Instead of the disciplines themselves, Mulholland identifies the key factor as "the inner dynamics of how we engage in the disciplines, the deep inner posture of being we bring to the disciplines."[48] He describes this posture by illustrating a potential experience of a "genuine" spiritual discipline:

> A genuine spiritual discipline . . . is an act of loving obedience that we offer to God with no strings attached. We simply offer it to God for God to do whatever God wants to do with it—even nothing at all! If we want to discover how serious we are about these kinds of spiritual disciplines, we need only ask ourselves, "Am I willing to offer to God this discipline of loving obedience day by day, week by week, month by month, year by year, and have God do nothing with it?" Only when we can answer "yes" to that are we really engaged in spiritual discipline.[49]

Mulholland's nuanced understanding of spiritual disciplines is reflected in his frequent utilization of the parallel expression native to his Wesleyan background of "means of grace," which he employs with comparable frequency to "spiritual disciplines,"[50] and the contextualization

---

46. Mulholland, *Invitation to a Journey*, 134.

47. Mulholland, *Invitation to a Journey*, 135–36.

48. Mulholland, *Invitation to a Journey*, 136. He describes these inner dynamics under the headings of silence, solitude, and prayer, commenting, "Usually these terms are associated with specific practices of spirituality, specific spiritual disciplines. . . . However, when used to describe the inner posture of being we bring to the disciplines, silence, solitude, and prayer take on powerfully new and disturbing dimensions that probe the heart of our being and behavior" (*Invitation to a Journey*, 136). This resembles Merton's distinction between interior and exterior solitude mentioned in chapter 3.

49. Mulholland, "If Christ," 31.

50. For Mulholland, "means of grace" is a broader term than "spiritual disciplines," but includes spiritual disciplines when they are practiced as intended. As examples, see Mulholland, "If Christ," 33–34; *Revelation: Holy Living*, 345; *Invitation to a Journey*, 39, 47, 50, 60, 76, 111, 133, 136, 146–47; *Shaped by the Word*, rev. ed, 94, 120, 124, 132; *Deeper Journey*, 99, 152; *Way of Scripture*, 32, 56, 65; "Wesleyan Doctrine of Scripture," 33. See also the previous discussion of Wesley's means of grace in chapter 2.

of spiritual disciplines as means of grace communicates this non-quietist and non-Pelagian understanding of Christian spiritual practice.

This willingness to engage in spiritual disciplines over time, even when there is no felt sense of the efficacy of the practice, is indicative of Mulholland's *contemplative* Mertonian accent, which has much more room for apophatic spiritual experience than is found in Wesley. Timothy M. Gallagher describes what it means to be contemplative as "progressive development of the capacity to notice the spiritual stirrings of [one's] heart,"[51] and although Wesley values the role of the affections in Christian experience—including the importance of recognizing assurance from the Holy Spirit that one is a child of God,[52] the apophatic capacity for valuing experiences that are void of consolations is underdeveloped in Wesley. As Albert C. Outler succinctly observes of Wesley, "He was not a contemplative man."[53]

Wesley's rejection of contemplative, apophatic spirituality and conflation of it with all of Christian mystical tradition is explored in chapter 4 and exemplified in his letter from June 27, 1766, to Charles Wesley, in which he expresses a lack of any sense of God's presence or activity. He writes,

> I do not feel the wrath of God abiding on me; nor can I believe it does. And yet, this is the mystery: [I do not love God. I never did]. Therefore [I never] believed in the Christian sense of the word. Therefore [I am only an] honest heathen, a proselyte of the Temple, one of the . . . "God-fearers." . . . And yet to be so

---

51. Gallagher, *Examen Prayer*, 118. Gallagher uses the phrase in a section titled "Developing the Contemplative Capacity," in reference to Ignatius of Loyola. He comments, "Classic theology teaches that the work of God's grace presupposes and further enriches all that is human. In terms of the examen, then, whatever increases our *human* capacity to notice experience around and within us simultaneously increases our capacity to notice, with the aid of God's grace, our *spiritual* experience as well" (Gallagher, *Examen Prayer*, 118).

52. See Wesley, *Bicentennial Works*, 1:267–313. See also Smith, *Voice of Jesus*, 42–47.

53. Outler, *John Wesley*, iv. Outler does not define "contemplative," and it is too much of an assumption to fully read Timothy M. Gallagher's description of the term into Outler's usage. Outler is juxtaposing contemplation and action, characterizing Wesley as fully on the active end of the spectrum. He continues, "The marks of incessant haste and urgency are everywhere in what he wrote and did. But this constant activity was everywhere informed and ordered by a clear and conscious understanding of the Christian truth, related always to the exigencies of his life and work" (Outler, *John Wesley*, iv). Nevertheless, this does not negate Gallagher's meaning of contemplative as applied to Wesley, and Outler's statement is true in a broader sense of the term than he indicates.

> employed of God; and so hedged in that I can neither get forward nor backward! Surely there never was such an instance before, from the beginning of the world! If I [ever have had] *that* faith, it would not be so strange. But [I never had any] other . . . awareness of the eternal or invisible world than [I have] now; and that is [none at all], unless such as fairly shines from reason's glimmering ray. [I have no] direct witness (I do not say that [I am a child of God]) but of anything invisible or eternal."[54]

Outler notes that this letter is exceptional for Wesley since "one of the remarkable features of Wesley's career after 1739 is the steadiness of his mood and the near total absence of emotional depressions."[55] In contrast, Merton's grounding in St. John of the Cross fostered his ability to view his experiences of lack of sense of consolation as natural and expected parts of his spiritual journey rather than departures from it. In contrast to Wesley's desperation resulting from a lack of sensed awareness of God, Merton's contemplative disciplines and their apophatic characteristics led him to understand contemplation as cultivating an awareness that "we are in the presence of God, that we live in Christ, that in the Spirit of God we 'see' God our Father without 'seeing.' We know him in 'unknowing.'"[56] For example, Merton describes contemplative prayer as

> sometimes quite difficult. If we bear with hardship in prayer and wait patiently for the time of grace, we may well discover that meditation and prayer are very joyful experiences. We should not, however, judge the value of our meditation by "how we feel." A hard and apparently fruitless meditation may in fact be much more valuable than one that is easy, happy, enlightened, and apparently a big success.[57]

Ironically, despite the high frequency of the term in Merton's writings, "contemplative" is a term Mulholland rarely uses in his publications, even though he is a frequently-referenced contributor to SFM's emphasis on contemplative reading of Scripture.[58] In one of his rare usages of the

---

54. Wesley, *Letters*, 5:15–17; Outler, *John Wesley*, 81–82. All brackets and punctuation are original to Telford, the editor of Wesley's *Letters*, indicating translations and expansions of Wesley's shorthand.

55. Outler, *John Wesley*, 80–81.

56. Merton, *Contemplative Prayer*, 34.

57. Merton, *Contemplative Prayer*, 34. Specifically, Merton is describing meditation.

58. For example, terms such as "contemplative," "contemplate," and "contemplation" are not present in any of the editions of *Shaped by the Word*, and the only instances of the terms in *Way of Scripture* are in Mulholland's quotations of others. As examples

term, however, Mulholland highlights the connection between the contemplative nature of formational reading of Scripture and its openness to either the fullness or emptiness of the experience of the practice, as he writes, "Instead of coming to the text with our agenda, we come in a posture of openness to God's agenda.... We take a contemplative posture that is open to ambiguity and mystery."[59]

This openness to mystery is indicative of the inextricable association between contemplative and *mystical* qualities in Mulholland's Mertonian accent. As Robert C. Pelfrey notes, "Mysticism ... means to follow the path of mystery,"[60] which Mulholland views as "one part of genuine spiritual pilgrimage."[61] Mulholland writes,

> Where one has all the right answers, all the easy answers, all the quick fixes, there is no room for mystery. There is no room for paradox. And if there is no room for mystery there is no room for God, because God is the ultimate mystery. One part of genuine spiritual pilgrimage is coming to the point where we let go of our limited concept of God. We let go of that box within which we have enclosed God, and we open ourselves to allow God to be whatever God wants to be in our life. When we do this, we also lose our former awareness and sense of God's presence. We lose our grasp upon God. Here, you see, is where faith enters into mystery, into the dark night of the soul. And here we need one another, in the strength of corporate spirituality, to encourage, to sustain, to support, to enable us to let go of our control of God, to let God be God, and to dwell in the mystery.[62]

Mulholland's openness to contemplative experience and mystical theology from within his Wesleyan tradition that can be opposed to them stems from his own conversion, which he describes as a "very mystical, a very relational experience":[63]

> Through a series of events in my life, [I realized] that I was hollow inside, that there was no center that held, that my life was

---

of works on contemplative reading in which he is cited, see Barton, *Sacred Rhythms*, 45–61; Rivera, *Introducción a las Disciplinas*, 51–60; Porter, "Biblical and Contemplative Spirituality," 141.

59. Mulholland, *Invitation to a Journey*, 111–12.
60. Pelfrey, *Untold Story*, xii.
61. Mulholland, *Invitation to a Journey*, 149.
62. Mulholland, *Invitation to a Journey*, 148–49.
63. Mulholland and Barton, "Spiritual Transformation," 23:38–24:00.

a façade out there. I had been turned off to Christianity years before—I knew there was nothing there. And so, I began . . . a frantic search for something to fill that void, reading all other religions, philosophy, and things like that. But I was not able to find anything. Finally, I decided, if there was no meaning to my life, then it wasn't worth living. So I decided [to commit] suicide. I was sitting at home, seeking to work up enough courage to go upstairs and put a shell in my rifle and put it through my head.

Then I noticed a little book in the couch, and I knew what it was when I saw it. It was Ralph Spalding Cushman's *Pocket Book of Faith*.[64] The pastor of the church had given every graduate one of those. Well, I'd had a bad experience with the pastor, and when I saw who it was from, I just slung it across the room. Apparently, it fell down the couch and worked its way out at the opportune time. . . . I was sure there was nothing in Christianity, but it wouldn't hurt to look. So, I noticed a section in this little book called "Faith in the Evening." . . . I sat in my bed and started working through this section. It began with a poem . . . and the poem was something like this, "Just as flood tides fill every nook and cranny of the bay, so the presence . . . of God can fill my life."[65]

That got my attention, because I had been looking for something to fill this black hole. And then the next thing was an examen, where [in] a series of questions, you went back and looked over your day . . . then there was a prayer of confession . . . so . . . I . . . knelt down and I began reading this prayer. And as I began reading this prayer, I suddenly *knew*, in—Paul talks about knowing the love of Christ that surpasses knowledge, that there's no way to get your mind around what this experience was. . . . I realized that there was a God and that God was in that room. And at the same time, I realized that this presence—because I had no idea who God was or what God was like—that this presence was the answer to this emptiness within, but that unless I invited this presence to come in, nothing was going to happen. And so not with my lips, but somewhere deep within, I

---

64. Cushman, *Pocket Book of Faith*.

65. The passage he references is not a poem but a quotation from Albert W. Palmer: "His love is round about me, and as flood tides from the ocean fill each cranny of the bay, so power and peace from God can fill my life as I rest quietly in Him" (Cushman, *Pocket Book of Faith*, 66–67). The conversation in which Mulholland relates this is more than sixty years after the occurrence, and the fact that he could remember the wording this closely to verbatim when asked about it conversationally indicates the depth to which it impacted him.

just said yes, and experienced that presence just sort of flooding my being.

So that was the mystical experience. And there have been times in my Christian journey when the inescapable reality of that experience has been the only thing that held me steady. I could not deny what had happened there.[66]

For Mulholland, as for the majority of Christian mystics, while such exceptional experiences are related to mysticism (and, therefore, referred to as "mystical experience"), experiences of any type do not constitute the whole, nor even the center of mysticism. Rather, as union with God was explored as a point of synthesis between Wesley and Merton in chapter 4, it is union that forms the center of Mulholland's mysticism. He says in a 2006 conference presentation,

> There are many different definitions of mystical experience, but ... I would suggest that mystical experience is a life of intimate, loving union with God. That it is that for which we were created. That it is this that is the unbelievable goal of the spiritual life, a life of loving union with God. It is that for which we hunger and thirst in the depths of our being. And it is that for which God is at work in us through his cruciform love. In every relationship of our life, in every situation and circumstance of our daily living, God is at work to draw us into that relationship of loving union with him.[67]

Mulholland titles the first chapter of *The Deeper Journey* as "The Goal," and devotes it to identification of the mystical emphasis on "a life of loving union with God at the depths of our being" as "the purpose of the Christian life."[68] This emphasis highlights how Mulholland's definition of Scripture explored above is not only non-fundamentalist and evangelical but also substantively mystical. In the same article in which he first published his definition of Scripture, he connects the mystical themes of mystery and union to his understanding of the nature of Scripture:

> While we wrestle with the mystery of God becoming human, how Jesus could be both fully human and fully divine, Christian tradition has recognized from the beginning that God was in Jesus. There is, however, another mystery in the Christian

---

66. Mulholland and Barton, "Spiritual Transformation," 26:13–29:58. Mulholland also tells the story in "NT 666," video of lecture 16, 51:54–58:30.

67. Mulholland, "Unbelievable Goal," 9.

68. Mulholland, *Deeper Journey*, 14.

experience, a companion to the Word become flesh: the mystery of the Word becoming "text." The Word becomes text in order to provide a place of transforming encounter with God so that the Word might become flesh in us in our world. The perennial discussions as to the nature of scripture, the character of its inspiration, its authority, its canonical status, are but partial and incomplete attempts to wrestle with this profound mystery in the same way that the Christological discussions of Christian history have wrestled in partial and incomplete ways with the mystery of the Word become flesh. . . . The Word become flesh is, ultimately, an unfathomable mystery. The Word become text is an equally dense enigma. Now if these two enigmatic realities are not enough to blow our minds, together they point to yet another and even more opaque mystery: the Word is to become flesh in us![69]

Lest this perspective be seen superficially and become susceptible to the critiques of individualism referenced above, it is critical to understand that for Mulholland and the sources he draws from in the Bible and Christian mystical tradition, "such a life of loving union with God results in Christlikeness—wholeness in the image of God. This is not a self-referenced, self-contained, achievement independent from our life with others in creation. . . . To be in the image of God, to be Christlike . . . is to be one in whom God's cruciform love becomes incarnate in relationships with others and in one's participation in the created order."[70]

Mulholland states this in an article published thirty years after his first lectures at the opening session of the URA in the context of addressing another iteration of the same paradox Merton addressed by identifying increased capacity for love as the purpose of his solitude. By the time Mulholland's article, "Spiritual Formation in Christ *and* Mission with Christ," was published in 2013, the similar inward versus outward tension was evident and, therefore, being countered in publications concerning "the false dichotomy between Christian spirituality and Christian mission."[71] In his article, Mulholland utilizes the metaphor of inhaling and exhaling to illustrate the interrelationship between formational and missional emphases:

---

69. Mulholland, "Biblical Spirituality," 209–10.
70. Mulholland, "Spiritual Formation in Christ," 13.
71. Porter, "Special Theme Issue," 3.

> The perennial tension between the contemplative life and the active life, between spiritual formation in Christ and mission with Christ, might be likened to the tension between breathing in and breathing out. Can there be any breathing in without breathing out? Can there be any breathing out without breathing in? One might say, "Yes"; but the consequences are less than desirable! There is a symbiotic reality here. There are not three classes of humans: "breathers in," "breathers out," and "breathers in and out."[72]

He continues,

> It seems clear that a spirituality that nurtures one in cruciform love (Christlikeness) is not only the core reality of being Christian, but also the source from which all genuine "doing" (mission) flows. Every advance in being formed in the image of Christ becomes incarnate and is confirmed by a corresponding advance in the Christlikeness of doing. To think of Christian spirituality and "mission" as separate and discrete aspects of the Christian life is a great mistake. They are the inseparable symbiosis of "breathing in" (spiritual formation) and "breathing out" (mission).[73]

Therefore, for Mulholland, it is not that attention to one's spiritual formation is important as preparation for ministry. Rather, the spiritual formation that each person is always experiencing is inevitably incarnated in their relationships and actions, making formation and ministry not only related movements, but the same movement. This echoes Merton's epiphany at Fourth and Walnut in Louisville that his solitude was for the sake of the strangers who passed by at the busy intersection, because solitude cultivated his capacity for love and clarity in his capacity to see others and the world.

The unitive nature of the inward and outward journey is particularly present in the writings of John of Ruusbroec, whom Merton read and referred to as "one of the greatest Christian mystics and the author of magnificent books on contemplation."[74] Ruusbroec refers to the ideal of Christian perfection in love as "the common life," as it is the life God lives

---

72. Mulholland, "Spiritual Formation in Christ," 13.
73. Mulholland, "Spiritual Formation in Christ," 16.
74. Merton, *Ascent to Truth*, 325. Merton also mentions reading Ruusbroec (spelled Ruysbroeck in Merton's writings) in journal entries of December 29, 1946, and January 18, 1947, in *Sign of Jonas*, 20, 23. Ruusbroec's influence on Merton is also explored in Harris, "Thomas Merton's Spiritual Formation," 190.

in the Trinity and in which humans are invited to participate.[75] Ruusbroec prefigures Mulholland's descriptions of cruciform love as he writes of "Christ as our model, for he gave himself completely to all in common, does so still, and will do so for all eternity. He was sent to earth for the common benefit of all who wished to turn to him."[76] Paradoxically, Ruusbroec includes this description of the outward orientation of Christ's life in his focus on the interior life of the Christian in the central section of his book, *The Spiritual Espousals*. For Ruusbroec (as also later for Merton and Mulholland), a Christian's journey inward through practices such as solitude is inherently identified with that person's journey outward in Christlike love for others. To apply Mulholland's phrase to Ruusbroec's insight, it is neither the inward nor outward movement that constitutes a person's "life in loving union with God," but it is the "inseparable symbiosis" of inward and outward movement that *is* a person's "common life" with the Father, Son, and Holy Spirit. Pelfrey comments, for Ruusbroec, "it is not a choice nor even a vacillation between solitary contemplation or communal charity, but one simultaneous movement,"[77] which also adequately describes Mulholland's concept of "formation in Christ *and* mission with Christ."

Thus, Mulholland states in the final public teaching prior to his death, "We tend to think of mystics as the 'weirdos' out there on the fringes of the faith . . . [but] they are at the center. . . . What they carry to us, what they proclaim to us, is the reality of a life hid with Christ in God."[78]

CASE STUDIES FROM MULHOLLAND'S MAJOR SPIRITUAL FORMATION WORKS

With the combination of Mulholland's Wesleyan accent in the SFM through the non-fundamentalist pietistic evangelical qualities of his

75. See Pelfrey, *Spiritual Formation*, 156–76.

76. Ruusbroec, *Spiritual Espousals*, 106. For an example comparison with Mulholland, he writes, "The deepest revelation of the essence of God's image is disclosed through the Cross. The Cross is not something God did; it is God's ultimate and crucial revelation of the essence of God's being: God is cruciform love. God's love is a radically other-referenced love, a love that seeks the wellbeing of the other and of all creation devoid of any self-referenced motives, a love that pours itself out for the redemption of others and all creation" (Mulholland, "Spiritual Formation in Christ," 13).

77. Pelfrey, email message to the author, November 3, 2020.

78. Mulholland, "Sake of Others," session two, 40:53–41:52.

works and his Mertonian accent through the non-quietist, contemplative mystical qualities, it now remains to explore Mulholland's major works in the SFM as case studies of his Wesleyan and Mertonian confluence. This exploration is organized below according to his three most noteworthy spiritual formation titles: first, *Shaped by the Word* represents the large extent of the influences of Wesley and Merton on Mulholland and his initial contribution to the SFM; second, *Invitation to a Journey*'s consideration of "the nature of the spiritual disciplines" includes a Mertonian interpretation of Wesley's doctrine of Christian perfection; and third, *The Deeper Journey* includes a Wesleyan exploration of the Mertonian themes of the true and false self.

Shaped by the Word (1985)

One glance at the table of contents of *Shaped by the Word* is all that is necessary to establish Wesley's influence on Mulholland when he made his initial major contribution to the burgeoning SFM through the 1983 lectures, The Place of Scripture in Spiritual Formation, that were published in the book in 1985. He dedicates an entire chapter to "Wesley's Guidelines for Reading Scripture" and includes an excerpt from Wesley as an appendix.[79] Any reader who encounters the thirty-eight references to Wesley in the text can conclude that Wesley is a major influence on Mulholland's approach.

The extensive influence of Merton on *Shaped by the Word*, in contrast, is less obvious to most of its readers. If the plausible assumption is accurate that significantly more readers have encountered *Shaped by the Word* since its 2000 revised edition than they did in the 15 years that passed in between its first and second editions,[80] Merton's impact upon the book is obscured to readers without a prior familiarity with Merton's *Opening the Bible* and *Seeds of Contemplation* or *New Seeds of Contemplation*. Merton's *Opening the Bible* is cited twenty-seven times in the first edition of *Shaped by the Word* (frequently enough that permission from the Merton Legacy Trust for republication of excerpts is noted on the copyright page), but it is never cited in the revised edition even though

---

79. Mulholland, *Shaped by the Word*, 119–28, 165–66.

80. Upper Room also published an "anniversary edition" in 2023. In contrast to the significant editorial changes between the 1985 first edition and 2000 revised edition, the body of the book remains the same between the 2000 and 2023 editions. The anniversary edition includes a new foreword by Steve Harper.

Mulholland's ideas in the revised edition are no less Mertonian. Because the first edition is very close to a transcript of Mulholland's The Place of Scripture in Spiritual Formation lectures, the editorial changes in the revised edition are understandable for readability, although they (presumably, unintentionally) went too far, resulting in the obscuration of the influence of *Opening the Bible*.

One example is a comparison of the passage in which Merton is first cited in the first edition with its parallel in the revised edition. In the first edition, Mulholland writes, "The Word is truly the mediator between us and God. The Word is 'for us' with respect to God, and it is also 'for God' with respect to us. This introduces the intrusive nature of the Word of God. The Word of God breaks into the midst of life. Merton speaks of the Word of God meeting us in encounter and event. Let me give you my definition of the Word of God."[81] The passage is almost verbatim in the revised edition but without the reference to Merton: "The Word is truly the mediator between us and God. The Word is 'for us' with respect to God, and it is also 'for God' with respect to us. This *dual purpose* introduces the intrusive nature of the Word of God. The Word of God breaks into the midst of life. ['Merton speaks . . . " sentence omitted.] Let me give you my definition of the Word of God."[82] This illustrates how one of the many citations of *Opening the Bible* is unnecessary to the flow of the writing and could be edited out, but doing so leaves the reader of the revision unaware of Merton's influence.[83]

Merton's fundamental influence on *Shaped by the Word* is evident beyond this issue with citations of *Opening the Bible*. One of Mulholland's central ideas in the book is that all people can view themselves as "words" of God. He writes,

> You are a "word" of God! Every human being is a word that God speaks into existence. Paul makes a profound statement in Ephesians 1:4 (paraphrased): "God chose us in Christ before the foundation of the world that we should be holy and blameless before God in love." I had read this passage for years, but suddenly I took notice of the word *chose*. It is composed from two

81. Mulholland, *Shaped by the Word*, 40.
82. Mulholland, *Shaped by the Word* (2000), 41. Changes indicated in italics.
83. This is no accusation of plagiarism. The ideas presented are genuinely Mulholland's. Merton's influence on those ideas is much more obvious in the first edition. Also, twenty-seven citations in a first edition then edited out of a revised edition would be a strange and ineffective method for plagiarizing another's thought.

Greek words, the preposition *ek* and the basic word *lektos*, which comes from *lego*. *Ek* means "out of" or "forth from." *Lego* means "to speak." It seems perfectly legitimate to translate the compound word as "spoken forth." After all, if we "choose" someone or something, do we not speak that person or object forth from among our other options? Thus Paul is saying that God "spoke us forth in Christ before the foundation of the world that we should be holy and blameless before God in love."[84]

He continues,

Our "word," this word with a small *w* that God is breathing forth, is to be incarnate in us. Our physical life, our psychological, mental, emotional life—our whole created being is the vehicle for the expression of that "word" God speaks us forth to be in the lives of others. We are created to be incarnate "words" of God. In all that we are and in all that we do with one another in the world, God is seeking to bring to full expression that "word" God is speaking us forth to be. But the "word" we are, this "word" incarnate in us, is constantly being shaped in us—in our incarnation. It is being shaped either positively or negatively—positively when our "word" is being shaped by the Word of God, negatively when our "word" is being garbled and distorted and debased by the values and structures of the world.[85]

Mulholland later explains,

The focal shaping of our "word" into wholeness in the image of Christ comes by allowing our "word" to be shaped by the Word of God. In a profound sense, our "word" is hidden in the Word; the essence of our being is rooted in the essence of God's nature. It is to this reality that being created in God's image points us (Gen. 1:26ff.). Who we are in the essence of our wholeness is an image of who God is. When we begin to allow our "word" to reverberate to the Word, we begin to experience increasing levels of wholeness in our being. We begin to experience that quality of wholeness in our interactions with others and our involvement in life for which we were spoken forth by God.[86]

---

84. Mulholland, *Shaped by the Word* (2000), 34. There are only minor edits from the first edition (*Shaped by the Word*, 34).

85. Mulholland, *Shaped by the Word* (2000), 35–36. There are only minor edits from the first edition (*Shaped by the Word*, 35–36).

86. Mulholland, *Shaped by the Word* (2000), 37. There are only minor edits from the first edition (*Shaped by the Word*, 37).

When Mulholland's explanation of this concept is viewed in relation to two passages from Merton in *New Seeds*, this idea that is fundamental to *Shaped by the Word* is evident as a Mertonian concept further developed through Mulholland's biblical exegesis and uniquely applied to his topic of formational reading of Scripture.

Merton writes,

> Contemplation is . . . the response to a call: a call from Him Who has no voice, and yet Who speaks in everything that is, and Who, most of all, speaks in the depths of our own being: for *we ourselves are words of His. But we are words that are meant to respond to Him, to answer to Him, to echo Him, and even in some way to contain Him and signify Him.* Contemplation is this echo. It is a deep resonance in the inmost center of our spirit in which our very life loses its separate voice and re-sounds with the majesty and the mercy of the Hidden and Living One. He answers Himself in us and this answer is divine life, divine creativity, making all things new. We ourselves become His echo and His answer.[87]

In another essay in *New Seeds*, he comments,

> *God utters me like a word containing a partial thought of Himself.* A word will never be able to comprehend the voice that utters it. But if I am true to the concept that God utters in me, if I am true to the thought of Him I was meant to embody, I shall be full of His actuality and find Him everywhere in myself, and find myself nowhere. I shall be lost in Him: that is, I shall find myself. I shall be "saved."[88]

Mulholland's background as an evangelical and his training as a New Testament scholar are evident in how he develops Merton's concept through his skills as a Wesleyan exegete. As explored below, he again employs this Wesleyan exegetical approach to Merton's concepts of the true and false self in *The Deeper Journey*.

---

87. Merton, *New Seeds*, 3; emphasis added. This is from the book's opening essay, "What Is Contemplation?" Merton wrote and added this after *Seeds of Contemplation*.

88. Merton, *New Seeds*, 37; emphasis added. Compare to the minor changes from *Seeds of Contemplation*, 31.

Invitation to a Journey *(1993)*

Between the instances in *Shaped by the Word* and *The Deeper Journey* of Mulholland's development of Mertonian ideas through his Wesleyan exegetical toolset, a similar dynamic is evident in a significant section of *Invitation to a Journey*. In this text, the dynamic is reversed as Mulholland interprets a fundamental Wesleyan doctrine through a Mertonian lens.

Mulholland dedicates the majority of his chapter on "The Nature of the Spiritual Disciplines" to his interpretation of the sixth through eighth chapters of Romans,[89] commenting that some of the pericope "is puzzling at first reading, but closer scrutiny discloses the nature of spiritual disciplines and reveals how we work and how God works to transform our deadness into life, our brokenness into wholeness, our bondage into freedom in Christ."[90] Mulholland's attention in most of this section of the book is on the meaning of Paul's references to the "dead body" in Rom 7:24 and 8:10 and the "body of sin" in Rom 6:6 and how God uses spiritual disciplines to bring life and wholeness instead. Mulholland states,

> Here is the great work of God in the process of spiritual formation. God is at work in the areas of our deadness to transform them into life in the image of Christ. This is the essential nature of our pilgrimage. Here is where God is working to conform each of us to the image of Christ for the sake of others. God's work is unique in each person, because none of us has exactly the same configuration of the dead body. Our "dead body," that complex structure of harmful habits, deeply ingrained attitudes, troubling perspectives, destructive ways of relating to others, unhealthy modes of reacting and responding to the world, is very individual. We may share some of the same general forms of deadness, but the nature of our particular deadness is always uniquely shaped to us. So Paul tells us that although this condition (spirit alive because of righteousness, body dead because of sin) is a normal part of Christian experience, it is also the base from which God works to move us toward wholeness in Christ.[91]

Mulholland believes that Paul describes two possible responses to this condition. First, people can "continue to allow the 'dead body' to rule

---

89. The chapter is in Mulholland, *Invitation to a Journey*, 120–34; the Romans passages are addressed in 120–30.

90. Mulholland, *Invitation to a Journey*, 121.

91. Mulholland, *Invitation to a Journey*, 128.

their lives [and] gradually slip back into the deadness out of which they were called to life."[92] Paul's second option is identified in Rom 8:13: "If, by the Spirit, you put to death the deeds of the body, you will live." Mulholland comments, "Here is where Paul puts his finger on the dynamics of that very personalized set of spiritual disciplines by which God raises our deadness into life, our brokenness into wholeness, and conforms us to the image of Christ for others."[93]

In the midst of this section of his chapter, Mulholland focuses for a few paragraphs on the verses preceding Paul's "piercing cry" of 7:24: "Wretched man that I am! Who will deliver me from *this body of death*?"[94] He describes the experience he is "sure . . . has been part of your own pilgrimage in Christ: the good you want to do, you do not do, while the evil you do not want to do is what you do."[95] He makes a claim that he is aware is contrary to "many in [his] own Wesleyan tradition, and particularly in its Holiness branch,"[96] who view Rom 7:14–25 as Paul's description of himself before his conversion. He writes, "Paul makes a most significant statement, one that is vital for our understanding of the reality he is conveying. He affirms [in 7:22], 'I delight in the law of God in my inmost being.'"[97] He then notes the similarity between this statement from Paul and Wesley's description of Christian perfection: "The will is entirely subject to the will of God and the affections wholly fixed on him,"[98] stating that he does not see the common Wesleyan interpretation of the passage as referring to a pre-conversion Paul as possible because, in 7:22 and throughout the passage, Paul's will is consistently described as genuinely oriented toward what is good.[99] Although Wesley interprets Paul's words as a description of "the whole process of a man reasoning, groaning, striving, and *escaping from the legal to the evangelical state*,"[100] Mulholland disagrees and states elsewhere that he views the passage as

---

92. Mulholland, *Invitation to a Journey*, 129.
93. Mulholland, *Invitation to a Journey*, 129.
94. Mulholland, *Invitation to a Journey*, 124–25.
95. Mulholland, *Invitation to a Journey*, 125, referencing Rom 7:14–25. Notably, this passage is also referenced in Mulholland, *Shaped by the Word*, 36–37, 96 and *Deeper Journey*, 24–27.
96. Mulholland, *Invitation to a Journey*, 124.
97. Mulholland, *Invitation to a Journey*, 123.
98. Wesley, "Thoughts on Christian Perfection," in Outler, *John Wesley*, 286.
99. Mulholland, *Invitation to a Journey*, 123.
100. See the note on Rom 7:14 in Wesley, *Explanatory Notes*, 392. Emphasis added.

"the witness of a *sanctified* believer. Paul's heart is totally given over to God."[101]

Mulholland's topic in *Invitation to a Journey* is the nature of spiritual disciplines and how they relate to the "complex network of habits and attitudes"[102] rather than his development of the Wesleyan doctrine of Christian perfection, and, therefore, the text does not explore in more depth the tension of his interpretation with prevalent Wesleyan views of sanctification. However, a 1989 lecture at ATS's "Holiness Emphasis Week," which is part of the development of his thought that became this chapter in *Invitation to a Journey*, does explore Mulholland's understanding as an alternative to the conventional Wesleyan view.[103]

As established in chapter 4, Wesley and Merton both understand the will's orientation toward love, rather than flawlessness, as constitutive of holiness in the lives of Christians. However, Mulholland observes an inconsistency in Wesley's assessment of Paul's recognition of his inability to fully do the good that he desires. Wesley's insistence that "omissions . . . shortcomings . . . mistakes in judgment and practice . . . defects of various kinds . . . and whatever infirmities necessarily flow from the corruptible state of the body are *no way contrary to love*"[104] is at variance with his view that the Romans passage must refer to experience other than that of a sanctified Christian, even though Paul wills what is good and delights in God's law in his inmost being.[105]

Although Merton does not engage Rom 7:14–25 in the exegetical manner of Wesley and Mulholland, a brief reference to 7:24–25 by Merton

---

101. Mulholland, "Holiness Emphasis," 18:04–18:24.

102. Mulholland, *Invitation to a Journey*, 125.

103. Mulholland, "Holiness Emphasis." The extent to which Mulholland's interpretation of Rom 7:14–25 differs from the conventional Wesleyan view is evident in the recorded questions and responses between him and the Wesleyan scholars who were present for the lecture. The first response is indicative, in which one of Mulholland's colleagues states, "I've just never in all my life, having been a part of the Holiness Movement and read extensively in it, ever heard Romans 7 being used as a testimony of one who's been entirely sanctified" (30:49–31:03). Another colleague says to Mulholland, "Whether you're completely right or wrong, I want to thank you for at least jumping in here and going for it" (52:37–52:52). The general tenor of the comments from others is that they were not swayed from the conventional interpretation.

104. Wesley, "Thoughts on Christian Perfection," in Outler, *John Wesley*, 286. Emphasis added.

105. Mulholland attributes the source of the difference between his interpretation of Paul and that of Wesley to the different usages of "sin" in Paul and Wesley. See Mulholland, *Invitation to a Journey*, 124; "Holiness Emphasis," 3:27–25:12.

in *The New Man* is illustrative of his view of the dynamics Mulholland explores in his respective section of *Invitation to a Journey*. Merton writes,

> All our strange ideas of conflict with God are born of the war that is within ourselves—the war between the "two laws"—the law of sin in our lower self and the law of God in our conscience. We are not fighting God, we are fighting ourselves. God, in His mercy, seeks to bring us peace—to reconcile us with ourselves. When we are reconciled to our true selves we find ourselves one with Him. "Who will deliver me from the body of this death? The grace of God through Jesus Christ our Lord" (Romans 7:24, 25). Grace is not a strange, magic substance which is subtly filtered into our souls to act as a kind of spiritual penicillin. Grace is unity, oneness within ourselves, oneness with God. Grace is the peace of friendship with God—and if it does not necessarily bring us "felt" peace, it nevertheless gives us every reason to be at peace, if we could only understand and appreciate what it means. Grace means that *there is no opposition* between man and God, and that man is able to be sufficiently united within himself to live without opposition to God. Grace is friendship with God. And more—it is sonship. It makes us the "beloved sons" of God in whom He is "well-pleased."[106]

What Merton here characterizes as "fighting ourselves" is akin to Mulholland's interpretation of Paul's concept of the "dead body"—"those old harmful habits, deeply ingrained attitudes, troubling perspectives, destructive ways of relating to others, unhealthy modes of reacting and responding to the world" that remain as a "normal" (but not "normative") part of Christian experience.[107] To Mulholland's point, it is understandable that such a complex combination of dynamics would result in the experience of "Romans 7 moments"[108] of not doing what one wants to

---

106. Merton, *New Man*, 41–42. See Thurston, "Thomas Merton," 14–18. The article does not deal directly with this passage of Romans, but Thurston describes Merton's thought as "startlingly Pauline in its assumptions" ("Thomas Merton," 14). She comments, "The whole of *The New Man* rests on Pauline assumptions about the regeneration of the human person in Christ. An index of Pauline texts in that volume would be extensive" ("Thomas Merton," 15). Mulholland assigned Merton's *The New Man* and *Opening the Bible* as required texts in a Doctor of Ministry course. See Mulholland, "DM 856."

107. Mulholland, *Invitation to a Journey*, 127.

108. See Mulholland, *Deeper Journey*, 24–26 for his description of one of his own experiences of a "Romans 7 moment."

do and vice-versa even after the will is oriented toward love of God and love of others.

Mulholland's recharacterization for Wesleyans of Rom 7:14–25 is indicative of the variety of experience only rarely indicated after 1739 in Wesley but often present in Merton's reflective writings. Even though Wesley's theology of sanctification is adamant that human holiness and shortcomings are not mutually exclusive, he rarely processes his own mistakes or errors in judgment after his major crisis of faith is resolved in the events leading up to and following his Aldersgate experience. Although Wesley and Merton are highly similar in their beliefs about grace, Wesley's aversion to apophatic theology and experience is naturally not characterized by Merton's statement in the passage just cited: "Grace is the peace of friendship with God—and if it does not necessarily bring us 'felt' peace, it nevertheless gives us every reason to be at peace."[109]

Merton's contemplative spirituality and high degree of transparency in his writings provide a lens through which Mulholland is able to view Rom 7:14–25 as normal experience of sanctified Christians even though it contrasts with convention in his Wesleyan tradition.[110] As an example, a predecessor of Merton's self-reflective writing style was Peter Abelard, of whom Merton comments in his journal, "After all these years I have a greater liking for Abelard than for St. Bernard. I understand him better, am closer to him. His weaknesses were great, his character had terrible flaws, he was vain and impressive. He did not control his vanity as Bernard did. It ruined him."[111] As this indicates, Merton could admire flawed people and was very aware of flaws within himself, but this is not antithetical to self-consecration to love as the focus of his sanctification. Another journal entry indicates a multifaceted combination of self-awareness, interior conflict, compassion for his own flaws and those of others around him, focus on love, desire for both solitude and community, and emphasis on spiritual disciplines as essential in his continuing sanctification:

> I see how easily I could go nuts and don't especially care. I see the huge flaws in myself and don't know what to do about them.

---

109. Merton, *New Man*, 42.

110. This is not to claim that Merton's reflective writings are the basis from which Mulholland offers his interpretation. Mulholland's primary basis is his biblical exegesis. However, he was well acquainted with Merton's writings by the time of his "Holiness Emphasis" lecture, and Merton's story can therefore be seen as a contributor to Mulholland's alternative Wesleyan perspective.

111. Merton, *Turning Toward the World*, 256.

> Die of them eventually, I suppose, what else can I do? I live a flawed and inconsequential life, believing in God's love. But faith can no longer be naive and sentimental. I cannot explain things away with it. Need for deeper meditation. I certainly see more clearly where I need to go and how (surprising how my prayer in community had really reached a dead end for *years* and stayed there—fortunately I could get out to the woods and my spirit could breathe). Still, Gethsemani too has to be fully accepted. My long refusal to fully identify myself with the place is futile (and identifying myself in some forlorn and lonesome way would be worse). It is simply where I am, and the monks are who they are: not monks but people, and the younger ones are more truly people than the old ones, who are also good in their own way.[112]

While Merton was respected by others in his monastery, they were also very aware of his flaws. This is evident in Merton's anxiety that he would be elected as abbot of Gethsemani after Dom James Fox announced his retirement in the fall of 1967. Mott comments,

> In his assessment of the abbatial elections, which would be held early in the New Year, Merton demonstrated a masterly degree of misreading and general maladroitness. He supposed there would be a strong movement to make him abbot, where there was little evidence for this. Much alarmed at the prospect, he included in his Sunday conference on December 17 [1967], a statement that he would not accept if he were elected. After this, Father Flavian teased him that the statement had made his election virtually certain—it would be read as a sign of the necessary humility.[113]

The community's regard for Merton included certitude on his shortcomings relative to the role of an abbot—perhaps beyond that of Merton toward himself. After election on January 13, 1968, "Merton discovered at least that he had been a poor prophet, totally misreading the spirit of the community. Father Flavian Burns was elected abbot 'by a large majority and surprisingly fast.'"[114] Nevertheless, members of his monastic community also saw him as "very much himself, very alive and very real. When you met him, spoke with him, had dealings with him, you never

---

112. Merton, *Dancing in the Water*, 328.
113. Mott, *Seven Mountains*, 503.
114. Mott, *Seven Mountains*, 506, citing the entry from January 15, 1967, in Merton, *Other Side*, 40.

felt you were dealing with something artificial: quite the opposite. He was nothing if not real. . . . What he said and what he did was rooted in love for God and man."[115]

To be very much one's self, alive, real, and rooted in love for God and others while also being one whose shortcomings are evident and not denied but acknowledged as part of the person who is loved by God, and to rely on God's grace through appropriate spiritual disciplines for continued growth in holiness, is to have a life consistent with conceptions of sanctification found in Wesley, Merton, and Mulholland. Merton's life and writings are valuably illustrative of how the "Romans 7 moment" of not doing the good that genuinely is one's desire can be seen in Mulholland's view as a normal part of the experience of sanctification rather than its prelude.

Mulholland's alternative understanding of the Wesleyan doctrine of Christian perfection and its inclusion of the tension characteristic of Merton described in Rom 7:14–25 is more consistent with views of sanctification generally represented in SFM literature than the conventional Wesleyan view that relegates such experience to non-sanctified people. This explains why sanctification can be seen as the central theological emphasis in the SFM, with Mulholland and many other Wesleyans involved in the movement, but without the SFM being characterized as a distinctively Wesleyan approach to growth in holiness. Porter comments on the non-sectarian emphasis on sanctification that is characteristic of the movement,

> The topic of spiritual formation within evangelicalism is simply the Protestant theological category of 'sanctification' *in a new key*. The Protestant theological category of "sanctification" has traditionally referred to the process of the believer being made holy, which is "to be conformed to the image of Christ" (Rom 8:29). While there have been various conceptions of this sanctification process within Protestantism, the underlying unity to these divergent views has been the attempt to spell out the nature and dynamics of growth in holiness (cf. 1 Pet 1:14–16). Partly due to distorted treatments of sanctification, alternative terms such as "spiritual formation," "spiritual theology," and "Christian spirituality" have become common within evangelical circles. While these terms and the plethora of viewpoints which accompany them often sound much different than typical evangelical presentations of sanctification, this should not detract us from

---

115. Kelty, "Man," 29.

the realization that what is being discussed under the heading of "spiritual formation" (at least within evangelical Protestantism) is none other than views regarding the nature and dynamics of growth in Christian holiness.[116]

The Deeper Journey (2006)

As explored above, there is plain evidence of Wesley's influence on Mulholland's thought in *Shaped by the Word*, while Merton's influence is present but obscured in the revised edition. Because Merton is not referenced in Mulholland's Wesleyan exegetical exploration of the theme of humans as words spoken by God in any of the book's editions, the influence is unlikely to be recognized unless readers are familiar with both Mulholland's work and the two brief passages in *Seeds of Contemplation* and *New Seeds* in which Merton describes the concept.

There is a significant similarity and a significant difference to this in Mulholland's work in *The Deeper Journey*. The similarity is that Mulholland again takes a Mertonian concept and develops it with scholarly exegesis within his Wesleyan theology. The difference is, rather than developing a pair of brief mentions of an idea from Merton, *The Deeper Journey* is structured around development of "one of the central themes that weaves its way through the writings of Thomas Merton . . . in passage after passage, in numerous works":[117] the twin concepts of the true self and false self.[118]

Shannon notes the various synonyms Merton uses for "false" in reference to the self—"'superficial,' 'empirical,' 'outward,' 'exterior,' 'alienated,' 'shadow,' 'smoke,' 'contingent,' 'imaginary,' 'private,' 'illusory,' and 'petty'"[119]—and he comments, "All these adjectives suggest, in various ways, that we are dealing with a self that is 'real,' but only at a very limited level of reality. The false self keeps us for the most part on the surface of reality."[120] Shannon also lists Merton's corresponding synonyms for the

---

116. Porter, "Sanctification," 129–30.

117. Shannon, "Thomas Merton," 298; See also Shannon, "Self."

118. Merton's influence on *Deeper Journey* is appropriately evident to readers with eight references in the text.

119. Shannon, "Self," 417.

120. Shannon, "Self," 417.

true self: "'inner and hidden self,' 'creative mysterious inner self,' 'inner self,' 'inmost self,' 'real self,' 'deepest most hidden self.'"[121]

While there is no conclusive argument that Merton or any other singular person originated the concepts of the true and false self, he is the source of their proliferation in the context of Christian spirituality. While there are predecessors who contributed to the concepts, Merton is the strongest nominee as the originator of the terminology as it came to be applied in the SFM.[122]

One of Merton's most well-known explorations of the true and false self is found in one of the critical essays referenced in chapter 4, titled "Things in Their Identity," in which Merton states, "For me to be a saint means to be myself. Therefore the problem of sanctity and salvation is in fact the problem of finding out who I am and of discovering my true self."[123] He continues, "To say I was born in sin is to say I came into the world with a false self. I was born into a mask," and, "Every one of us is shadowed by an illusory person, a false self."[124] He states near the end of the essay,

> The secret of my identity is hidden in the love and mercy of God. But whatever is in God is really identical with Him, for His infinite simplicity admits no division and no distinction. Therefore I cannot hope to find myself anywhere except in Him. Ultimately the only way that I can be myself is to become identified with Him in Whom is hidden the reason and fulfillment of my existence. Therefore there is only one problem on which all my existence, my peace and my happiness depend: to discover myself in discovering God. If I find Him I will find myself and if I find my true self I will find Him.[125]

Likewise, in the work of Merton that Mulholland references most often (*Opening the Bible*), Merton writes,

> The great question of the New Testament, the question which includes all others, is *who* is Christ and what does it mean to encounter him? The rest follows: *how* is one to share in this event and enter into the Christ-life, how does one participate

---

121. Shannon, "Self," 418.

122. For an exploration of the history of the usage of the terms, see Vaden, "False Self."

123. Merton, *New Seeds*, 31.

124. Merton, *New Seeds*, 33–34.

125. Merton, *New Seeds*, 35–36.

in the existence of the Son of Man? . . . The New Testament's answer is "in the word of the Cross," by which the shallow self, the ego-self which clings to a relatively superficial and limited freedom centered in its own satisfaction, surrenders to the ultimate Christ-self, the New Man created in justice and holiness of truth (Ephesians 4:24), in which our freedom is moved not by ego-fantasy but by the Spirit of Christ speaking out of the inmost ground of our being in our encounter with our brother. In this obedience to the Spirit of God who has now identified himself by grace with our own spirit, we reach the peak of freedom and exist entirely *for others,* no longer held back by our own petty limitations.[126]

The Deeper Journey is Mulholland's work that most extensively seeks to explore this conception of sanctification, and he organizes the work around his "basic premise . . . that loving union with God is the essence of Christian life in the world" and "that the deeper journey into this loving union with God passes through" the "false self" and the "religious false self" before coming to the "Christ self" with "its twofold rhythm of wholeness: putting off the vices . . . and putting on the virtues."[127] As to be expected, Mulholland's primary method of exploration of the themes is through biblical exegesis. He dedicates the first chapter to exploration of "a life of loving union with God at the depths of our being" as "the purpose of the Christian life"[128] through exegesis of multiple New Testament texts with particular attention to John 17:20–23[129] and examples from Christian history.[130] He then begins chapter 2 by using Jer 17:5–10 to illustrate

> a reality that threads its way from Genesis through Revelation. [Jeremiah] reveals there are two fundamental ways of being human in the world: trusting in our human resources and abilities or a radical trust in God. You cannot be grasped by or sustained

---

126. Merton, *Opening the Bible*, 79–80.
127. Mulholland, *Deeper Journey*, 20.
128. Mulholland, *Deeper Journey*, 14.
129. Mulholland, *Deeper Journey*, 12–17.

130. Mulholland, *Deeper Journey*, 17–20. The last of the examples he cites from Christian history is Merton, referencing his statement, "This Spirit of God, dwelling in us, given to us, to be as it were our own Spirit, enables us to know and experience, in a mysterious manner, the reality and presence of the divine mercy in ourselves. So the Holy Spirit is intimately united to our own inmost self, and His presence in us makes our 'I' the 'I' of Christ and of God.'" See Merton, *Inner Experience*, 46; Mulholland, *Deeper Journey*, 19–20.

in the deeper life in God—being like Jesus—until you are awakened at the deep levels of your being to this essential reality. You might describe these two ways of being in the world as the "false self" and the "true self."[131]

He then explores instances of the false self in the early chapters of Genesis (3–11) and states that the false self's "essence is a mode of being in the world decentered from life in God, although seeking to retain God on its own terms; a mode of being that creates its own structures of identity, meaning, value, and purpose; and a mode of being that determines for itself the nature of its own being."[132] Mulholland then uses most of his second chapter to describe the "basic attributes" of the false self under the categories of the false self as "fearful," "possessive," "manipulative," "destructive," "self-promoting," "indulgent," and "distinction-making."[133]

Whereas Mulholland's chapter on the false self is his expansion of Merton's concept, chapters 3 and 4 of *The Deeper Journey* are instances of Mulholland's further development of Merton's categories. Rather than the binary of the true self and false self as prevalent in Merton, Mulholland uses his third chapter to explore an additional category: the "religious false self."[134] He comments, "Our religious false self presumes, because we are religious, that everything is fine in our relationship with God.... Our religious false self may be religious in religiosity, devoted in discipleship and sacrificial in service—without being in loving union with God."[135] He then explores this high level of religious activity apart from union with God through the example of Matt 7:22–23 as profiles of people who are

> so busy *being in the world for God* that they failed to *be in God for the world*. There is a great difference between these two ways. A religious false self will expend amazing amounts of energy and resources to be in the world for God. But, you see, we are called to be in God for the world, and this is costly. It requires the abandonment of the whole self-referenced structure of our false self, and, especially, the religious false self.... For those of us on an intentional spiritual journey, our awareness

---

131. Mulholland, *Deeper Journey*, 23.

132. Mulholland, *Deeper Journey*, 29. In a URA lecture, Mulholland attributes his usage of the term "false self" to Merton: "I like to use Merton's term, the 'false self,' because it encompasses so much.... It focuses on the whole being and the ... manifold nature of that being." See Mulholland, "Sustaining Life," session 1.

133. Mulholland, *Deeper Journey*, 30–42.

134. Mulholland, *Deeper Journey*, 46–67.

135. Mulholland, *Deeper Journey*, 47.

of the deadly and debilitating nature of the religious false self is essential. Rigorous religious practices, devoted discipleship, sacrificial service, deeper devotional activities may do nothing more than turn a nominally religious false self into a fanatically religious false self.[136]

Mulholland prefaces his exploration of the religious false self under the same attributes as the false self by summarizing,

> The essential difference between a false self and a religious false self is that the latter brings God into its life. Our religious false self may begin with a genuine experience with God. But then . . . we attempt to integrate our experience with God into the structures of our life in ways that are minimally disruptive to our status quo. . . . Whenever we attempt to have God in our life on our terms, we are a religious false self.[137]

Although Merton does not make such a distinction between a false self and a religious false self, the seeds of the concept can be seen in his descriptions of religious qualities that a false self can adopt, such as his identification of "the disease which is spiritual pride . . . that gets into the hearts of the saints and eats away their sanctity before it is mature. There is something of this worm in the hearts of all religious men."[138] Merton also comments in *Life and Holiness*,

> We obey the "flesh" when we follow the norms of prejudice, complacency, bigotry, group-pride, superstition, ambition, or greed. Hence even an apparent holiness, based not on sincerity of heart but on hypocritical display, is of the "flesh." Whatever may be the "inclination of the flesh," even when it seems to point to heroic and dazzling actions admired by men, it is always death in the sight of God. It is not directed to him but to men around us. . . . For the "flesh" is our external self, our false self. The "spirit" is our real self, our inmost being united to God in Christ.[139]

---

136. Mulholland, *Deeper Journey*, 47–48. See also Mulholland, "Spiritual Formation in Christ," 15, in which he characterizes the first group in the parable as "trying to 'breathe out' without first 'breathing in.'"

137. Mulholland, *Deeper Journey*, 49.

138. Merton, *New Seeds*, 48–49.

139. Merton, *Life and Holiness*, 67.

In Mulholland's fourth chapter, he develops the term "true self" into "Christ self," based largely on his interpretation of Col 3:3.[140] The two terms are interchangeable for him, but "Christ self" is indicative of his perspective on Christ's relationship to the false self:

> We usually think of these as polar opposites, and, to be sure, there is a sense in which this is true. Our false self certainly is not our Christ self; we are not in loving union with God even though we may be a highly developed religious false self. The relationship between these two selves is a divine mystery. Christ dwells in the depths of our false self as the crucified one, yet at the same time as the risen Lord and our new life, our Christ self.[141]

He reiterates, "God comes to us *in our false self* in order to offer God's self to us to be our true life."[142] Mulholland's development of Merton's concept of the true self into the Christ self is a clarification that distinguishes Mulholland's understanding of the true self from the usages of the term in secular psychology and spiritualities other than those within Christianity.[143]

Whereas *Shaped by the Word* and *Invitation to a Journey* have a combined fifty-nine references to Wesley, *The Deeper Journey* is the rare work from Mulholland that does not mention him. Nevertheless, Mulholland's background as a Wesleyan New Testament scholar is the source of the book's substance. Mulholland's characteristic non-fundamentalist, evangelical biblical exegesis is the primary focus of each chapter, the emphasis on spiritual disciplines reflects the pietistic emphasis that makes this book Mulholland's third major published contribution to the SFM, and the more than forty mentions in the book of themes of holiness, sanctification, and perfect love establish *The Deeper Journey* as a model example of the kind of Wesleyanism that has been highly influential on the SFM from its beginning.

---

140. Mulholland, *Deeper Journey*, 86.
141. Mulholland, *Deeper Journey*, 77.
142. Mulholland, *Deeper Journey*, 74.
143. As examples, see Vaden, "False Self," 156–226 on the work of D. W. Winnicott and Susan Harter.

CASE STUDY FROM MULHOLLAND'S MAJOR BIBLICAL STUDIES WORK

The publication of *Invitation to a Journey* in 1993 is a significant turning point in the trajectory of Mulholland's writings. In the years prior, the majority of his works were on topics of biblical studies, and from *Invitation to a Journey* and afterward, most of his published works were on topics of spiritual formation. Judging by the quantity of published reviews of his works, Mulholland's publishing efforts in *Shaped by the Word*, *Invitation to a Journey*, and *The Deeper Journey* had significantly wider impact than did his publishing in biblical studies.[144] Nevertheless, Mulholland never held a position as a professor of spiritual formation, but retired from ATS as a professor emeritus of New Testament.[145] As a final exploration of his contribution to the SFM as a confluence of his Wesleyan and Mertonian influences, it is informative to consider his final major (book-length) work—his second commentary on Revelation—and the insights it offers regarding his contribution to the SFM since it was the final book he published before his death.[146]

As the New Testament scholar who made a foundational contribution to the SFM, it is unsurprising yet still significant that his 2011 *Revelation* displays scholarly exegesis in combination with each of the qualities of the SFM explored above. Mulholland's "Wesleyan accent" is evident in his identification of "three major themes in John's vision."[147] First, although Revelation is an intriguing text to fundamentalists, Mulholland notes the *non-fundamentalist* nature of the book: "John tells us that his vision is 'a revelation from Jesus Christ' (1:1). This is the title of the writing [and] . . . the primary theme of the vision. This is not a vision of 'end times' . . . [nor] of the 'rapture.' It is a vision of Jesus the

---

144. Of eleven published reviews of his works, all but two are on his spiritual formation titles. The other two are of his 1990 commentary, *Revelation: Holy Living in an Unholy World*.

145. ATS's announcement of Mulholland's death is indicative of both his status as a professor emeritus of New Testament and the wide reach of his spiritual formation works because of the irony that the institution in which he taught New Testament only mentions his publications in spiritual formation. See ATS, "Asbury Seminary Announces Passing."

146. Mulholland, *Revelation*. All three of Mulholland's major spiritual formation works (*Shaped by the Word*, *Invitation to a Journey*, and *Deeper Journey*) were republished in later editions after his death, but the 2011 *Revelation* is his last first edition of a book. The earlier commentary is Mulholland, *Revelation: Holy Living*.

147. Mulholland, *Revelation*, 412–13.

Messiah."[148] Next, Mulholland echoes the *pietistic* emphasis on the holy community of God's people in the midst of a fallen world: "New Jerusalem is John's image for the realm of God's people.... Fallen Babylon is John's image for the realm of rebellion against God.... John's vision is a clarion call to the followers of Jesus to live their lives as faithful citizens of New Jerusalem in the midst of their fallen Babylon world."[149] Finally, the crucicentrism characteristic of *evangelicalism* is central in Mulholland's identification of the theme of "the role of the cross in what God has done and will accomplish.... John's vision is a revelation of the meaning of the cross of Jesus the Messiah."[150]

Mulholland's Mertonian accent in the commentary is more inconspicuous but still substantively present. Highlighting the more subtle non-quietist, contemplative, and mystical elements in the commentary[151] is unnecessary here because Mulholland's two citations of Merton, combined with the highly atypical inclusion of Merton's voice in an exegetical commentary of Revelation by an evangelical scholar, is indicative of the depth of Merton's influence on Mulholland.[152] The juxtaposition of references to Merton in the context of exegesis of Revelation is epitomized in the readings either about or from Merton that Mulholland uses to open all but the first of the twenty-three sessions of his 2009 ATS course on Revelation.[153] While the juxtaposition would be noteworthy even if it were only a devotional pause before beginning class, Mulholland clearly sees more of a connection between his interpretation of Revelation and Merton's perspective. This is evident as he opens the final session of the course, in which he covers the exegesis of Rev 21:18—22:21 by reading this passage from Merton:

> If there is a "problem" for Christianity today, it is the problem of the identification of "Christendom" with certain forms of culture and society, certain political and social structures which

---

148. Mulholland, *Revelation*, 412.

149. Mulholland, *Revelation*, 412–13.

150. Mulholland, *Revelation*, 412.

151. The most evident of these is the mystical emphasis on union. See Mulholland, *Revelation*, 441, 464, 526, 582.

152. Mulholland, *Revelation*, 412, 464. No other scholar's citation of Merton in a commentary on Revelation was found. See also Mulholland, "Entry Point Notes," 1640. Mulholland *Revelation*, 558 also cites Wesley, although that is not peculiar for a Wesleyan biblical studies scholar.

153. Mulholland, "NT 666." All but the last of these readings (see the next note) are from Finley, *Merton's Palace of Nowhere*.

for fifteen-hundred years have dominated Europe and the West. The first monks were men who, already in the fourth century, began to protest against this identification as a falsehood and a servitude. Fifteen hundred years of European Christendom, in spite of certain definite achievements, have not been an unequivocal glory for Christendom. The time has come for judgment to be passed on this history. I can rejoice in this fact, believing that the judgment will be a liberation of the Christian faith, from servitude to an involvement in the structures of the secular world. And that is why I think certain forms of Christian "optimism" are to be taken with reservations in so far as they lack the genuine eschatological consciousness of the Christian vision and concentrate upon the naive hope of merely temporal achievements.[154]

After reading the passage, Mulholland comments, "What Merton is speaking of here is New Jerusalem living in a fallen Babylon world. His concern is that Christendom has [cooperated] with the fallen Babylon world. So, we see that what John is dealing with here is something that we deal with all the time."[155]

CONCLUSION

Mulholland's foundational contribution to the SFM is thus a confluence of his Wesleyan and Mertonian influences. Attention to Mulholland's voice in the SFM in his spiritual formation works and commentary on Revelation, with both his non-fundamentalist, pietistic, evangelical, Wesleyan accent and his non-quietist, contemplative, mystical Mertonian accent, is, therefore, indicative of fundamental characteristics of the SFM during the thirty-two years from Mulholland's 1983 The Place of Scripture in Spiritual Formation lectures at the URA until his death in 2015.

---

154. Merton, "Preface," 66; Mulholland, "NT 666," lecture 23, 0:12–1:20.
155. Mulholland, "NT 666," lecture 23, 1:20–1:39.

APPENDIX

Key Figures, Organizations, and Influencers of the Spiritual Formation Movement

INTRODUCTION

THE FOLLOWING LIST IS organized into two sections: direct contributors from 1970 to 1989 and critical influences from the second half of the twentieth century. Accordant with the textual analysis and timeline from chapter one, the primary criteria for inclusion in the list of direct contributors is whether the person or organization adopted the usage of the term "spiritual formation" as applicable to everyone (rather than only in reference to an aspect of ministerial preparation as it had been previously used in Roman Catholicism) in publishing or organizational efforts during the SFM's transitional phase (1970s) or the first decade of the organizational phase (1980s). Some additional entries are included despite not using the terminology through these means, but because their impact is attested to by other contributors to the movement.

Two criteria for inclusion in the list of critical influences are either, first, that the individual or organization's work during the 1950s or 1960s surfaced through the research of the preceding chapters as directly influencing what later became the SFM, or, second, that the individual or organization was influential on the SFM during the 1970s or 1980s from within a tradition distinct from the SFM.

While the research into these lists is thorough, it is understood that the lists are intended to be initial contributions to identifications of historical associations with the SFM and further research is needed for the lists to approach being exhaustive.

Mentions of works that are included in the bibliography are referenced by the titles only in this list. Otherwise, full publication information is included.

DIRECT CONTRIBUTORS FROM 1970 TO 1989

Asbury Theological Seminary: non-denominational Wesleyan seminary in Wilmore, Kentucky. Asbury was involved in the pre-SFM relational phase in the 1960s through relationships faculty members developed with Thomas Merton. Merton visited the seminary on January 10, 1962, and a memorial service was held for Merton in Asbury's chapel on January 14, 1969. Asbury was the first Protestant seminary to have a department of prayer and spiritual life, which began in 1964 and was renamed the department of spiritual formation in 1984. Asbury made significant faculty hires for the early organizational phase of the SFM of Reginald Johnson in 1978, Mulholland in 1979, and Steve Harper in 1980.

Dunnam, Maxie (1934–): Methodist pastor, author, and leader of the Upper Room and Asbury Theological Seminary. Dunnam participated in Douglas V. Steere's Ecumenical Institute of Spirituality and was world editor of the Upper Room from 1975–1982. He published the first book by a Protestant to have "spiritual formation" in its title consistent with SFM usage—*Alive in Christ: The Dynamic Process of Spiritual Formation* in 1982. Dunnam later became president of Asbury Theological Seminary in 1994. See also his *The Workbook on Spiritual Disciplines* (1984); and *The Workbook on Becoming Alive in Christ* (Nashville: Upper Room, 1986).

Edwards, Tilden: Episcopal priest who participated in Douglas V. Steere's Ecumenical Institute of Spirituality and founded the Shalem Institute for Spiritual Formation in Washington, DC, in 1978. Although Edwards and Shalem are less connected to evangelicalism than others in the SFM, they are examples of early adoption of the terminology of spiritual formation as its SFM usage, and Shalem became a spiritual direction training institution accessible to evangelicals. See his *Living in the Presence: Disciplines for the Spiritual Heart* (San Francisco: Harper and Row, 1987).

Foster, Richard J. (1942–): Quaker scholar and minister whose publication of *Celebration of Discipline* is credited by some for launching the SFM, followed by numerous publications on spiritual disciplines and spiritual formation, culminating in his work as editor of *The Renovaré Spiritual Formation Bible* (San Francisco: HarperSanFrancisco, 2005). While a professor at Friends University, he founded Renovaré with James Bryan Smith in 1988 and promoted Renovaré's emphasis on spiritual formation groups.

Friends University: nondenominational Christian university in Wichita, Kansas, historically associated with the Quakers (Society of Friends). See entries for Richard J. Foster, James Bryan Smith, and Renovaré.

Fuller Theological Seminary: nondenominational evangelical seminary based in Pasadena, California, which began offering courses on spiritual formation taught by Dallas Willard in 1989. Fuller was fundamentalist in its origins, then influenced by leading neo-evangelicals and was central in the development of the Church Growth Movement.

HarperSanFrancisco: imprint of Harper and Row, whose publications included numerous SFM-related titles in the 1970s and 1980s. Particularly important for the SFM during this period were Foster, *Celebration of Discipline* (1979); Willard, *In Search of Guidance: Developing a Conversational Relationship with God* (1983); *The Spirit of the Disciplines* (1988). The imprint also published the edited series of Merton's journals.

Harper, Steve: Wesleyan scholar, author, and professor of spiritual formation. Harper was hired to teach spiritual formation and Wesley studies at Asbury Theological Seminary in 1980. He led the process of Asbury's renaming of its department of prayer and spiritual life to the department of spiritual formation in 1984. See his *Devotional Life in the Wesleyan Tradition* (Nashville: Upper Room, 1983); *Embrace the Spirit: An Invitation to Friendship with God*. Spiritual Formation Series (Wheaton, IL: Victor Books, 1987).

Hinson, E. Glenn (1931–): professor of church history and spirituality at The Southern Baptist Theological Seminary, Louisville, Kentucky; Baptist Theological Seminary, Richmond, Virginia; Wake Forest

University, Winston-Salem, North Carolina. Hinson participated in the Ecumenical Institute of Spirituality and repeatedly served as faculty at the Upper Room Academy of Spiritual Formation from its first session in 1983. He authored the first Protestant article to adopt previous Roman Catholic usage of "spiritual formation" in his "The Spiritual Formation of the Minister as a Person." See also his *A Serious Call to a Contemplative Lifestyle* (Philadelphia: Westminster, 1974); *Doubleday Devotional Classics*. Vol. 1 (Garden City, NY: Doubleday, 1978).

Houston, James M. (1922–): founding principal of Regent College in 1970, professor of spiritual theology, and mentoring influence to numerous other contributors to the SFM. Houston contributed significantly to the reintroduction among evangelicals of the language of spiritual theology and recovery of spiritual direction among them. See his *The Transforming Friendship: A Guide to Prayer* (Oxford: Lion, 1989).

InterVarsity Press: evangelical publisher founded in 1947 and publisher of numerous books associated with the SFM. Significant publications for the early years of the SFM include Richard F. Lovelace, *Dynamics of Spiritual Life: An Evangelical Theology of Renewal* (1979); Eugene H. Peterson, *A Long Obedience in the Same Direction: Discipleship in an Instant Society* (Downers Grove, IL: InterVarsity, 1980); Peterson, *Run with the Horses: The Quest for Life at its Best* (1983); and later, included Mulholland, *Invitation to a Journey* (1993) and *The Deeper Journey* (2006). In 2006, InterVarsity began its imprints including Formatio, which focuses on spiritual formation titles, and IVP Academic, which includes scholarly spiritual formation contributions.

Job, Rueben P. (1928–2015): United Methodist bishop, world editor of the Upper Room, and author of influential guides to spiritual formation. See his *A Journey Toward Solitude and Community: A Guided Retreat in Spiritual Formation* (Nashville: Upper Room, 1982); *A Guide to Prayer for Ministers and Other Servants*, with Norman Shawchuck (Nashville: Upper Room, 1983); *How to Conduct a Spiritual Life Retreat*, with Shawchuck and Robert G. Doherty (Nashville: Upper Room, 1986).

Johnson, Reginald: professor of spiritual formation and dean of the chapel at Asbury Theological Seminary. See his *Celebrate My Soul: Discover the Potential of Your God-Given Personality.* Spiritual Formation Series (Wheaton, IL: Victor, 1988).

Johnson, Suzanne: professor of Christian education at Perkins School of Theology. See her *Christian Spiritual Formation in the Church and Classroom* (Nashville: Abingdon, 1989).

Lovelace, Richard F. (1930–2020): professor of church history at Gordon-Conwell Theological Seminary. His 1973 article "The Sanctification Gap" was a landmark publication for the development that became the SFM. See also his *Dynamics of Spiritual Life: An Evangelical Theology of Renewal* (Downers Grove, IL: InterVarsity, 1979).

May, Gerald G. (1940–2005): psychiatrist and faculty at the Shalem Institute for Spiritual Formation. See his *Pilgrimage Home: The Conduct of Contemplative Practice in Groups* (New York: Paulist, 1979); *Will and Spirit: A Contemplative Psychology* (San Francisco: HarperSanFrancisco, 1982); and *Care of Mind, Care of Spirit* (1982).

Mogabgab, John S. (1946–2014): member of the advisory group that founded the Upper Room Academy for Spiritual Formation and later its theologian in residence. He was a teaching assistant to and close friend of Henri J. M. Nouwen. Mogabgab was the editor of *Weavings: A Journal of the Christian Spiritual Life*, which was published by the Upper Room from 1986–2017, and he was the husband of Marjorie J. Thompson.

Morris, Danny E. (1933–2021): United Methodist pastor, staff member of the Upper Room, and founding director of the Upper Room Academy for Spiritual Formation. See Pfaff, *Light and Fire: A Spiritual Biography of Danny E. Morris.*

Mulholland, M. Robert, Jr. (1936–2015): professor of New Testament and vice president at Asbury Theological Seminary. Mulholland served as a faculty member at seventeen sessions of the Upper Room Academy for Spiritual Formation, including the opening lectures of the first Academy on The Place of Scripture in Spiritual Formation, the transcripts of which became his *Shaped by the Word* (1985). Later major works in spiritual formation were

Invitation to a Journey (1993) and *The Deeper Journey* (2006). His work is influential on the later work of Ruth Haley Barton and the Transforming Center.

Muto, Susan Annette: (1942–): Cofounded the Epiphany Association of Pittsburgh, Pennsylvania, with Adrian van Kaam in 1988 and continues as the dean and executive director of the Epiphany Academy of Formative Spirituality. See her *A Practical Guide to Spiritual Reading* (Denville, NJ: Dimension, 1976); *Tell Me Who I Am: Questions and Answers on Christian Spirituality*, with van Kaam (Denville, NJ: Dimension, 1977); *Am I Living a Spiritual Life? Questions and Answers on Formative Spirituality*, with van Kaam (Denville, NJ: Dimension, 1978); *Renewed at Each Awakening: The Formative Power of Sacred Words* (Denville, NJ: Dimension, 1979); *Practicing the Prayer of Presence*, with van Kaam (Denville, NJ: Dimension, 1980); *Blessings That Make Us Be: A Formative Approach to Living the Beatitudes* (New York: Crossroads, 1982); *Celebrating the Single Life: A Spirituality for Single Persons in Today's World* (Garden City, NY: Doubleday, 1982); *Pathways of Spiritual Living* (1984); *Meditation in Motion* (Garden City, NY: Image, 1986); *Commitment: Key to Christian Maturity*, with van Kaam (Mahwah, NJ: Paulist, 1989).

Oden, Thomas C. (1931–2016): Methodist professor of theology at Drew University in Madison, New Jersey. He was among the earliest Protestants to adopt the language of spiritual formation in the 1970s in reference to psychological and theological integration. See his *The Intensive Group Experience: The New Pietism* (Philadelphia: Westminster, 1972); *Game Free: A Guide to the Meaning of Intimacy* (New York: Harper and Row, 1974); and *Crisis Ministries*. Classical Pastoral Care 4 (New York: Crossroad, 1986). He later served as one of the general editors of the *Renovaré Spiritual Formation Bible*.

Palmer, Parker (1939–): Quaker sociologist, educator, and founder of the Center for Courage and Renewal. His "circles of trust" are group experiences similar to group spiritual direction. See his *To Know as We Are Known: A Spirituality of Education* (San Francisco: Harper and Row, 1983).

Peterson, Eugene H. (1932–2018): Presbyterian pastor, prolific author, and the James M. Houston Professor of Spiritual Theology at Regent College from 1993–1998. He did not often use the term "spiritual formation," but wrote extensively on spiritual theology and his works were highly influential in the SFM. Although he was not a participant in the Ecumenical Institute of Spirituality, he was influenced by a relationship with Douglas V. Steere. His works from the respective period from publishers in this list include *A Long Obedience in the Same Direction: Discipleship in an Instant Society* (Downers Grove, IL: InterVarsity, 1980); *Run with the Horses: The Quest for Life at its Best* (Downers Grove, IL: InterVarsity, 1983); *Earth and Altar: The Community of Prayer in a Self-Bound Society* (Downers Grove, IL: InterVarsity, 1985); *Reversed Thunder: The Revelation of John and the Praying Imagination* (San Francisco: HarperSanFrancisco, 1988); and *Answering God: The Psalms as Tools for Prayer* (San Francisco: Harper and Row, 1989).

Regent College: interdenominational graduate theological school in Vancouver, BC. The school was founded in 1968 with the unique focus of theological education of laity. James M. Houston became the first principal in 1970. Houston and Eugene H. Peterson are professors emeriti of spiritual theology.

Renovaré: founded in 1988 by Richard J. Foster and James Bryan Smith through their relationship at Friends University. Dallas Willard also became a frequent teacher at Renovaré events. During its early years, the organization's focus was conferences encouraging participation in spiritual formation groups in local churches, later adding publishing of spiritual formation resources.

Shalem Institute for Spiritual Formation: see entries for Tilden Edwards and Gerald G. May.

Smith, James Bryan (1961–): cofounded Renovaré with Richard J. Foster in 1988. He later published numerous spiritual formation resources, beginning with *A Spiritual Formation Workbook: Small Group Resources for Spiritual Growth* (San Francisco: HarperSanFrancisco, 1991) and became the professor of religion and Dallas Willard Chair for Spiritual Formation at Friends University.

Stanger, Frank (1914–1986): professor at and then president of Asbury Theological Seminary from 1962–1982, during which time Asbury hired Reginald Johnson, Steve Harper, and M. Robert Mulholland Jr. as faculty. Stanger visited Thomas Merton with fellow Asbury professor Howard F. Shipps in June 1960. See his *Spiritual Formation in the Local Church* (Grand Rapids: Zondervan, 1989).

Thompson, Marjorie J.: Presbyterian pastor, faculty for the Upper Room Academy for Spiritual Formation, director of Upper Room's Pathways Center for Spiritual Leadership, and was married to John Mogabgab. See her *Family: The Forming Center: A Vision of the Role of Family in Spiritual Formation* (Nashville: Upper Room, 1989).

Upper Room: ecumenical ministry of Discipleship Ministries (formerly Global Board of Discipleship) of the United Methodist Church based in Nashville, Tennessee. Its daily devotional guide (titled *The Upper Room*) has been in publication since 1935. Individuals in the organization adopted language of spiritual formation while Maxie Dunnam was world editor from 1975–1982. The organization is the home of multiple spiritual formation ministries, including the Upper Room Chapel, the Walk to Emmaus, the Upper Room Academy for Spiritual Formation, and Upper Room Books.

Weborg, C. John (1937–): professor of theology and coordinator of spiritual formation at North Park Theological Seminary of Chicago, Illinois. He developed programs in spiritual formation and spiritual direction at the seminary beginning in 1975. See his *Alive in Christ, Alert to Life* (Chicago: Covenant, 1985).

Willard, Dallas (1935–2013): professor of philosophy at the University of Southern California. Through his close friendship with Richard J. Foster, he became a featured speaker at Renovaré events, and his published works were increasingly influential as the SFM progressed after the first decade of its organizational phase. Willard was influential on many subsequent contributors to the SFM, including James Bryan Smith, Steven L. Porter, Gary W. Moon, John Ortberg, Jan Johnson, and John Mark Comer. His works that were influential on the SFM published during the respective years of this list are "Discipleship: For Super-Christians Only?" (1980);

In Search of Guidance: Developing a Conversational Relationship with God (San Francisco: HarperSanFrancisco, 1983); *The Spirit of the Disciplines* (1988).

CRITICAL INFLUENCES ON THE SFM FROM THE SECOND HALF OF THE TWENTIETH CENTURY

Bloesch, Donald G. (1928–2010): Bloesch was professor of theology at the University of Dubuque Theological Seminary in Dubuque, Iowa, and an ordained minister in the United Church of Christ. He was raised in the Evangelical and Reformed Church, which became part of the United Church of Christ, and he had a pietist background that was reflected in some emphases he shared with the SFM, particularly as seen in his *Crisis of Piety: Essays Toward a Theology of the Christian Life* (Grand Rapids: Eerdmans, 1968). However, he did not adopt terminology of spiritual formation and was often critical of some of the characteristics of the movement, as in his *Spirituality Old and New: Recovering an Authentic Spiritual Life* (Downers Grove, IL: IVP Academic, 2007).

Day, Albert Edward (1884–1973): Methodist pastor in Ohio, Pennsylvania, Maryland, and California. He founded the New Life Movement, which became the Disciplined Order of Christ. His *Discipline and Discovery* (Nashville: Upper Room, 1947) served as the rule of life for the order. He wrote extensively on spiritual life and ministry, including (from 1950 and afterward) his *An Autobiography of Prayer* (Shaker Heights, OH: Disciplined Order of Christ, 1952); *Dialogue and Destiny* (New York: Harper and Brothers, 1961); *Letters on the Healing Ministry* (Nashville: Methodist Evangelistic Materials, 1964); *The Cup and the Sword* (Nashville: Parthenon, 1962); *The Captivating Presence* (Nashville: Parthenon, 1971).

Disciplined Order of Christ: founded in 1945 by Albert Edward Day and initially called the New Life Movement. Members made annual commitments to the practice of spiritual disciplines and participation in a small group, with opportunities to attend an annual retreat. Day's *Discipline and Discovery* served as their rule of life. The order existed as an organization into the late 1990s.

Doherty, Catherine de Hueck (1896–1985): Russian immigrant who founded the Friendship House in Harlem and then the Madonna House in Toronto. She developed a friendship with Thomas Merton while he volunteered with her in Harlem. Her model of solitude as a spiritual practice, adapted from Russian hermits (*poustiniks*), encouraged monthly solitude for people active in ministry, which Merton admired and became echoed in the SFM. See her *Poustinia: Christian Spirituality of the East for Western Man* (1975).

Ecumenical Institute of Spirituality (EIOS): annual gathering of eighteen to twenty-five scholars from a variety of Christian traditions, begun in 1965 by Douglas V. Steere and Godfrey Diekman. Participants who became influential in the SFM included Maxie Dunnam, E. Glenn Hinson, and Tilden Edwards. See Hinson, ed. *Spirituality in Ecumenical Perspective* (Louisville: Westminster John Knox, 1993).

Evangelical Order of the Burning Heart: see Carl H. Lundquist.

Institute of Formative Spirituality: see Adrian van Kaam.

Iona Community: see George MacLeod.

Jones, E. Stanley (1884–1973): Methodist missionary to India, evangelist, and prolific author. Jones wrote numerous devotional books on the spiritual life including his *Abundant Living* (Nashville: Abingdon, 1942); and *Growing Spiritually* (Nashville: Abingdon-Cokesbury, 1953). He founded a movement of Christian Ashrams that began in India, spread internationally, and included times of solitude and silence for participants in a manner beyond that which was typical of the pietistic evangelicalism of the time but became more prevalent in the SFM.

Laubach, Frank (1884–1970): American missionary to the Philippines who developed the "Each One Teach One" method of promoting world literacy. His writings on prayer were highly influential on Dallas Willard.

Lewis, C. S. (1898–1963): tutor in English and literature at Oxford who famously converted from atheism to Christianity. His fiction and non-fiction writings on apologetics and spirituality became highly influential in Protestant Christianity, including the SFM, especially *Mere Christianity* (New York: Macmillan, 1943); *The Great Divorce* (New York: Macmillan, 1946); and *The Screwtape Letters* (New York: Macmillan, 1961)

Lundquist, Carl H.: Swedish-American Baptist pietist and president of Bethel College and Seminary from 1954 to 1982. He founded the Evangelical Order of the Burning Heart, which encouraged Christians to commit to prayer, Bible reading, and spiritual discipline and meeting in small pietistic *ecclesiola in ecclesia* groups.

MacLeod, George (1895–1991): began reconstruction of the ancient monastery on the island of Iona in 1938 and founded the Iona Community as an ecumenical ministry influenced by the rhythms of monasticism and emphasizing a combination of prayer and social service. He began a friendship with D. Elton Trueblood, who was impacted by his 1948 visit to Iona, and the Iona model influenced Trueblood's concept of *The Company of the Committed* and the resulting Yokefellow Movement.

Manning, Brennan (1934–2013): former Franciscan priest who left the priesthood, married, struggled with alcoholism, and wrote influential books on the depth of God's love for sinful people. Manning became a popular writer and speaker among evangelicals, and his synthesis of the Protestant emphasis on salvation by grace with contemplative spirituality from his Roman Catholic background resonated with the themes of the SFM.

Merton, Thomas (1915–1968): Trappist monk at the Abbey of Our Lady of Gethsemani in Trappist, Kentucky. Merton wrote extensively on prayer and contemplation, extending the contemplative life as available to all rather than limited to those with monastic vocations. He eventually sought to live as a Trappist hermit, which did not have precedent in his order. His writings on solitude and eventual semi-eremitical life directly influenced the inclusion of solitude as a standard discipline in SFM literature. In the 1960s, Merton began to write frequently on social issues and developed ecumenical relationships, some of which eventually had direct influence on the SFM—particularly through faculty at two Protestant seminaries in Kentucky, E. Glenn Hinson of The Southern Baptist Seminary and Howard F. Shipps at Asbury Theological Seminary.

Newbigin, Lesslie (1909–1998): missionary, theologian, and apologist from the Church of Scotland. His apologetic criticisms of classical liberalism contributed to the intellectual strength of Protestants who sought expressions of evangelicalism that avoided both theological liberalism and fundamentalism.

Nouwen, Henri J. M. (1932–1996): Dutch Roman Catholic priest who resided in the United States and Canada. He studied theological integration with psychology, which led to teaching at Notre Dame, Yale, and Harvard. He was heavily influenced by Merton, and his writings on spirituality became highly popular among Protestants and widely read among contributors to and participants in the SFM.

Pinnock, Clark H. (1937–2010): Canadian Baptist theologian and professor of Christian interpretation at McMaster Divinity College whose writings on the Bible shifted during the 1970s away from fundamentalist views of inerrancy toward an alternative "high view" of Scripture, adding intellectual foundation to the nonfundamentalist evangelicalism that became characteristic of the SFM. Later, Pinnock's work in pneumatology and open theism resonated with the relational and inherently pneumatological theology of the SFM. Pinnock taught at Regent College from 1974–1977 and gave lectures at Asbury Theological Seminary in 1996. See his *The Scripture Principle* (San Francisco: Harper and Row, 1984); *Flame of Love: A Theology of the Holy Spirit* (Downers Grove, IL: InterVarsity, 1996); and *Most Moved Mover: A Theology of God's Openness* (Grand Rapids: Baker Academic, 2001).

Steere, Douglas V. (1901–1995): Quaker philosopher and cofounder of the Ecumenical Institute of Spirituality, through which he influenced multiple others who contributed to the SFM, including E. Glenn Hinson, Tilden Edwards, and Maxie Dunnam. Steere's writing and teaching integrated Catholic and Protestant spiritualities, exemplified by his creation of the EIOS, participation in the Second Vatican Council as an observer-delegate on behalf of the Religious Society of Friends, and his relationship with Thomas Merton (whom he invited to participate in the EIOS, but the request was denied by Merton's abbot). Steere wrote about contemplative spirituality and its disciplines of retreat, silence, and solitude in a manner uncharacteristic of Protestants prior to the SFM. See his *Together in Solitude* (New York: Crossroad, 1982).

Tozer, A. W. (1897–1963): evangelical pastor and author from the Christian and Missionary Alliance whose writings were contemplative beyond those of most popular evangelicals of his time. See his *The Pursuit of God* (Harrisburg, PA: Christian, 1948); and *The Knowledge of the Holy* (New York: Harper and Brothers, 1961).

Trueblood, D. Elton (1900–1994): Quaker philosopher and colleague of Douglas V. Steere at Haverford College. Following his visit to George MacLeod at the Iona Community, he founded the Yokefellow Movement, which encouraged *ecclesiola* groups based on a mutual commitment to spiritual disciplines. He encouraged regular solitude among his readers and group members, similar to what would become an emphasis in the SFM but was rare among pietistic evangelicals prior to the SFM. Trueblood was instrumental in the publication of Richard J. Foster's landmark book for the SFM, *Celebration of Discipline*, both through his relationship with Foster and by recommending it to his own publisher. See his *Alternative to Futility* (New York: Harper and Brothers, 1948); and *The Company of the Committed* (San Francisco: Harper and Row, 1961).

van Kaam, Adrian (1920–2007): Dutch Roman Catholic priest and psychologist who founded the Institute of Formative Spirituality at Duquesne University in 1979. Van Kaam's work and the Institute promoted research in "formative spirituality," including publishing a journal and offering a PhD. Susan Muto joined his faculty, and after the Institute separated from Duquesne, it reorganized as van Kaam and Muto co-founded the Epiphany Association Academy of Formative Spirituality.

Yokefellow Movement: see D. Elton Trueblood

Bibliography

Abbott, Walter M., ed. *Documents of Vatican II*. New York: Guild 1966.
Abraham, William J. *The Coming Great Revival: Recovering the Full Evangelical Tradition*. San Francisco: Harper and Row, 1984.
———. *The Logic of Evangelism*. London: Hodder and Stoughton, 1989.
Addington, Bethany. Review of *Invitation to a Journey*, by M. Robert Mulholland Jr. *Christian Education Journal* 14 (2017) 210–13.
Allert, Craig D. *A High View of Scripture? The Authority of the Bible and the Formation of the New Testament*. Grand Rapids: Baker Academic, 2007.
Apel, William D. "'Who Stands Fast?' Dietrich Bonhoeffer and Thomas Merton on Obedience." *The Merton Seasonal* 23 (1998) 3–10.
Arnold, Klaus. "Pietism." In *Global Wesleyan Dictionary of Theology*, edited by Al Truesdale et al., 408–10. Kansas City: Beacon Hill, 2013.
ATS. "Asbury Seminary Announces Passing of Dr. M. Robert Mulholland." https://asburyseminary.edu/news/passing-of-robert-mulholland/.
Axmacher, Elke. *Praxis Evangelorium. Theologie und Frömmigkeit bei Martin Moller*. Göttingen: Vandenhoeck and Ruprecht, 1989.
Bailey, Raymond. *Thomas Merton on Mysticism*. Garden City, NY: Doubleday, 1975.
Balmer, Randall. *The Making of Evangelicalism: From Revivalism to Politics and Beyond*. Waco, TX: Baylor University Press, 2010.
Barry, William A., and William J. Connolly. *The Practice of Spiritual Direction*. San Francisco: HarperSanFrancisco, 1982.
Barton, Ruth Haley. "A Biblical Perspective on Spiritual Transformation." In *Pursuing God's Will Together: A Discernment Practice for Leadership Groups*, 240–45. Downers Grove, IL: InterVarsity, 2012.
———. "Dr. M. Robert Mulholland, Jr. 1936–2015, Honoring a Beloved Friend and Teacher." Transforming Center. Dec. 21, 2015. https://transformingcenter.org/2015/12/bob-mulholland-december-20-2015.
———. Foreword to *Invitation to a Journey: A Road Map for Spiritual Formation*, expanded ed., by M. Robert Mulholland Jr. Downers Grove, IL: InterVarsity, 2016.
———. *Invitation to Solitude and Silence: Experiencing God's Transforming Presence*. Downers Grove, IL: InterVarsity, 2004.
———. *Life Together in Christ: Experiencing Transformation in Community*. Downers Grove, IL: InterVarsity, 2014.
———. *Sacred Rhythms: Arranging Our Lives for Spiritual Transformation*. Downers Grove, IL: InterVarsity, 2006.

———. *Strengthening the Soul of Your Leadership: Seeking God in the Crucible of Ministry*. Downers Grove, IL: InterVarsity, 2008.

Baum, Gregory. "Ecumenism at Vatican II and Fifty Years Later." *Ecumenism* 173 (2009) 27–30.

Beasley-Topliffe, Keith. "Formation, Spiritual." In *The Upper Room Dictionary of Christian Spiritual Formation*, edited by Keith Beasley-Topliffe, 107–10. Nashville: Upper Room, 2003.

———. *Surrendering to God: Living the Covenant Prayer*. Brewster, MA: Paraclete, 2001.

Bebbington, D. W. *Evangelicalism in Modern Britain: A History From the 1730s to the 1980s*. New York: Routledge, 2005.

Benefiel, Margaret. *Soul at Work: Spiritual Leadership in Organizations*. New York: Seabury, 2015.

Bengel, Johann Albrecht. *Abriß der so Gennanten Brüdergemeine*. Stuttgart: Johann Benedict Mekler, 1751.

Black, Gary, Jr. *The Theology of Dallas Willard: Discovering Protoevangelical Faith*. Eugene, OR: Pickwick, 2013.

Blaising, Craig A. "Spiritual Formation in the Early Church." In *The Christian Educator's Handbook on Spiritual Formation*, edited by Kenneth O. Gangel and James C. Wilhoit, 21–36. Grand Rapids: Baker, 1994.

Bloesch, Donald G. "The Crisis of Piety." *The Covenant Quarterly* 25 (1967) 3–11.

———. *Spirituality Old and New: Recovering Authentic Spiritual Life*. Downers Grove, IL: IVP Academic, 2007.

Bochen, Christine M. Introduction to *Learning to Love: Exploring Solitude and Freedom: 1966–1967*, by Thomas Merton. The Journals of Thomas Merton 6, edited by Christine M. Bochen. San Francisco: HarperSanFrancisco, 1997.

Bonhoeffer, Dietrich. *Life Together and Prayerbook of the Bible*. Dietrich Bonhoeffer Works 5. Minneapolis: Fortress, 1996.

———. *A Testament to Freedom: The Essential Writings of Dietrich Bonhoeffer*. Rev. ed., edited by Geffrey B. Kelly and F. Burton Nelson. San Francisco: HarperSanFrancisco, 1995.

Bourgeault, Cynthia. "Merton in Love." *The Merton Seasonal* 27 (2002) 20–25.

Brown, Dale W. *Understanding Pietism*. Grand Rapids: Eerdmans, 1978.

———. "The Wesleyan Revival From a Pietist Perspective." *Wesleyan Theological Journal* 24 (1989) 7–17.

Bundy, David, and J. Steven O'Malley. Foreword to *The Presence of God in the Christian Life: John Wesley and the Means of Grace*, by Henry H. Knight III. Pietist and Wesleyan Studies 3. Metuchen, NJ: Scarecrow, 1992.

Burkholder, Benjamin J. "Bonhoeffer's Account of the Conscience and How It Can Inform Formation Today." *Journal of Spiritual Formation and Soul Care* 15 (2022) 70–91.

Burton-Christie, Douglas. "Rediscovering Love's World: Thomas Merton's Love Poems and the Language of Ecstasy." *Cross Currents* 39 (1989) 64–82.

———. "The Work of Loneliness: Solitude, Emptiness, and Compassion. *Anglican Theological Review* 88 (2006) 25–45.

Caldwell, Robert W., III. *Theologies of the American Revivalists: From Whitefield to Finney*. Downers Grove, IL: IVP Academic, 2017.

Campbell, Ted A. "Are United Methodists Reaping What John Wesley Sowed?" *Firebrand*. Apr. 5, 2022. https://firebrandmag.com/articles/are-united-methodists-reaping-what-john-wesley-sowed.

Carr, Anne E. *A Search for Wisdom and Spirit: Thomas Merton's Theology of the Self*. Notre Dame: University of Notre Dame Press, 1988.

Cashen, Richard Anthony. *Solitude in the Thought of Thomas Merton*. Kalamazoo, MI: Cistercian, 1981.

Chan, Simon. "Pietism." In *Global Dictionary of Theology: A Resource for the Worldwide Church*, edited by William A. Dyrness et al., 655–57. Downers Grove, IL: IVP Academic, 2008.

———. "Quietism." In *Dictionary of Christian Spirituality*, edited by Glen G. Scorgie et al., 706–7. Grand Rapids: Zondervan, 2011.

———. "Spiritual Theology." In *Dictionary of Christian Spirituality*, edited by Glen G. Scorgie et al., 52–57. Grand Rapids: Zondervan, 2011.

———. *Spiritual Theology: A Systematic Study of the Christian Life*. Downers Grove, IL: InterVarsity, 1998.

Chandler, Diane J. *Christian Spiritual Formation: An Integrated Approach for Personal and Relational Wholeness*. Downers Grove, IL: IVP Academic, 2014.

Chilcote, Paul Wesley. *Recapturing the Wesleys' Vision: An Introduction to the Faith of John and Charles Wesley*. Downers Grove, IL: IVP Academic, 2004.

Coe, John H. "Approaches to the Study of Christian Spirituality." In *Dictionary of Christian Spirituality*, edited by Glen G. Scorgie et al., 34–39. Grand Rapids: Zondervan: 2011.

Collier, Winn. *A Burning in My Bones: The Authorized Biography of Eugene H. Peterson*. Colorado Springs, CO: Waterbrook, 2021.

Collins, Kenneth, J., "Introduction." In *Exploring Christian Spirituality: An Ecumenical Reader*, edited by Kenneth J. Collins, 9–18. Grand Rapids: Baker Academic, 2000.

———. *The Theology of John Wesley: Holy Love and the Shape of Grace*. Nashville: Abingdon, 2007.

Colón-Emeric, Edgardo A. *Wesley, Aquinas, and Christian Perfection: An Ecumenical Dialogue*. Waco, TX: Baylor University Press, 2009.

Coombs, Marie Theresa, and Francis Kelly Nemeck. *Discerning Vocations to the Apostolic Life, the Contemplative Life, and the Eremitic Life*. Eugene, OR: Cascade, 2018.

The Country-Parson's Advice to His Parishioners. London: Benj. Tooke, 1680.

Cunningham, Lawrence. "Ecumenism and Christian Spirituality." Review of *Invitation to a Journey*, by M. Robert Mulholland Jr. *Commonweal* 121 (1994) 41–43.

Cushman, Ralph Spaulding. *The Pocket Book of Faith*. Nashville: Upper Room, 1945.

Dahill, Lisa E. *Reading from the Underside of Selfhood: Bonhoeffer and Spiritual Formation*. Princeton Theological Monograph Series 95. Eugene, OR: Pickwick, 2009.

Day, Albert Edward. *Discipline and Discovery*. Nashville: Disciplined Order of Christ, 1988.

Dayton, Donald W. "Some Doubts About the Usefulness of the Category 'Evangelical.'" In *The Variety of American Evangelicalism*, edited by Dayton and Robert K. Johnston, 245–51. Downers Grove, IL: InterVarsity, 1991.

Dayton, Donald W., and Douglas M. Strong. *Rediscovering an Evangelical Heritage: A Tradition and Trajectory of Integrating Piety and Justice*. 2nd ed. Grand Rapids: Baker Academic, 2014.

de Guibert, Joseph. *The Theology of the Spiritual Life*. Translated by Paul Barrett. New York: Sheed and Ward, 1953.

Doble Research Associates, Inc. "The Academy for Spiritual Formation, An Analysis of the Views of Pastors Who Attended: A Report to The Upper Room Ministries." Nashville: Upper Room Ministries, 2004.

Doherty, Catherine de Hueck. *Poustinia: Christian Spirituality of the East for Western Man*. Notre Dame: Ave Maria, 1975.

Dorrien, Gary. *The Remaking of Evangelical Theology*. Louisville: Westminster John Knox, 1998.

Du Mez, Kristin Kobes. *Jesus and John Wayne: How White Evangelicals Corrupted a Faith and Fractured a Nation*. New York: Liveright, 2021.

Dunnam, Maxie. *Alive in Christ: The Dynamic Process of Spiritual Formation*. Nashville: Abingdon, 1982.

———. *The Workbook on Spiritual Disciplines*. Nashville: Upper Room, 1984.

Duquin, Lorine Hanley. *They Called Her the Baroness: The Life of Catherine de Hueck Doherty*. Staten Island, NY: Alba House, 1995.

Egan, Keith J. "Contemplation." In *The New Westminster Dictionary of Christian Spirituality*, edited by Philip Sheldrake, 211–13. Louisville: Westminster John Knox, 2005.

Ehmer, Hermann. "Johann Albrecht Bengel (1687–1752)." In *The Pietist Theologians: An Introduction to Theology in the Seventeenth and Eighteenth Centuries*, edited by Carter Lindberg, 224–38. Malden, MA: Blackwell, 2005.

Fea, John. *Believe Me: The Evangelical Road to Donald Trump*. Grand Rapids: Eerdmans, 2018.

Fee, Gordon D. "On Getting the Spirit Back into Spirituality." In *Life in the Spirit: Spiritual Formation in Theological Perspective*, edited by Jeffrey P. Greenman and George Kalantzis, 36–44. Downers Grove, IL: IVP Academic, 2010.

Finley, James. *Merton's Palace of Nowhere*. Notre Dame: Ave Maria, 2003.

Finney, Charles G. "Letter to Readers." In *Principles of Discipleship*. Bethany House, 1988.

———. *Principles of Discipleship*, edited by Louis Gifford Parkhurst, Jr. Minneapolis, MN: Bethany House, 1988.

Fitzgerald, Frances. *The Evangelicals: The Struggle to Shape America*. New York: Simon and Schuster, 2017.

Forest, Jim. *Living with Wisdom: A Life of Thomas Merton*. Rev. ed. Maryknoll, NY: Orbis, 2008.

Foster, Richard J. *Celebration of Discipline: The Path to Spiritual Growth*. 20th anniv. ed. San Francisco: HarperSanFrancisco, 1998.

———. *Celebration of Discipline: The Path to Spiritual Growth*. San Francisco: HarperSanFrancisco, 1978.

———. "A Place to Stand: The Theology Behind the Renovaré Covenant." Renovaré. https://renovare.org/articles/a-place-to-stand.

———. *Streams of Living Water: Celebrating the Great Traditions of the Christian Faith*. San Francisco: HarperSanFrancisco, 1998.

Foster, Richard J., and Kathryn A. Helmers. *Life with God: Reading the Bible for Spiritual Transformation*. New York: HarperOne, 2008.
Fries, Adelaide L. *The Moravians in Georgia, 1735–1740*. Winston-Salem, NC: Edwards and Broughton, 1905.
"From Other Lands: Spiritual Formation of Youth Leaders." *Orate Fratres* 17 (1943) 456–57.
Fry, Timothy, ed. and trans. *RB 1980: The Rule of St. Benedict in Latin and English with Notes*. Collegeville, MN: Liturgical, 1981.
Gallagher, Eugene. *Catholic Action: The Spiritual Formation of Laymen and Their Role in the Apostolate*. Washington, DC: Georgetown University College of the Arts and Sciences, 1950.
Gallagher, Timothy M. *The Examen Prayer: Ignatian Wisdom for Our Lives Today*. New York: Crossroad, 2006.
Gallie, W. B. *Philosophy and the Historical Understanding*. 2nd ed. New York: Schocken, 1968.
Gannon, Thomas M., and George W. Traub. *The Desert and the City: An Interpretation of the History of Christian Spirituality*. Chicago, IL: Loyola University Press, 1969.
Gilbert. Kathy L. "Bishop Job, Who Helped People Deal with Death, Dead at 86." UM News, Jan. 4, 2015. https://www.umnews.org/en/news/bishop-job-who-helped-people-deal-with-death-dead- at-861.
Gillespie, John M. "Surprised by Similarity: C. S. Lewis and Thomas Merton on the Self." *Sehnucht: The C. S. Lewis Journal* 17 (2023) 109–35.
González, Justo L. *The Reformation to the Present Day*. Vol. 2 of *The Story of Christianity*. Rev. ed. New York: HarperOne, 2010.
Graham, Billy. *Hear My Heart: What I Would Say to You*. New York: Howard, 2014.
Grayston, Donald, ed. *Thomas Merton's Rewritings: The Five Versions of* Seeds / New Seeds of Contemplation *as a Key to the Development of His Thought*. Lewiston, NY: Edwin Mellen, 1989.
Greenman, Jeffrey P. "Spiritual Formation in Theological Perspective." In *Life in the Spirit: Spiritual Formation in Theological Perspective*, edited by Jeffrey P. Greenman and George Kalantzis, 23–35. Downers Grove, IL: IVP Academic, 2010.
Griffin, John Howard. *Follow the Ecstasy: Thomas Merton, the Hermitage Years, 1965–1968*. Fort Worth, TX: Latitudes, 1983.
Hahn, Hans-Christoph, and Hellmut Reichel. *Zinzendorf und die Herrnhuter Brüder: Quellen zur Geschichte der Brüder-Unität von 1722 bis 1760*. Hamburg, Germany: Wittig, 1977.
Hammond, Geordan. "Restoring Primitive Christianity: John Wesley and Georgia, 1735–1737." PhD diss., University of Manchester, 2008.
———. "Versions of Primitive Christianity: John Wesley's Relations with the Moravians in Georgia, 1735–1737." *Journal of Moravian History* 6 (2009) 31–60.
Hanson, Bradley. "Pietism." In *The New Westminster Dictionary of Christian Spirituality*, edited by Philip Sheldrake, 490–91. Louisville: Westminster John Knox, 2005.
Harper, Steve. *The Way to Heaven: The Gospel According to John Wesley*. Grand Rapids: Zondervan, 2003.
Harris, Daniel Ethan. "The Peculiar Difficulty of the Methodist Pastor." Firebrand. Feb. 28, 2023. https://firebrandmag.com/articles/the-peculiar-difficulty-of-the-methodist-pastor.

———. "Thomas Merton's Spiritual Formation and Writings on Racism: From Harlem, Through Louisville, to Birmingham." *Journal of Spiritual Formation and Soul Care* 15 (2022) 184–204.

Hart, Patrick. Introduction to *The Asian Journal of Thomas Merton*, by Thomas Merton, edited by Naomi Burton et al. New York: New Directions, 1973

Heath, Elaine A. "Ecstasy: Mysticism and Mission in the Wesleyan Tradition. Oxford Institute of Methodist Theological Studies. July 2007. https://oxford-institute.org/wp-content/uploads/2013/04/2007-5-heath.pdf.

———. *Naked Faith: The Mystical Theology of Pheobe Palmer.* Princeton Theological Monograph Series 108. Eugene, OR: Pickwick, 2009.

Heath, Elaine A., and Scott T. Kisker. *Longing for Spring: A New Vision for Wesleyan Community.* New Monastic Library. Eugene, OR: Cascade, 2010.

Heitzenrater, Richard P. *Mirror and Memory: Reflections on Early Methodism.* Nashville: Kingswood, 1989.

———. *Wesley and the People Called Methodists.* 2nd ed. Nashville: Abingdon, 2013.

Henderson, D. Michael. *John Wesley's Class Meeting: A Model for Making Disciples.* Napannee, IN: Francis Asbury, 1997.

Hinson, E. Glenn. *Baptist Spirituality: A Call for Renewed Attentiveness to God.* Macon, GA: Nurturing Faith, 2013.

———. "Expansive Catholicism: Merton's Ecumenical Perceptions." *Cistercian Studies* 14 (1979) 290–304.

———. *Love at the Heart of Things: A Biography of Douglas V. Steere.* Wallingford, PA: Pendle Hill, 1998.

———. *A Miracle of Grace: An Autobiography.* Macon, GA: Mercer University Press, 2012.

———. "The Spiritual Formation of the Minister as a Person." *Review and Expositor* 70, (1973) 73–85.

———, ed. *Spirituality in Ecumenical Perspective.* Louisville: Westminster John Knox, 1993.

———. *Spiritual Preparation for Christian Leadership.* Nashville: Upper Room, 1999.

Holt, Bradley P. *Thirsty for God: A Brief History of Christian Spirituality.* 3rd ed. Minneapolis: Fortress, 2017.

Horton, Michael. *Putting Amazing Back Into Grace: An Introduction to Reformed Theology.* Nashville: Thomas Nelson, 1991.

———. *Rediscovering the Holy Spirit.* Grand Rapids: Zondervan, 2017.

Howard, Evan B. *The Brazos Introduction to Christian Spirituality.* Grand Rapids: Brazos, 2008.

———. *A Guide to Christian Spiritual Formation: How Scripture, Spirit, Community, and Mission Shape Our Souls.* Grand Rapids: Baker Academic, 2018.

Hower, Robert G. Review of *Invitation to a Journey*, by M. Robert Mulholland Jr. *Evangelical Journal* 13 (1995) 46–48.

Hoyer, George W. *Toward a Program of Spiritual Formation at Lutheran and Protestant Theological Seminaries.* St. Louis, MO: Concordia Theological Seminary, 1970.

Hummel, Daniel G. *The Rise and Fall of Dispensationalism: How the Evangelical Battle over the End Times Shaped a Nation.* Grand Rapids: Eerdmans, 2023.

Illg, Thomas. "Johann Arndt." In *Protestants and Mysticism in Reformation Europe*, edited by Ronald K. Rittgers and Vincent Evener, 309–27. Boston: Brill, 2019.

Janssen, Al. Review of *Ecclesiastical Training: Being a Short Treatise on the Spiritual Formation of Aspirants to the Priesthood*, by Francis Bourne. *Ephemerides Theologicae Lovanienses* 4 (1927) 250–51.

Job, Rueben P. *A Journey Toward Solitude and Community, Leader's Guide*. Nashville: Upper Room, 1984.

John Paul II. *Shepherds After My Own Heart: Post-Synodal Apostolic Exhortation of His Holiness John Paul II on the Formation of Priests in the Circumstances of the Present Day*. Vatican Translation. Sherbrooke, QC: Ediciones Paulines, 1992.

Johansen, Paul. "What a Friend We Have in Henri: Reflections on the Influence of Henri Nouwen on Protestant Evangelicals." In *Turning the Wheel: Henri Nouwen and our Search for God*, edited by Jonathan Bengtson and Gabrielle Earnshaw, 32–46. Maryknoll, NY: Orbis, 2007.

Johnson, Gregory O. "From Morning Watch to Quiet Time: The Historical and Theological Development of Private Prayer in Anglo-American Protestant Instruction." PhD diss., Saint Louis University, 2007.

Jones, Beth Felker. *God the Spirit: Introducing Pneumatology in Wesleyan and Ecumenical Perspective*. Wesleyan Doctrine Series 5. Eugene, OR: Cascade, 2014.

Jones, E. Stanley. *Abundant Living*. Nashville: Abingdon, 1980.

Jones, W. Paul. *The Art of Spiritual Direction: Giving and Receiving Spiritual Guidance*. Nashville: Upper Room, 2002.

Kelty, Matthew. "The Man." In *Thomas Merton, Monk: A Monastic Tribute*, edited by Patrick Hart, 21–38. Garden City, NY: Image, 1976.

Kidder, Richard. *The Life of the Reverend Anthony Horneck*. London: Aylmer, 1698.

Kinghorn, Kenneth Cain. *The Story of Asbury Theological Seminary*. Lexington, KY: Emeth, 2010.

Kisker, Scott T. *Foundation for Revival: Anthony Horneck, the Religious Societies, and the Construction of an Anglican Pietism*. Pietist and Wesleyan Studies 24. Lanham, MD: Scarecrow, 2008.

———. "John Wesley's Puritan and Pietist Heritage Reexamined." *Wesleyan Theological Journal* 34 (1999) 271–75.

Kloepfer, John W. "Muto, Susan Annette." In *The Upper Room Dictionary of Christian Spiritual Formation*, edited by Keith Beasley-Topliffe, 193–94. Nashville: Upper Room, 2003.

Knight, Henry H., III. *The Presence of God in the Christian Life: John Wesley and the Means of Grace*. Pietist and Wesleyan Studies 3. Metuchen, NJ: Scarecrow, 1992.

Lane, Belden C. "Merton's Hermitage: Bachelard, Domestic Space, and Spiritual Transformation." *Spiritus* 4 (2004) 123–50.

Lauridson, James R. "Merton and the Feminine: A Reflection." *The Merton Seasonal* 15 (1990) 3–5.

Lea, Thomas D. Review of *Revelation*, by M. Robert Mulholland Jr. *Criswell Theological Review* 5 (1990) 110–12.

Lentfoehr, Thérèse. "The Solitary." In *Thomas Merton, Monk: A Monastic Tribute*, edited by Patrick Hart, 59–77. Garden City, NY: Image, 1976.

———. "The Spiritual Writer." In *Thomas Merton, Monk: A Monastic Tribute*, edited by Patrick Hart, 105–24. Garden City, NY: Image, 1976.

Licona, Michael R. *Jesus, Contradicted: Why the Gospels Tell the Same Story Differently*. Grand Rapids: Zondervan Academic, 2024.

Lindsell, Harold. *The Battle for the Bible*. Grand Rapids: Zondervan, 1976.

Lindsey, Hal. *The Late Great Planet Earth*. Grand Rapids: Zondervan, 1970.
Lindström, Harald. *Wesley and Sanctification*. Nappanee, IN: Francis Asbury, 1996.
"The Lost Chord of Evangelism," *Christianity Today* 1 (1957) 26–27.
Lovelace, Richard F. *Dynamics of Spiritual Life: An Evangelical Theology of Renewal*. Expanded ed. Downers Grove, IL: IVP Academic, 2020.
———. "The Sanctification Gap." *Theology Today* 29 (1973) 363–69.
Loyer, Kenneth Milton. "'And to Crown it All': John Wesley on Union with God in the New Creation." *Methodist Review* 1 (2009) 109–25.
Malits, Elena. *The Solitary Explorer: Thomas Merton's Transforming Journey*. San Francisco: Harper and Row, 1980.
Markofski, Wes. *New Monasticism and the Transformation of American Evangelicalism*. New York: Oxford University Press, 2015.
Marsden, George M. "The Evangelical Denomination." In *Evangelicals: Who They Have Been, Are Now, and Could Be*, edited by Mark A. Noll et al., 17–30. Grand Rapids: Eerdmans, 2019
———. *Fundamentalism and American Culture*. 3rd ed. New York: Oxford University Press, 2022.
———. *Reforming Fundamentalism: Fuller Seminary and the New Evangelicalism*. Grand Rapids: Eerdmans, 1987.
Martyn, Stephen. "The Journey to God: Union, Purgation, and Transformation Within *The Ascent of Mount Carmel* and *A Plain Account of Christian Perfection*." *Asbury Journal* 67 (2012) 139–57.
Matthews, Rex D. "John Wesley's Idea of Christian Perfection Reconsidered." *Wesleyan Theological Journal* 50 (2015) 25–67.
Matthews-Younes, Anne. *A History of the Christian Ashrams in North America*. 2nd ed. Potomac, MD: E. Stanley Jones Foundation, 2018.
Matthias, Markus. "Gab es eine Frömmigkeitkrise um 1700?" In *Frömmigkeit oder Theologie*, edited by Hans Otte and Hans Schneider, 27–36. Göttingen: Vandenhoeck and Ruprecht, 2007.
May, Gerald G. *Care of Mind / Care of Spirit: Psychiatric Dimensions of Spiritual Direction*. San Francisco: Harper & Row, 1982.
McGarry, Joseph. "Con-Formed to Christ: Dietrich Bonhoeffer and Christian Formation." *Journal of Spiritual Formation and Soul Care* 5 (2012) 226–42.
McGavran, Donald A. "My Pilgrimage in Mission." *International Bulletin of Missionary Research* 10 (1986) 53–58.
———. *Understanding Church Growth*. Grand Rapids: Eerdmans, 1970.
McGinn, Bernard. "The Letter and the Spirit: Spirituality as an Academic Discipline." In *Minding the Spirit: The Study of Christian Spirituality*, edited by Elizabeth A. Dreyer and Mark S. Burrows, 25–41. Baltimore, MD: Johns Hopkins University Press, 2005.
McGregor, Michael M. Foreword to *A Course in Christian Mysticism: Thirteen Sessions with the Famous Trappist Monk*, by Thomas Merton, edited by Jon M. Sweeney. Collegeville, MN: Liturgical, 2017.
McKinley, E. H. *A History of the Disciplined Order of Christ, 1945–1990*. Nashville: Disciplined Order of Christ, 1990.
McKnight, Scot. *The King Jesus Gospel: The Original Good News Revisited*. Rev. ed. Grand Rapids: Zondervan, 2016.
Merton, Thomas. *The Ascent to Truth*. San Diego, CA: Harvest, 1981.

———. *The Asian Journal of Thomas Merton*, edited by Naomi Burton et al. New York: New Directions, 1973.
———. *Basic Principles of Monastic Spirituality*. Springfield, IL: Templegate, 1957.
———. "Cell." *Paternost* 5 (1967) 332–38.
———. "Christian Solitude, Notes on an Experiment." *Current* 7 (1967) 14–28.
———. *Conjectures of a Guilty Bystander*. New York: Image, 2014.
———. *Contemplation in a World of Action*. Image ed. Garden City, NY: Image, 1973.
———. *Contemplative Prayer*. New York: Image, 1996.
———. *A Course in Christian Mysticism: Thirteen Sessions with the Famous Trappist Monk*, edited by Jon M. Sweeney. Collegeville, MN: Liturgical, 2017.
———. *Dancing in the Water of Life: 1963–1965*. The Journals of Thomas Merton 5, edited by Robert E. Daggy. San Francisco, HarperSanFrancisco, 1997.
———. *Disputed Questions*. San Diego, CA: Harvest, 1985.
———. *Entering the Silence: 1941–1952*. The Journals of Thomas Merton 2, edited by Jonathan Montaldo. San Francisco: HarperSanFrancisco, 1996.
———. *Faith and Violence: Christian Teaching and Christian Practice*. Notre Dame: University of Notre Dame, 1968.
———, ed. *Gandhi on Non-Violence*. New York: New Directions, 1965.
———. *Honorable Reader: Reflections on My Work*, edited by Robert E. Daggy. New York: Crossroad, 1989.
———. *The Inner Experience: Notes on Contemplation*, edited by William H. Shannon. San Francisco: HarperSanFrancisco, 2003.
———. *Learning to Love: Exploring Solitude and Freedom: 1966–1967*. The Journals of Thomas Merton 6, edited by Christine M. Bochen. San Francisco: HarperSanFrancisco, 1997.
———. *Life and Holiness*. New York: Doubleday, 1964.
———. *Love and Living*, edited by Naomi Burton Stone and Patrick Hart. San Diego, CA: Harvest/HBJ, 1985.
———. *The New Man*. New York: Farrar, Straus, and Giroux, 1961.
———. *New Seeds of Contemplation*. New York: New Directions, 1962.
———. *No Man Is an Island*. Garden City, NY: Image, 1967.
———. *Opening the Bible*. Collegeville, MN: Liturgical, 1986.
———. *The Other Side of the Mountain: 1967–1968*. The Journals of Thomas Merton 7, edited by Patrick Hart. San Francisco: HarperSanFrancisco, 1998.
———. *Passion for Peace: The Social Essays*, edited by William H. Shannon. New York: Crossroad, 1995.
———. *Peace in the Post-Christian Era*. Maryknoll, NY: Orbis, 2004.
———. "Perfection, Christian." In *Catholic Encyclopedia for School and Home* 8:328–32. New York: McGraw-Hill, 1965.
———. "Preface to the Japanese Edition of *The Seven Storey Mountain*." In *Honorable Reader: Reflections on My Work*, edited by Robert E. Daggy, 59–67. New York: Crossroad, 1989.
———. *The Rule of Saint Benedict*, edited by Patrick F. O'Connell. Initiation to the Monastic Tradition 4. Monastic Wisdom Series 19. Collegeville, MN: Liturgical, 2009.
———. *A Search for Solitude: Pursuing the Monk's True Life, 1952–1960*. The Journals of Thomas Merton 3, edited by Lawrence S. Cunningham. San Francisco: HarperSanFrancisco, 1996.

———. *Seeds of Contemplation*. Rev. ed. New York: New Directions, 1960.
———. *Seeds of Contemplation*. Norfolk, CT: New Directions, 1949.
———. *Seeds of Destruction*. New York: Farrar, Straus, and Giroux, 1964.
———. *The Seven Storey Mountain*. 50th anniv. ed. Orlando, FL: Harvest, 1998.
———. *The Sign of Jonas*. New York: Harcourt, Brace, 1953.
———. *The Silent Life*. New York: Farrar, Straus, and Giroux, 1957.
———. "The Solitary Life." *Cistercian Studies* 4 (1969) 213–17.
———. "Spiritual Direction." *The Merton Seasonal* 32 (2007) 3–17.
———. *Spiritual Direction and Meditation*. Collegeville, MN: Liturgical, 1960.
———. *Thomas Merton: A Life in Letters: The Essential Collection*, edited by William H. Shannon and Christine M. Bochen. New York: HarperOne, 2008.
———. *Thomas Merton: Spiritual Master*, edited by Lawrence S. Cunningham. Mahwah, NJ: Paulist, 1992.
———. *Thoughts in Solitude*. New York: Farrar, Straus, and Giroux, 1958.
———. *Turning Toward the World: The Pivotal Years, 1960–1963*. The Journals of Thomas Merton 4, edited by Victor A. Kramer. San Francisco: HarperSanFrancisco, 1996.
———. *A Vow of Conversation: Journals 1964–1965*, edited by Naomi Burton Stone. New York: Farrar, Straus, and Giroux, 1988.
———. *The Waters of Siloe*. New York: Harcourt, Brace, 1949.
———. *What Ought I to Do? Sayings of the Desert Fathers*. Lexington, KY: Stamperia del Santuccio, 1959.
———. *The Wisdom of the Desert*. New York: New Directions, 1960.
Merton, Thomas, and Catherine de Hueck Doherty. *Compassionate Fire: The Letters of Thomas Merton and Catherine de Hueck Doherty*, edited by Robert A. Wild. Notre Dame: Ave Maria, 2009.
Moon, Gary W. *Becoming Dallas Willard: The Formation of a Philosopher, Teacher, and Christ Follower*. Downers Grove, IL: InterVarsity, 2018.
Mott, Michael. *The Seven Mountains of Thomas Merton*. Boston, MA: Houghton Mifflin, 1984.
Mueller, Gustav E. "The Hegel Legend of 'Thesis-Antithesis-Synthesis.'" *Journal of the History of Ideas* 19 (1958) 411–14.
Mulholland, M. Robert, Jr. "The Anatomy of Trust." *Weavings* 5 (1990) 25–32.
———. "Biblical Spirituality as Incarnation of the Word." *Leaven: A Journal of Christian Ministry* 12 (2004) 209–214.
———. *The Deeper Journey: The Spirituality of Discovering Your True Self*. Downers Grove, IL: InterVarsity, 2006.
———. *The Deeper Journey: The Spirituality of Discovering Your True Self*. Expanded ed. Downers Grove, IL: InterVarsity, 2016.
———. "Discerning the Body." *Weavings* 8 (1993) 20–26.
———. "DM 856 Incarnating the Word." Syllabi. Jan. 2001. https://place.asbury seminary.edu/syllabi/884/.
———. "Entry Point Notes: Revelation." In *The Spiritual Formation Bible*, edited by Timothy K. Jones, 1641–63. Grand Rapids: Zondervan, 1999.
———. "For the Sake of Others." Transforming Center Retreat. Mundelein, IL, July 26–28, 2015. Four sessions. MP4 videos.
———. Foreword to *Coming Home to Your True Self: Leaving the Emptiness of False Attractions*, by Albert Haase. Downers Grove, IL: InterVarsity, 2008.

———. "Holiness Emphasis Lectures, 1989 (Part 2)." ATS. Holiness Emphasis Conference 1989. MP3 audio. https://place.asburyseminary.edu/atsconferences/247/.

———. "If Christ Is in You: Growing From Death to Life." *Weavings* 4 (1989) 26–34.

———. *Invitation to a Journey: A Road Map for Spiritual Formation*. Downers Grove, IL: InterVarsity, 1993.

———. *Invitation to a Journey: A Road Map for Spiritual Formation*. Expanded ed. Downers Grove, IL: InterVarsity, 2016.

———. "Invitation to an Academic Journey of Spiritual Formation." In *Building a Culture of Faith: University-Wide Partnerships for Spiritual Formation*, edited by Cary Balzer and Rod Reed, 125–38. Abilene, TX: Abilene Christian University Press, 2012.

———. "Life at the Center—Life at the Edge." *Weavings* 13 (1998) 25–31.

———. "Losing Ourselves in Silence and Peace." In *Rhythm and Fire: Experiencing the Holy in Community and Solitude*, edited by Jerry P. Haas and Cynthia Langston Clark, 77–79. Nashville: Upper Room, 2008.

———. "The Markan Opponents of Jesus." ThD diss., Harvard Divinity School, 1977.

———. "NT 520: New Testament Introduction." Syllabi. Jan. 2002. https://place.asburyseminary.edu/syllabi/2483/.

———. "NT 666: The Book of Revelation." ATS. Spring 2009. Class recordings. 23 videos. https://www.biblicaltraining.org/learn/institute/nt666-revelation.

———. "The Place of Scripture in Spiritual Formation." Upper Room Academy for Spiritual Formation I, Nashville, TN. May 17–22, 1983. 5 Sessions. 6 Cassette Tapes.

———. "Reading the Scripture Devotionally." In *The Spiritual Formation Bible*, xx–xxii. Grand Rapids: Zondervan, 1999.

———. *Revelation*. Cornerstone Biblical Commentary 18. Carol Stream, IL: Tyndale, 2011.

———. *Revelation: Holy Living in an Unholy World*. Grand Rapids: Francis Asbury, 1990.

———. Review of *Christian Spiritual Formation: An Integrated Approach for Personal and Relational Wholeness*, by Diane J. Chandler. *Journal of Spiritual Formation and Soul Care* 8 (2015) 205–7.

———. *Shaped by the Word: The Power of Scripture in Spiritual Formation*. Nashville: Upper Room, 1985.

———. *Shaped by the Word: The Power of Scripture in Spiritual Formation*. Rev. ed. Nashville: Upper Room, 2000.

———. *Shaped by the Word: The Power of Scripture in Spiritual Formation*. Anniv. ed. Nashville: Upper Room, 2023.

———. "Spiritual Formation." Course recordings. ATS. June–July, 2012. Video Recordings.

———. "Spiritual Formation in Christ *and* Mission with Christ." *Journal of Spiritual Formation and Soul Care* 6 (2013) 11–17.

———. "Spiritual Reading of Scripture." *Weavings* 3 (1988) 46–59.

———. "Spirituality of the New Testament." Upper Room Academy for Spiritual Formation XVIII. Sinsinawa, WI. Nov. 11–16, 2002. 5 Sessions. 5 Cassette Tapes.

———. "Sustaining Life in the Spirit: New Testament Communities and Our Communities." Upper Room Academy for Spiritual Formation XIV. Sinsinawa, WI. March 12–17, 2001. 5 Sessions. 5 Cassette Tapes.

———. "The Unbelievable Goal of the Spiritual Life Part 1." Lecture Audio and Transcript. Biola University, La Mirada, CA. Sept. 26, 2006. https://digitalcommons.biola.edu/isf-lect-pre/32/.

———. "The Wesleyan Doctrine of Scripture (As Contrasted with Fundamentalism)." In *Square Peg: Why Wesleyan's Aren't Fundamentalists*, edited by Al Truesdale, 27–38. Kansas City, MO: Beacon Hill, 2012.

———. "The Word Became Text: The Nature of Spiritual Reading." In *The Pastor's Guide to Personal Spiritual Formation*, 83–95. Kansas City, MO: Beacon Hill, 2005.

Mulholland, M. Robert, Jr., and Marjorie J. Thompson. *The Way of Scripture, Participant's Book*. Nashville: Upper Room, 2010.

Mulholland, M. Robert, Jr., and Ruth Haley Barton. "Spiritual Transformation for the Sake of Others: A Conversation with Dr. M. Robert Mulholland, Jr. and Dr. Ruth Haley Barton." Wheaton, IL: Transforming Center, 2015. DVD.

Muto, Susan. *Pathways to Spiritual Living*. Garden City, NY: Image, 1984.

Murray, Andrew. *The Inner Chamber and the Inner Life*. London: Hodder and Stoughton, 1905.

Nagler, Arthur Wilford. *Pietism and Methodism: Or the Significance of German Pietism in the Origin and Early Development of Methodism*. Nashville: Methodist Episcopal Church, South, 1918.

Nelson, James. "John Wesley and the Georgia Moravians." *Transactions of the Moravian Historical Society* 23 (1984) 17–46.

Newby, James R. *Elton Trueblood: Believer, Teacher, and Friend*. San Francisco: Harper and Row, 1990.

Noll, Mark A. "Where We Are and How We Got Here." *Christianity Today* 50 (2006) 42–49.

Noll, Mark A., et al., eds. *Evangelicals: Who They Have Been, Are Now, and Could Be*. Grand Rapids: Eerdmans, 2019.

O'Connell, Patrick F. "Hermitage." In *The Thomas Merton Encyclopedia*, edited by William H. Shannon et al., 197–200. Maryknoll, NY: Orbis, 2002.

———. "Love." In *The Thomas Merton Encyclopedia*, edited by William H. Shannon et al., 268–71. Maryknoll, NY: Orbis, 2002.

Oden, Thomas C. *Christ and Salvation*. Vol. 2 in *John Wesley's Teachings*. Grand Rapids: Zondervan, 2012.

Ogden, Schubert Miles. "'Love Divine, All Loves Excelling': Some Theological Reflections on the Witness of a Hymn." *Methodist History* 56 (2018) 235–41.

Okholm, Dennis. "Rule of St. Benedict." In *Dictionary of Christian Spirituality*, edited by Glen G. Scorgie et al., 723–24. Grand Rapids: Zondervan, 2011.

Olson, Roger E. *The Westminster Handbook to Evangelical Theology*. Louisville: Westminster John Knox, 2004.

Olson, Roger E., and Christian T. Collins Winn. *Reclaiming Pietism: Retrieving an Evangelical Tradition*. Grand Rapids: Eerdmans, 2015.

O'Rourke, Elaine. "Spirit (or Will or Heart)." In *A Dallas Willard Dictionary*. 2nd ed., 237–42. Independently Published, 2016.

Ortberg, John. *The Life You've Always Wanted: Spiritual Disciplines for Ordinary People*. Grand Rapids: Zondervan, 1997.

Outler, Albert C., ed. *John Wesley*. New York: Oxford University Press, 1964.

Padgett, Alan G., "The Church Growth Movement: A Wesleyan Critique." In *The Mission of the Church in Wesleyan Perspective: The World Is My Parish*, ed. Alan G. Padgett, 137–47. Lewiston, NY: Edwin Mellen, 1992.

Patterson, William P. *A Heartening Word for Mr. Fearing: Or, Cheer for Doubting Pilgrims*. Philadelphia, PA: Westminster, 1897.

Paulsell, William Oliver. "The Ecumenical Dimension of Thomas Merton. *Mid-Stream* 23 (1984) 176–84.

———, ed. *Merton and the Protestant Tradition*. Louisville, KY: Fons Vitae, 2016.

Pearson, Paul M. "The Extraordinary Success of *The Seven Storey Mountain*." *Bellarmine Magazine*. Fall 2023. https://www.bellarmine.edu/magazine/magazine-fall-2023/article/magazine-2023/2023/05/08/the-seven-storey-goldmine-the-extraordinary-success-of-thomas-mertons-autobiography/.

Pelfrey, Robert C. *Spiritual Formation as the Hero's Journey in John of Ruusbroec*. Contemporary Theological Explorations in Mysticism. New York: Routledge, 2022.

———. *An Untold Story: Heroism, Mysticism, and the Quest for the True Self*. Eugene, OR: Cascade, 2023.

Peters, Greg. "On Spiritual Theology: A Primer." *Journal of Spiritual Formation and Soul Care* 4 (2011) 5–26.

Peterson, Eugene H. *The Contemplative Pastor: Returning to the Art of Spiritual Direction*. Grand Rapids: Eerdmans, 1989.

———. *The Pastor: A Memoir*. New York: HarperOne, 2011.

Pettit, Paul, ed. *Foundations of Spiritual Formation: A Community Approach to Becoming Like Christ*. Grand Rapids: Kregel, 2008.

Pfaff, Nancy. *Light and Fire: A Spiritual Biography of Danny E. Morris*. Franklin, TN: Providence House, 2002.

Pickett, J. Waskom. *Christian Mass Movements in India*. New York: Abingdon, 1933.

Pinnock, Clark H. *Flame of Love: A Theology of the Holy Spirit*. Downers Grove, IL: InterVarsity, 1996.

Podmore, Colin. *The Moravian Church in England, 1728–1760*. Oxford Historical Monographs. Oxford: Clarendon, 1998.

Porter, Steven L. "Biblical and Contemplative Spirituality." In *Embracing Contemplation: Reclaiming a Christian Spiritual Practice*, edited by John H. Coe and Kyle C. Strobel, 139–65. Downers Grove, IL: IVP Academic, 2019.

———. "In Memoriam: M. Robert Mulholland, Jr. (1936–2015)." *Journal of Spiritual Formation and Soul Care* 9 (2016) 2–4.

———. "Introduction to the Inaugural Issue." *Journal of Spiritual Formation and Soul Care* 1 (2008) 5–7.

———. "Introduction to the Special Theme Issue: Christian Spirituality and Christian Mission: On Not Trying to be More Generous Than God." *Journal of Spiritual Formation and Soul Care* 6 (2013) 3–10.

———. "Sanctification in a New Key: Relieving Evangelical Anxieties Over Spiritual Formation." *Journal of Spiritual Formation and Soul Care* 1 (2008) 129–48.

Principe, Walter. "Toward Defining Spirituality." In *Exploring Christian Spirituality: An Ecumenical Reader*, edited by Kenneth J. Collins, 43–59. Grand Rapids: Baker Academic, 2000.

Rademacher, Nicholas. "'Allow Me to Disappear . . . in the Fetid Slums': Catherine de Hueck, Catholic Action, and the Growing End of Catholic Radicalism." *Catholic Historian* 32 (2014) 71–100.

Regent College. "James M. Houston." https://www.regent-college.edu/faculty/past/james-houston.

Rescher, Nicholas. *Dialectics: A Classical Approach to Inquiry.* Piscataway, NJ: Transaction, 2007.

Reside, Graham. "Renovaré: Professional Pilgrims in a Post-Industrial World: A Sociological Study of a Contemporary Evangelical Spiritual Formation Movement." PhD diss., Emory University, 2003.

Review of *The Deeper Journey*, by M. Robert Mulholland Jr. *Publishers Weekly* 252 (2005) 61.

Rieger, Joerg, "Sanctification." In *The Cambridge Dictionary of Christian Theology*, edited by Ian A. McFarland et al., 458–60. Cambridge: Cambridge University Press, 2011.

Rios, Jeremy M. "Bonhoeffer and Bowen Theory: A Theological Anthropology of the Collective-Person and its Implications for Spiritual Formation." *Journal of Spiritual Formation and Soul Care* 13 (2020) 176–92.

Ritschl, Albrecht. *Die Geschichte des Pietismus.* 3 vols. Bonn, Germany: Adolph Marcus, 1880–1886.

Rivera, Roberto Amparo. *Introducción a las disciplinas Espirituales.* Nashville: Abingdon, 2008.

Robb, Michael Stewart. *The Kingdom Among Us: The Gospel According to Dallas Willard.* Minneapolis: Fortress, 2022.

Rolheiser, Ronald. *The Holy Longing: The Search for a Christian Spirituality.* New York: Doubleday, 1999.

Ruffle, Doug. "Going Deeper as We Go Wider." Discipleship Ministries of the United Methodist Church. May 28, 2019. https://www.umcdiscipleship.org/blog/going-deeper-as-we-go-wider-becoming-who-god-wants-you-to-be.

Ruusbroec, John. *The Spiritual Espousals and Other Works.* Translated by James A. Wiseman. Classics of Western Spirituality. Mahwah, NJ: Paulist, 1985.

Sánchez M., Leopoldo A., *Sculptor Spirit: Models of Sanctification from Spirit Christology.* Downers Grove, IL: IVP Academic, 2019.

Schmidt, Martin. *John Wesley: A Theological Biography.* Translated by Norman P. Goldhawk. 2 vols. Nashville: Abingdon, 1972.

Schneiders, Sandra M. "A Hermeneutical Approach to the Study of Christian Spirituality." In *Minding the Spirit: The Study of Christian Spirituality*, edited by Elizabeth A. Dreyer and Mark S. Burrows, 49–60. Baltimore, MD: Johns Hopkins University Press, 2005.

Schwanda, Tom. "Evangelical Spiritual Disciplines: Practices for Knowing God." *Journal of Spiritual Formation and Soul Care* 10 (2017) 220–36.

———. "To Gaze on the Beauty of the Lord: The Evangelical Resistance and Retrieval of Contemplation." In *Embracing Contemplation: Reclaiming a Christian Spiritual Practice*, edited by John H. Coe and Kyle C. Strobel, 95–117. Downers Grove, IL: IVP Academic, 2019.

Scorgie, Glen G. "Overview of Christian Spirituality." In *Dictionary of Christian Spirituality*, edited by Glen G. Scorgie et al., 27–33. Grand Rapids: Zondervan, 2011.

———. "Patterns of the Wind: Reflections on Christian Spirituality over the Past Century." *Spiritus: A Journal of Christian Spirituality* 22 (2022) 23–40.
Sears, Johnny. "Contemplation in a World of Action: Thomas Merton, Douglas Steere, E. Glenn Hinson, and The Academy for Spiritual Formation." *Baptist History and Heritage* 53 (2018) 68–79.
Shannon, William H. "Contemplation." *The Thomas Merton Encyclopedia*, edited by William H. Shannon et al., 79–84. Maryknoll, NY: Orbis, 2002.
———. Introduction to *Passion for Peace: The Social Essays*, by Thomas Merton, edited by William H. Shannon. New York: Crossroad, 1995.
———. "Reflections on Thomas Merton's Article 'Notes for a Philosophy of Solitude.'" *Cistercian Studies Quarterly* 29 (1994) 83–99.
———. "Self." In *The Thomas Merton Encyclopedia*, edited by William H. Shannon et al., 417–20. Maryknoll, NY: Orbis, 2002.
———. *Silent Lamp: The Thomas Merton Story*. New York: Crossroad, 1992.
———. "Solitude." In *The Thomas Merton Encyclopedia*, edited by William H. Shannon et al., 443–44. Maryknoll, NY: Orbis, 2002.
———. "Thomas Merton and the Discovery of the Real Self." *Cistercian Studies* 13 (1978) 298–308.
———. *Thomas Merton's Paradise Journey: Writings on Contemplation*. Cincinnati, OH: St. Anthony Messenger, 2000.
Shewmaker, John B. "The Spirituality of Discovering Your True Self." Review of *The Deeper Journey*, by M. Robert Mulholland Jr. *The Catholic Library World* 77 (2006) 50.
Shipps, Howard F. "Post-Reformation Trends Toward Ecumenicity." *The Asbury Seminarian* 6 (1967) 8–14.
———. "A Service in Memory of Thomas Merton." ATS, Jan. 14, 1969. https://place.asburyseminary.edu/ecommonsatschapelservices/4642/.
Simon, John S. *John Wesley and the Religious Societies*. London: Epworth, 1921.
Simpson, Gillian. "Solitude and Religion: The Spaces Between." In *The Bloomsbury Handbook of Solitude, Silence, and Loneliness*, edited by Julian Stern et al., 116–28. New York: Bloomsbury Academic, 2022.
Smith, Gordon T. *Beginning Well: Christian Conversion and Authentic Transformation*. Downers Grove, IL: InterVarsity, 2001.
———. *Called to be Saints: An Invitation to Christian Maturity*. Downers Grove, IL: IVP Academic, 2014.
———. *Transforming Conversion: Rethinking the Language and Contours of Christian Initiation*. Grand Rapids: Baker Academic, 2010.
———. *The Voice of Jesus: Discernment, Prayer, and the Witness of the Spirit*. Downers Grove, IL: InterVarsity, 2003.
———. *Welcome, Holy Spirit: A Theological and Experiential Introduction*. Downers Grove, IL: IVP Academic, 2021.
Smith, James Bryan. *A Spiritual Formation Workbook: Small-Group Resources for Nurturing Spiritual Growth*. Rev. ed. New York: HarperOne, 1999.
———. "Techniques Without Transformation." *Christianity Today* 66 (2022) 42–48.
Smith, Timothy L. "The Doctrine of the Sanctifying Spirit: Charles G. Finney's Synthesis of Wesleyan and Covenant Theology." *Wesleyan Theological Journal* 13 (1978) 92–113.

———. *Revivalism and Social Reform: American Protestantism on the Eve of the Civil War.* New York: Harper and Row, 1957.

Smith, Warren Thomas. "Eighteenth Century Encounters: Methodist-Moravian." *Methodist History* 24 (1986) 141–56.

Spangenberg, August G. *The Life of Nicholas Lewis Count Zinzendorf.* Translated by Samuel Jackson. London: Samuel Holdsworth, 1838.

Stanger, Frank Bateman. "Methodism's Ecumenical Perspective." *The Asbury Seminarian* 6 (1952) 21–48.

Steere, Douglas V. *Together in Solitude.* New York: Crossroad, 1985.

Stetzer, Ed. "The Evolution of Church Growth, Church Health, and the Missional Church: An Overview of the Church Growth Movement from, and Back to, Its Missional Roots." *Journal of the American Society for Church Growth* 17 (2006) 87–112.

Stoeffler, F. Ernest, ed. *Continental Pietism and Early American Christianity.* Grand Rapids: Eerdmans, 1976.

Tan, Siang-Yang, and Douglas H. Gregg. *Disciplines of the Holy Spirit: How to Connect to the Spirit's Power and Presence.* Grand Rapids: Zondervan, 1997.

Taylor, James. *The Remnant in Relation to Prophetic Testimony: Notes of Readings and Addresses at Indianapolis, U.S.A., 1910.* London: G. Morrish, 1910.

Teahan, John F. "Solitude: A Central Motif in Thomas Merton's Life and Writings." *Journal of the American Academy of Religion* 50 (1982) 522.

Thomas, Gary. *Sacred Pathways: Discover Your Soul's Path to God.* Grand Rapids: Zondervan, 2000.

Thomas Merton Center. "Manuscript Results for Subject: Contemplation." https://merton.org/Research/Manuscripts/Subject.aspx?id=57.

———. "Manuscript Results for Subject: Monastic and Religious Life." https://merton.org/Research/Manuscripts/Subject.aspx?id=88.

———. "Theses and Dissertations (Page One)." https://merton.org/Research/Theses/#1.

Thompson, Marjorie J. *Soul Feast: An Invitation to the Christian Spiritual Life.* Louisville: Westminster John Knox, 1995.

Thornton, Edward E. Review of *Shaped by the Word*, by M. Robert Mulholland Jr. *Review and Expositor* 83 (1986) 655–57.

Thurston, Bonnie B. "'I Never Had a Sister': Merton's Friendships with Women." *The Merton Seasonal* 17 (1992) 4–8.

———. *Shaped by the End You Live For: Thomas Merton's Monastic Spirituality.* Collegeville, MN: Liturgical, 2020.

———. "Thomas Merton and St. Paul." *The Merton Seasonal* 34 (2009) 14–18.

Tisby, Jemar. "Are Black Christians Evangelicals?" In *Evangelicals: Who They Have Been, Are Now, and Could Be*, edited by Mark A. Noll et al., 262–72. Grand Rapids: Eerdmans, 2019.

Towns, Elmer L. "The Rise and Decline of the Church Growth Movement." *Great Commission Research Journal* 4 (2013) 159–81.

Tozer, A. W. *The Best of A. W. Tozer*, edited by Warren W. Wiersbe. Grand Rapids: Baker, 1979.

Tracy, Wesley D. "Spiritual Direction in the Wesleyan-Holiness Tradition." In *Spiritual Direction and the Care of Souls: A Guide to Christian Approaches and Practices,* edited by Gary W. Moon and David G. Benner, 115–36. Downers Grove, IL: InterVarsity, 2004.

Tracy, Wesley D., et al. *The Upward Call: Spiritual Formation and the Holy Life*. Kansas City, MO: Beacon Hill, 1994.

Transforming Center. "About Us." https://transformingcenter.org/about-us/.

———. "Transforming Community." https://transformingcenter.org/transforming-community/.

Troelstch, Ernst. *The Social Teaching of the Christian Churches*. Translated by Olive Wyon. Vol. 1. New York: Harper Torchbook, 1960.

Trousdale, Whitney M. "The Moravian Society, Fetter Lane—London." *Proceedings of the Wesley Historical Society* 17 (1929) 29–35.

Trueblood, Elton. *Alternative to Futility*. New York: Harper and Brothers, 1948.

———. *The Company of the Committed*. New York: Harper Brothers, 1961.

———. *While It Is Day: An Autobiography*. New York: Harper and Row, 1974.

Tuttle, Robert G., Jr. *Mysticism in the Wesleyan Tradition*. Grand Rapids: Francis Asbury, 1989.

Tyson, John R. *The Way of the Wesleys: A Short Introduction*. Grand Rapids: Eerdmans, 2014.

Underhill, Evelyn. *The Essentials of Mysticism and Other Essays*. New York: E. P. Dutton, 1920.

———. *A Study in the Nature and Development of Man's Spiritual Consciousness*. 3rd ed. New York: E. P. Dutton, 1911.

Upper Room Academy for Spiritual Formation. "Mission, Vision, Research, and History." The Upper Room. https://academy.upperroom.org/about/.

———. *Two-Year Academy Leadership Manual*. Nashville: Upper Room, n.d.

Vaden, Matthew Brett. "The False Self and the True Self: A Christian Perspective." PhD diss., The Southern Baptist Theological Seminary, 2015.

van Kaam, Adrian. *The Life Journey of a Joyful Man of God: The Autobiographical Memoirs of Adrian van Kaam*, edited by Susan Muto. Eugene, OR: Resource, 2001.

Vincent, David. *A History of Solitude*. Medford, MA: Polity, 2020.

Wallmann, Johannes. "Johann Arndt (1555–1621)." In *The Pietist Theologians: An Introduction to Theology in the Seventeenth and Eighteenth Centuries*, edited by Carter Lindberg, 21–37. Malden, MA: Blackwell, 2005.

Walsh, J. D. "Origins of the Evangelical Revival." In *Essays in Modern Church History: In Memory of Norman Sykes*, edited by G. V. Bennett and J. D. Walsh, 132–62. London: Adam and Charles Black, 1966.

Walvoord, John F. Review of *Revelation*, by M. Robert Mulholland Jr. *Bibliotheca Sacra* 147 (1990) 500–501.

Ward, Benedicta, trans. *The Desert Fathers: Sayings of the Early Christian Monks*. Penguin Classics. New York: Penguin, 2003.

Watson, David Lowes. *Class Leaders: Recovering a Tradition*. Eugene, OR: Wipf and Stock, 2002.

———. *The Early Methodist Class Meeting: Its Origins and Significance*. Eugene, OR: Wipf & Stock, 2002.

Watson, Kevin M. *The Class Meeting: Recovering a Forgotten (and Essential) Small Group Experience*. Wilmore, KY: Seedbed, 2014.

———. *Pursuing Social Holiness: The Band Meeting in Wesley's Thought and Popular Methodist Practice*. New York: Oxford University Press, 2014.

Watson, J. B., Jr., and Walter H. Scalen, Jr. "'Dining with the Devil': The Unique Secularization of American Evangelical Churches." *International Social Science Review* 83 (2008) 171–80.

Weisgram, Stephanie. Review of *Shaped by the Word*, by M. Robert Mulholland Jr. *Sisters Today* 57 (1986) 616.

Wesley, John. *The Bicentennial Edition of the Works of John Wesley*, edited by Frank Baker et al. 35 vols. Nashville: Abingdon, 1976–.

———. *A Collection of Hymns for the People Called Methodists*. Leeds, England: Hardisty and Lund, 1815.

———. *Explanatory Notes Upon the New Testament*. New York: J. Soule and T. Mason, 1818.

———. *Hymns for Those That Seek, and Those That Have Redemption in the Blood of Jesus Christ*. Bristol: Felix Farley, 1747.

———. *The Journal of the Rev. John Wesley, A.M.*, edited by Nehemiah Curnock. Vol. 2. New York: Eaton and Mains, 1909.

———. *The Letters of the Rev. John Wesley, A.M.*, edited by John Telford. 8 vols. London: Epworth, 1931.

———. *The Works of John Wesley*, edited by Thomas Jackson. 14 vols. 3rd ed. Grand Rapids: Baker, 2007.

Wesley, Samuel. "An Account of the Religious Society Begun in Epworth, in the Isle of Axholm Lincolnshire, Feb: 1, An: Dom: 1701–2." In *Two Hundred Years: The History of the Society for Promoting Christian Knowledge*, edited by W. O. B. Allen and Edmund McClure, 89–93. London: SPCK, 1898.

Wesley, Susanna. *Susanna Wesley: The Complete Writings*, edited by Charles Wallace Jr. New York: Oxford University Press, 1997.

Wesley, T. J. "The Impact of Completion of the Upper Room's Two Year Academy for Spiritual Formation Upon the Ministry of Ordained Participants." DMin diss., ATS, 2004.

Westerhoff, John. *Spiritual Life: The Foundation for Preaching and Teaching*. Louisville: Westminster John Knox, 1994.

Wheatcroft, G. Richard. Review of *Invitation to a Journey*, by M. Robert Mulholland Jr. *Weavings* 11 (1996) 43–45.

Whitney, Donald S. *Spiritual Disciplines for the Christian Life*. Colorado Springs: NavPress, 1991.

Wilhoit, James C. "Only God's Love Counts: Van Kaam's Formation Theology." *Journal of Spiritual Formation and Soul Care* 1 (2008) 168–81.

Willard, Dallas. "Discipleship: For Super-Christians Only?" *Christianity Today* 24 (1980) 24–25, 27.

———. *The Divine Conspiracy: Rediscovering Our Hidden Life in God*. San Francisco: HarperSanFrancisco, 1998.

———. Foreword to *Invitation to Solitude and Silence: Experiencing God's Transforming Presence*, by Ruth Haley Barton. Downers Grove, IL: InterVarsity, 2004.

———. *The Great Omission: Reclaiming Jesus's Essential Teachings on Discipleship*. New York: HarperOne, 2006.

———. *Renovation of the Heart: Putting on the Character of Christ*. Colorado Springs: NavPress, 2002.

———. "The Spirit Is Willing: The Body as a Tool for Spiritual Growth." In *The Christian Educator's Handbook on Spiritual Formation*, edited by Kenneth O. Gangel and James C. Wilhoit, 225–33. Grand Rapids: Baker, 1994.

———. *The Spirit of the Disciplines: Understanding How God Changes Lives*. San Francisco: HarperSanFrancisco, 1988.

———. "Spiritual Formation in Christ: A Perspective on What it Is and How It Might Be Done." In *The Great Omission: Reclaiming Jesus's Essential Teachings on Discipleship*, 68–79. New York: HarperOne, 2006.

Williams, Claudia. "The Role of Scripture in Spiritual Formation: Calvin and Barth Critique two Postmodern Perspectives." MA thesis, Wheaton College Graduate School, 2008.

Williams, Joel Stephen. Review of *Invitation to a Journey*, by M. Robert Mulholland Jr. *Restoration Quarterly* 39 (1997) 189–90.

Willimon, William H. *Why Jesus?* Nashville: Abingdon, 2010.

Winnicott, D. W. *The Maturational Processes and the Facilitating Environment*. New York: Routledge, 2018.

Witherington, Ben, III. *The Problem with Evangelical Theology: Testing the Exegetical Foundations of Calvinism, Dispensationalism, Wesleyanism, and Pentecostalism*. Rev. ed. Waco, TX: Baylor University Press, 2016.

———. *A Shared Christian Life*. Nashville: Abingdon, 2012.

Woodward, Josiah. *An Account of the Rise and Progress of the Religious Societies in the City of London and of the Endeavours for the Reformation of Manners*. 6th ed. London: Downing, 1744.

Wynkoop, Mildred Bangs. *A Theology of Love: The Dynamic of Wesleyanism*. 2nd ed. Kansas City, MO: Beacon Hill, 2015.

Yates, Kelly Diehl. *The Limits of a Catholic Spirit: John Wesley, Methodism, and Catholicism*. Eugene, OR: Pickwick, 2021.

Yeide, Harry, Jr. *Studies in Classical Pietism: The Flowering of the Ecclesiola*. Studies in Church History 6. New York: Peter Lang, 1997.

Zeller, Winfried. "Protestantiche Frömmigkeit im 17. Jahrhundert." In *Theologie und Frömmigkeit. Gesammelte Aufsätze*, ed. Bernd Jaspert, 85–116. Marburg, Germany: Elwert, 1971.

Zirlott, Cynthia I. "Van Kaam, Adrian L." In *The Upper Room Dictionary of Christian Spiritual Formation*, edited by Keith Beasley-Topliffe, 282. Nashville: Upper Room, 2003.

Index of Names and Subjects

á Kempis, Thomas, 57
Abbey of Gethsemani. *See* Gethsemani.
Abelard, Peter, 174
Abraham, William J., 19–21, 26, 32n73
Academy for Spiritual Formation. *See* Upper Room
activism, 19, 20n12, 26, 97, 105, 138n85; *See also* Bebbington, David W.
Adams, James Luther, 50
Aldersgate, John Wesley's experience at, 15, 61n70, 63, 174
Allert, Craig D., 147n6
amillennialism. *See* eschatology, amillennial.
Anglican religious societies. *See* pietism, Anglican.
Apel, William D., 123n31
apophatic spirituality, 139–40, 144n114, 158–59, 174; *see also* desert spirituality
Aquinas, Thomas, 127–28
Arminian, 22–25
Arminius. *See* Arminian.
Arndt, Johann, 48n12
Asbury Theological Seminary (ATS), 3–4, 37–38, 41, 43, 76, 149n18, 151n24, 172, 183–84, 188–89, 191, 194, 197–98
Bailey, Raymond, 138n83, 138n85
Balmer, Randall, 22–25, 27–29
bands (band meetings):

Moravian, 50, 58, 60–61, 64–65, 68, 72n120–21, 81–82; Methodist, 50–51, 68, 70, 72–73, 75, 82, 121n27, 122n28, 123n32, 127, 144
Baptists. *See* denominations, Baptist
Barry, William A., 120n17
Barton, Ruth Haley, 1n1, 3n10, 11n41, 12n43, 78–79, 112n129, 149n16, 154n34, 160n58,n63, 162n66, 192; *see also* Transforming Center
Baum, Gregory, 37
Baxter, Richard, 45
Beasley-Topliffe, Keith, 40n108
Bebbington, David W., 19–20, 105n102
Bebbington's quadrilateral. *See* Bebbington, David W., activism, biblicism, conversionism, crucicentrism
Bellarmine University. *See* Merton Center.
Benedict. *See* monasticism, Benedictine; *Rule of St. Benedict*
Benedictine monasticism. *See* monasticism, Benedictine.
Benefiel, Margaret, 40n104
Bengel, Johann Albrecht, 50n22, 79–82, 152,
Bernard of Clairvaux, 96n58, 131n59, 174
Beveridge, William, 57n54

biblicism, 19, 20n12, 26, 42, 147; *See also* Bebbington, David W.
Black Christians, 26n39
Black, Gary, Jr., 5n19, 7n26, 18–19n6, 19n8, 20n20
Blaising, Craig A., 113n135
Bloesch, Donald G., 45–46, 83–86; *See also* crisis of piety
Bochen, Christine M., 101, 102n89
Böhler, Peter, 50, 63–64, 79
Bonhoeffer, Dietrich, 6, 85–86, 111n126, 115n145
Bourgeault, Cynthia, 102n89–90
Brown, Dale W., 49n19
Burkholder, Benjamin J., 6n25
Burns, Flavian, 175
Burton-Christie, Douglas, 101n84, 102n89–90
Caldwell, Robert W., 22n20, 24–25
Calvin, John, 221; *See also* Calvinism
Calvinist (Calvinism). *See* soteriology, Calvinist; *See also* Calvin, John.
Camaldolese monasticism. *See* monasticism, Camaldolese
Campbell, Ted A., 123n32
Carruth, Thomas A., 76
Carthusians. *See* monasticism, Carthusian
Cashen, Richard Anthony, 89–90, 93n47, 95n56, 96–97
Catholicism. *See* denominations, Roman Catholicism
Chan, Simon, 13, 28n51, 47n9, 138n83, 156n42
Chandler, Diane J., 45
Chilcote, Paul Wesley, 69n104
Christian perfection:
  Aquinas on, 128;
  as fulfillment of creation, 134–37;
  as perfection in love 130–34;
  contrasted with perfectionism 133–34; 170–77;
  intended for all 128–30;
  Merton on, 120n18, 128, 127, 130–37, 170–77;
  Moravian view of, 65–66 ;
  Mulholland's view of ;
  Ruusbroec on, 164–65;
  Wesleyan view of, 30, 74, 125–26, 128–37, 142, 171;
  Wesley's synonyms for, 125–26n39, 142;
  William Law on, 59n62
Christianity Today, 23, 31n67
Church Growth Movement (CGM), 14, 21, 28–29, 32–34
Cistercians. *See* monasticism, Cistercian
class meetings, 15, 50–51, 55, 68, 70n112, 71, 73–76, 82, 120, 122, 123n32, 127, 144
classical evangelicalism. *See* evangelicalism, classical
Coe, John H., 28
Collier, Winn, 5n19
Collins Winn, Christian T., 45n3, 47–49, 50n22, 77n137, 122n28, 150–52
Collins, Kenneth J., 7n27, 141n99
Colón-Emeric, Edgardo A., 128, 130, 132n63, 140
Communion. *See* Lord's Supper
Connolly, William J., 120n17
contemplation, 87–90, 130, 139, 158n53, 159, 164–65, 169
contemplative, 77n141, 87–90, 94, 96, 97, 100, 107n114, 144, 146, 158–60, 164, 174
conversion, 28–33, 46–47, 58–59, 65–66, 68, 86, 117, 160–62, 171
conversionism, 19, 20n12, 26; *see also* Bebbington, David W.
Country-Parson's Advice to His Parishioners, The, 56, 203
crisis of piety, 45, 83, 85–86; *see also* Bloesch, Donald G.
crucicentrism (cruciform), 20, 26, 47, 153, 162–63, 165; *see also* Bebbington, David W.
Cunningham, Lawrence S., 92n43
Cushman, Ralph Spalding, 161
Dahill, Lisa, 6n25

Darby, John Nelson, 22; *see also* eschatology, premillennial
Day, Albert Edward, 45, 109–10, 195
Dayton, Donald W., 19n7, 21n15, 28n50
de Guibert, Joseph, 156
denominations, 25;
 Anglican, 15, 50–57, 60–64, 69–71, 74, 81–82, 123–24;
 Baptist, 25, 27n48, 31n70, 38, 41, 46, 189, 197, 198;
 Lutheran, 45n3, 46–47, 65, 122n28;
 Methodist, 2n5, 25, 46, 50–57, 68–82, 109, 118–25, 188, 190–92, 194–96;
 Presbyterian, 25, 46, 193, 194;
 Puritan, 29, 46, 49n19, 49–50n20, 125n38;
 Quaker (Society of Friends), 25, 39, 89n31, 112, 138n85, 189, 192, 193, 198, 199;
 Roman Catholic, 4–5, 21, 35–37; 39–40, 41n110, 86, 113–14, 116–18, 122–25, 126, 141n99, 197–99;
 see also ecumenism
desert spirituality, 91, 94, 96, 99, 101, 103, 107, 111, 132;
 criticism of, 83–85, 116
discipline, 1, 6, 9–11, 17n1, 45–46, 50–57, 69–71, 74–79, 81–82, 109–15, 121, 124, 152, 155–59, 170–77, 182;
 as insufficient, 58–68
Disciplined Order of Christ, 109–10, 195; *see also* Day, Albert Edward
dispensationalism, 24, 26, 27n47; *see also* eschatology, premillennial
Doble Research Associates, 2–3
Dobson, James, 23
Doherty, Catherine du Hueck, 105–13, 196; *see also* poustinia
Dorrien, Gary, 19n7, 21, 22n22, 23n26, 27n47, 42n115, 46–47, 144

Du Mez, Kristin Kobes, 18n5, 23n27
Dunnam, Maxie, 3n12, 9n32, 38–40, 113–14, 188, 194, 196, 198
Duquesne University. *See* Institute of Formative Spirituality
Duquin, Lorine Hanley, 106
ecclesiola (*ecclesiola in ecclesia*), 4, 48–50, 52, 57, 60, 71, 75, 76, 122, 123, 144, 150, 152, 197, 199
ecclesiology, 11, 26–27, 31–32, 143
Ecumenical Institute of Spirituality (EIOS), 36, 39–41, 112–13, 188–90, 193, 196, 198; *see also* Steere, Douglas V.
ecumenical movement. *See* ecumenism.
ecumenism, 23n26, 24, 36–39, 41, 47–49, 77, 109, 110n124, 117n5, 118
Edwards, Jonathan, 22–25, 29
Edwards, Tilden, 39–40, 188
Egan, Keith J., 87
Ehmer, Hermann, 80
Emerging Church Movement, 18–19n6
entire sanctification. *See* Christian perfection
Epiphany Association, 40, 192, 199; *see also* Institute of Formative Spirituality; van Kaam, Adrian; Muto, Susan
Epworth, 51, 53–55, 56, 57, 70–71
eremitical monasticism, 92n43, 101–6, 108; *See also* monasticism, Carthusian; monasticism, Camaldolese
eschatology, 22–27, 29, 42, 80n152, 142n105, 152, 185;
 amillennial, 24;
 postmillennial, 22–23;
 premillennial, 22–24, 26n40, 26n42, 27
essentially contested concept, 19–20
Eucharist. *See* Lord's Supper
Evangelical Order of the Burning Heart, 109, 197; *See also* Lundquist, Carl H.

INDEX OF NAMES AND SUBJECTS

evangelicalism, 18–34, 42–43, 46–47, 109–12 144, 147, 176, 184;
   classical, 21, 46, 144;
   emphatic and historical descriptions of, 19–21;
   modern conservative (fundamentalist), 18, 20n14, 21, 27, 144, 147, 198;
   non-fundamentalist, 14–15, 21, 25–28, 42, 143–44, 146–50, 155, 162, 165, 182–83, 185;
   pietistic 18, 21, 26, 34, 42, 44–82, 83–85, 110–12, 115, 143–44, 150–55;
   post-evangelicalism,19n6;
   post-fundamentalist, 20n14, 31n68;
   turning points in, 22–25
evangelism, 31–33, 39
faith, 45, 47, 58–68, 70, 82, 97, 125n38, 138, 141
false self. *See* self, true and false
Falwell, Jerry, 23, 27
Fea, John, 23n27
Fee, Gordon D., 14n50
Fetter Lane Society, 60, 64, 66–70, 72n121, 74, 138
Finkenwalde Seminary. *See* Bonhoeffer, Dietrich
Finney, Charles G., 22–25, 28–31, 34
Fitzgerald, Frances, 18n5, 23n27
Forest, Jim, 92n39, 93n47, 102n89
Foster, Richard J., 3–4, 12, 18n4, 25n36, 39–40, 41n111, 78n143, 109n123, 189, 193, 194, 199;
   Celebration of Discipline, 27, 113, 189, 199;
   see also Renovaré
Foundery Society, 70–75, 82, 138
Fox, James, 91–92, 98, 175
Francke, August Hermann, 48–50, 152
Friends University, 4, 189, 193
Fries, Adelaide L., 60n66–67
Fuller Theological Seminary, 189; *see also* McGavran, Donald G.

fundamentalism, 20n14, 22–23, 26–27, 32n73–74, 147n6;
   theological commitments of, 26;
   fundamentalist-modernist controversy, 21, 23;
   the SFM as non-fundamentalist, 14–15, 21, 25–28, 42, 143–44, 146n5, 146–55;
   see also evangelicalism, modern conservative
Gallagher, Timothy M., 158
Gallie. W. B., 19n7
Gandhi, Mahatma, 100–1
Gannon, Thomas M., 138n83
General Rules, 68, 74–75, 121–22
Gethsemani, Abbey of, 37–38, 84n4, 90–93, 100, 131n59, 175, 197; *see also* Mount Olivet
González, Justo L., 47
grace:
   growth in, 30, 118, 120, 134, 176;
   in definitions of spiritual formation, 11–14;
   means of, 52n27, 67, 69–70, 74, 85–6, 155–59;
   Merton's understanding of, 130, 132, 138, 140, 141–44, 173–74, 176;
   Wesley's understanding of, 67, 69–70, 85n6, 129, 138, 140, 141–44, 176
Graham, Billy, 22, 23n26, 27, 29–32, 34
Grayston, Donald, 135n76
Great Awakenings, 20n14, 22, 23n26, 49n19; *see also* Finney, Charles G.
Greenman, Jeffrey P., 9n32, 11–13, 27n49
Gregg, Douglas H., 113n135
Griffin, John Howard, 102n89
Hamilton, Victor P., 129–30n51
Hammond, Geordan, 59n59, 60n66, 138n83, 140
Harper, Steve, 3n12, 38n91, 41n111, 76, 141n99, 166n80, 188, 189, 194

INDEX OF NAMES AND SUBJECTS   225

HarperSanFrancisco, 189
Hart, Patrick, 93n47
Harter, Susan, 182n143
Haverford College, 112, 199; *see also* Trueblood, D. Elton and Steere, Douglas V.
Heath, Elaine A. 125n37, 139–40n91, 143
Heitzenrater, Richard P., 50n24, 55n47–48, 56n49–50, 57n52, 57n54, 59n59, 59n61, 62n74, 64n83, 65, 81n155, 124n34
Henderson, D. Michael, 68n102, 70n111–13, 71n116, 71n118, 72n119, 74–75
Henry, Carl F. H., 22, 27
hermitage. *See* Mount Olivet
Herrnhut. *See* pietism, Moravian
Hinson, E. Glenn, 18n4, 31, 38–39, 41, 105, 113n135, 118n9, 189–90, 196, 197, 198
holiness. *See* Christian perfection
Holt, Bradley P., 86n12
Holy Club (Oxford Society), 55–57, 64, 71
Holy Spirit (pneumatology), 10–14, 30n61, 31, 36, 58, 78, 120, 131, 138n87, 141, 142, 147, 149, 150, 158, 165, 179n130, 198
Horneck, Anthony, 50–55, 64, 70–71
Horton, Michael, 141n101
Houston, James M., 3–4, 25n36, 190, 193
Howard, Evan B., 9–10n35, 41n111, 155n39
Hoyer, George W., 40
Hummel, Daniel G., 22n22, 27n47
Hutton, James, 66, 72n120
Hybels, Bill, 32n73–74
Ignatius of Loyola, 158n51
Illg, Thomas, 45n3
inerrancy, biblical, 26–28, 42–43, 46, 147n6, 198
Institute of Formative Spirituality, 36, 40–41; *see also* van

Kaam, Adrian; and Muto, Susan
InterVarsity Press, 190
Job, Rueben P., 2, 113n135, 190
John of Ruusbroec, 164–65
John of the Cross, 139–40, 159
Johnson, Gregory O., 109n121
Johnson, Reginald, 38n91, 76, 188, 191, 194
Johnson, Suzanne, 191
Jones, Bob, Sr., 22
Jones, E. Stanley, 111, 196
Jones, W. Paul, 119–24
Keller, Tim, 32n73
Kelty, Matthew, 93n45
Kidder, Richard, 51n27, 52n28, 52n31, 53n32
Kinghorn, Kenneth Cain, 38n90–91, 76
Kisker, Scott T. 47n9, 49n19, 50n22, 51n26–27, 52n28, 52n31, 53n33–34, 54n37, 55, 125n37
Kloepfer, John W., 41n109
Knight, Henry H., III, 67n99, 68n100, 69, 70n108, 75, 85n6, 138
LaHaye, Tim, 23, 27
Lane, Belden C., 102n89
Laubach, Frank, 196
Lauridson, James R., 102n90, 103
Law, William, 57n54–55, 59n62, 64
Lax, Robert, 126–27
Leech, Kenneth, 145
Lentfoehr, Thérèse, 89, 97n64
Lewis, C. S., 196
Licona, Michael R., 147n6
Lindsell, Harold, 27
Lindsey, Hal, 27
Lindström, Harald, 126n39
Lord's Supper, 67, 70, 71, 85n6
love:
    as central to Christian perfection, 130–34;
    as the goal of solitude, 93–97
Lovelace, Richard F., 28–29, 45, 46, 86, 190, 191
Lundquist, Carl H., 109n123, 197

Machen, J. Gresham, 22
MacLeod, George, 197
Malits, Elena, 100n82
Manning, Brennan, 197
Markofski, Wes, 5n17, 18n5–6
Marsden, George M., 19n9, 22n22–24, 26n40, 27, 32n74
Martyn, Stephen, 142–43
Matthews, Rex D., 125–26, 128n47, 129n50, 133
maturity, 9–10n35, 30n61, 31, 58, 66, 69, 79, 133
May, Gerald G., 9, 11, 191
McGarry, Joseph, 6n25
McGavran, Donald, 32–34; see also Church Growth Movement (CGM)
McGinn, Bernard, 10
McGregor, Michael M., 142–43
McKinley, E. H., 109n123, 110
McKnight, Scot, 31, 32n71
means of grace. See grace, means of
Merton, Thomas, 5, 37–38, 41, 83–115, 116–44, 145–46, 148–50, 155–85:
  impact of *Seven Storey Mountain*, 86, 97, 117;
  in Louisville (at Fourth and Walnut), 95;
  in love with "M.," 102–3;
  meaning of solitude for, 90–108;
  New Seeds of Contemplation, 87n19, 88n20, 97n64, 99, 135n76, 136, 176, 169, 178, 181n138;
  "Notes for a Philosophy of Solitude," 90, 95, 97–98;
  on contemplation, 87–90;
  on social issues, 99–101;
  on true and false self, 177–82;
  Opening the Bible, 148n12, 149n14, 166–67, 173n106, 178–79;
  resistance to Protestantism, 117;
  Seeds of Contemplation, 94–96, 97n64, 99, 135n76, 166, 169n87–88, 177;
  solitude as essential in, 89–90

Methodist:
  band meetings, 50–51, 68, 70, 72–73, 75, 82, 121n27, 122n28, 123n32, 127, 144;
  class meetings, 15, 50–51, 55, 68, 70n112, 71, 73–76, 82, 120, 122, 123n32, 127, 144;
  societies (United Societies), 50–51, 55, 57, 68–72, 81–82;
  see also, denominations, Methodist
modern conservative evangelicalism. See evangelicalism, modern conservative
Mogabgab, John S., 191
Molinos, Michael, 156
Molther, Philipp Heinrich, 66–67
monasticism, 83–90, 106, 119–24:
  cenobitic, 91, 106, 119;
  contemplative, 83–90, 91n36, 94–97, 100, 107n114, 158;
  eremitical, 92n43, 101–8;
  new, see New Monasticism;
  see also religious orders: Benedictine, Camaldolese, Carthusian, Cistercian
Moody, Dwight L., 22, 23n26, 31
Moon, Gary W., 5n19, 194
Moravian pietism. See pietism, Moravian
Morris, Danny E., 39, 110, 191
Moser, Johann Jakob, 152
Mott, Michael, 92n42, 93n45, 98n70, 102n89, 103, 105n103, 175
Mount Olivet, 93, 99–101, 104–8
Mulholland, M. Robert, Jr. (Bob), 1–9, 25n36, 27n48, 38n91, 41–43, 76–82, 113n135, 115, 116, 145–85, 191–92;
  conversion experience, 160–62;
  Deeper Journey, 153n30, 157n50, 162, 173n108, 177–82, 183, 190, 191–92;
  definition of scripture, 149;
  definition of spiritual formation, 9, 12, 17–18, 154;

INDEX OF NAMES AND SUBJECTS   227

evangelical characteristics of,
   20n12, 24;
his Mertonian "accent," 155–65;
his Wesleyan "accent," 146–55;
"Holiness Emphasis Lectures,"
   156, 172;
Invitation to a Journey, 8n29,
   9n32–33, 17, 20n12,
   21n17, 42, 77n132, 81n157,
   115n142–44, 145n2, 146,
   154–57, 160n59,61–62, 166,
   170–77, 182, 183, 191–99;
on Christian Perfection, 170–77;
on mysticism, 160–65;
on the religious false self,
   180–82;
on spiritual disciplines, 170–77;
"Place of Scripture in Spiritual
   Formation," 2, 39, 145, 155,
   166, 185;
Revelation commentaries,
   20n12, 24, 154n34, 157n50,
   183–85;
Shaped by the Word, 2, 5n20,
   8n29, 9n33, 12n42, 17, 145–
   46, 147n8, 149n13, 149n16,
   150n20, 153, 154n33–34,
   155, 157n50, 159n58, 166–
   69, 170, 171n95, 177, 182,
   183n146;
"Wesleyan Doctrine of Scripture
   (as Contrasted with
   Fundamentalism)," 145n2,
   148–50, 157n50
Murray, Andrew, 111
Muto, Susan, 40–41, 113n135, 192,
   199
mutual relational knowledge, 58–68,
   69, 72, 74–76, 82
mysticism, 83–86, 138–40, 142–44,
   146, 158, 160–66, 184–85;
   false mysticism, *see* quietism
Nagler, Arthur Wilford, 49n19–20
Nelson, Robert, 57n54
neo-evangelicalism, 21, 22, 28–34,
   189; *see also* Graham, Billy
New Monasticism, 5n17, 19–20n6
Newbigin, Lesslie, 198

Newby, James R., 109n120, 109n123
Noll, Mark A., 19n9, 23n25, 32n73
Nouwen, Henri J. M., 4–5, 191, 198
O'Connell, Patrick F., 96n62, 131n59
Oden, Thomas C., 125n38, 130n51,
   141, 192
Oetinger, F. C., 152
Ogden, Schubert Miles, 129n49–50
Okholm, Dennis, 119
Olson, Roger E., 19n7, 20n14,
   25n37–38, 26, 27n44, 27n48,
   45n3, 47–49, 50n22, 77n137,
   122n28, 150–52
Ortberg, John, 113n135, 194
Outler, Albert C., 58n57, 61n70,
   63n78, 65n89, 66n92,
   125n37, 158–59, 171n98,
   172n104
Oxford society. *See* Holy Club
Padgett, Alan G., 32–33, 34n80
Palmer, Albert W., 161n65
Palmer, Parker, 192
Paulsell, William Oliver, 118n9
Pearson, Paul M., 117n6
Pelagianism, 156–58
Pelfrey, Robert C., 160, 165
perfection, Christian. *See* Christian
   perfection
perfectionism (sinless perfection),
   65–66, 69n106, 132, 133n69
Peterson, Eugene H., 3–4, 25n36,
   42n114, 113n135, 190, 193
Pettit, Paul, 12
Pfaff, Nancy, 5
Pickett, J. Waskom, 32–34
pietism, 14–15, 45–82, 122n28, 123,
   150–52;
   Anglican, 15, 51–57;
   hallmarks of, 47–49, 150–51;
   Moravian, 15, 50–51, 58–68,
      69–70, 73–76, 81–82,
      122n28;
   Württemberg, 79–82
pietistic evangelicalism. *See*
   evangelicalism, pietistic
Pinnock, Clark H. 14n51, 198
pneumatology. *See* Holy Spirit
Podmore, Colin, 60–61, 64

228 INDEX OF NAMES AND SUBJECTS

Pope John Paul II, 36
Porter, Steven L., 1, 3, 21n17, 28,
    81n156, 151n23, 160n58,
    163n71, 176–77, 194
postmillennialism. *See* eschatology,
    postmillennial
poustinia, 106–9, 112, 196; *see also*
    Doherty, Catherine du
    Hueck
premillennialism. *See* eschatology,
    premillennial
Presbyterians. *See* denominations,
    Presbyterian
Principe, Walter, 8
Protestant Reformation, 5, 20n14,
    21, 28, 31, 46–47, 144
Pseudo-Dyonisius, 140
Puritans. *See* denominations,
    Puritan
Quakers. *See* denominations,
    Quaker
quietism, 67, 85n6, 137–40, 141,
    143, 144, 146n5, 156
Rademacher, Nicholas, 105n104
Reformation. *See* Protestant
    Reformation
Reformed theology, 23n26, 24–25,
    46–47, 86, 141n101, 150,
    195
Regent College, 3–4, 42n114, 190,
    193, 198
religious orders, 119–25;
    Benedictine, 107n114, 121–22,
        125, 139;
    Camaldolese, 92, 114n107,
        108n116;
    canon law in, 122–24;
    Carthusian, 91n37, 92–93,
        108n116;
    Cistercian (and Trappist), 93,
        96, 107n114, 119, 121–24,
        131n59, 197;
    Franciscan, 78, 124;
    Methodism characterized
        as, 50–51, 68–69, 70, 82,
        119–25;
    rules of life in, 119, 121–22,
        124–25;
    spiritual direction in, 119–21
Religious Right, 22–25, 27, 42
Renovaré, 3–4, 5n18, 18n6, 19n8,
    40, 41, 77–78, 109n123, 189,
    192, 193, 194; *see also* Foster,
    Richard J.
Reside, Graham, 5n18, 18n6,
    40n105, 77n138–40, 78n143
revivalism, 23n26, 29, 31n68
Rieger, Joerg, 125n38
Rios, Jerry M., 6n25
Ritschl, Albrecht, 122n28
Rivera, Roberto Amparo, 160n58
Robertson, Pat, 23
Rolheiser, Ronald, 7
Roman Catholics. *See*
    denominations, Roman
    Catholic
Ruffle, Doug, 199n15
rule of life, 51, 119, 121–22, 124–25,
    195
Rule of St. Benedict, 119, 121–22
Ruusbroec, John. *See* John of
    Ruusbroec
Ruysbroeck, John. *See* John of
    Ruusbroec
salvation. *See* soteriology
Sánchez M., Leopaldo A., 14
sanctification gap, 28–29, 31n68,
    32, 42–43, 44, 65, 76, 86; *see
    also,* Lovelace, Richard F.
Sanders, Fred, 1, 3
Scalen, Walter H., Jr., 19n8, 32n74
Schmidt, Martin, 122n28
Schneiders, Sandra M., 7, 10n38
Schwanda, Tom, 83n2, 109n121
Scofield, Cyrus I., 22
Scorgie, Glen G., 10–11
Sears, Johnny, 2n3, 24n28, 39,
    41–42n112, 77n135
Second Vatican Council, 24, 36–37,
    39, 41, 198
self: religious false, 180–82; true and
    false, 177–82
Shalem Institute for Spiritual
    Formation, 40, 188, 191, 193
Shannon, William H., 87–89, 92n39,
    93n46, 95, 97–100, 177–78

INDEX OF NAMES AND SUBJECTS 229

Shipps, Howard F., 37–38, 41, 105, 116, 118n9, 194, 197
Siang-Yang Tan, 113n135
Simon, John S., 56–57
Simpson, Gillian, 114–15
Smith, Gordon T., 14, 58, 62, 66, 135
Smith, James Bryan, 77, 113, 189, 193, 194
Smith, Timothy L., 30n64
Smith, Warren Thomas, 138n84
Society for Promoting Christian Knowledge (SPCK), 53
Society of Friends. *See* denominations, Quaker
solitude:
    as essential in Merton, 89–90;
    in the SFM, 113–14;
    meaning of for Merton, 90–108;
    recommendations of one day per month in, 112
soteriology, 22, 24n30, 25, 31, 66
Southern Baptist Theological Seminary, The, 38, 189; *see also* Hinson, E. Glenn
Spangenberg, August, 50, 60–61, 64–67, 72n121, 79
Spener, Philip Jakob, 45, 48, 49n19, 50n22, 52
spirit, 6–7
spiritual direction, 9n35, 78, 119–21, 123–24, 188, 190, 192
spiritual disciplines. *See* discipline
spiritual formation, 6–14;
    usage of the term in publishing, 35–36;
    usage of the term in Roman Catholicism, 35–37
Spiritual Formation Movement (SFM), 1–6, 9, 17–28, 32n74, 33n79, 34–43, 44, 46–47, 50, 75–82, 84–90, 104–5, 108, 110–15, 116–18, 137–38, 143–44, 145–46, 150–55, 165–66, 176–78, 182–85, 187–99;
spiritual theology, 6, 13–15, 176
spirituality, 6–14, 119–25
Squire, Aelred, 145n1

Stanger, Frank, 37–38, 76, 118n9, 194
Steere, Douglas V., 39–41, 112–13, 115n145, 188, 193, 196, 198, 199
Stetzer, Ed, 32n72, 32n74
Stoeffler, F. Ernest, 80
Strong, Douglas M., 28
Sunday, Billy, 31
Taylor, Jeremy, 57n54, 64
Teahan, John F., 89n31, 96n58, 96n62
Thomas, Gary, 113n135
Thompson, Marjorie J., 113n135, 191, 194
Thornton, Edward E., 17n3, 42n113
Thurston, Bonnie B., 88–89, 102n90, 173n106
Tisby, Jemar, 26n39
Towns, Elmer, 32n74
Tozer, A. W., 111n126, 199
Tracy, Wesley D., 9n32, 120–21n21
Transforming Center, 3, 42n112, 78–79, 145–46, 192; *see also* Barton, Ruth Haley
Traub, George W., 138n83
Troelstch, Ernst, 124
Trousdale, Whitney M., 64n81, 72n121
Trueblood, D. Elton, 108–13, 115n145, 197, 199
Trump, Donald, 23n25
Tuttle, Robert G., Jr., 138n83, 140n96
Tyson, John R., 133
Underhill, Evelyn, 111n126, 143n107
union with God, 8, 14, 36, 89–90, 91n36, 120, 139, 140–44, 148n10, 153, 162–65, 179–82, 184n151
Upper Room (Upper Room Academy for Spiritual Formation, URA), 2–4, 4n13, 5n16, 39, 41–43, 76–77, 112, 145, 148, 163, 166n80, 180n132, 185, 188, 190, 191, 194

Vaden, Matthew Brett, 178n122, 182n143
van Kaam, Adrian, 4–5, 40, 192, 199
Vatican II. *See* Second Vatican Council
Wallace, Charles, Jr., 54, 55n43
Wallmann, Johannes, 48
Walsh, J. D., 57n54, 59n62
Warren, Rick, 32n73–74
Watson, David Lowes, 50, 53n34, 55n42, 59–61, 71, 74, 122
Watson, J. B., Jr, 19n8, 32n74
Watson, Kevin M., 52n27, 60n64, 72n121, 74, 121
Weborg, John C., 194
Weisgram, Stephanie, 2n6, 42n113
Wesley, Charles, 129, 158
Wesley, John, 44–82, 116–44, 145–60, 162, 165–66, 169–72, 174–77, 182–85;
 against Roman Catholicism, 116–18;
 Aldersgate experience, 15, 61n70, 63, 174;
 "General Rules," 68, 74–75, 121–22;
 on Christian perfection, 30, 74, 125–26, 128–37, 142, 171,
 on means of grace, 67, 69–70, 85n6, 129, 138, 140, 141–44, 176;
 see also Methodist
Wesley, Samuel, 53–54
Wesley, Susanna, 54–55, 71
Wesley, T. J., 5n18
Westerhoff, John, 113n135
Wheatcroft, G. Richard, 17n3
Whitefield, George, 22, 24
Whitney, Donald S., 113n135
Wilhoit, James C., 40n108
Willard, Dallas, 3–9, 12n47, 14n50, 18n4, 18n6, 25n36, 33n79, 34, 44–46, 113n135, 114, 189, 193, 194, 196
Williams, Claudia, 5n20, 150n20
Willimon, William H., 84–85, 116
Winnicott, D. W., 182n143
Witherington, Ben, III, 22n22, 84–85, 116, 151–52, 155
Woodward, Josiah, 51n25, 51n26, 52n28–31, 53
Württemberg Pietism, *see* pietism, Württemberg
Wynkoop, Mildred Bangs, 130–31, 134–35
Yates, Kelly Diehl, 116n1, 117
Yeide, Harry, Jr., 47n9, 48–50, 79n149–50, 80n151, 122n28, 123n33, 151–52
Yokefellow Movement. *See* Trueblood, D. Elton
Zeller, Winfried, 45n3
Zinzendorf, Nicholas Ludwig von, 45, 50, 64–65, 66n92, 79–80, 152
Zirlott, Cynthia I., 40n107

Index of Scripture References

OLD TESTAMENT

Genesis
3–11	180

2 Chronicles
34:14	66

Jeremiah
17:5–10	179

Lamentations
3:40	66

Joel
2:12	66

NEW TESTAMENT

Matthew
7:22–23	180
22:37–39	133
25:31–46	153

John
3:16	29
17:20–23	179

Acts
2:37	66

Romans
5:1–2	62
5:5	62, 73
6–8	170–77
6:6	170
7:14–25	171–76
7:24	170–73
8:10	170
8:13	171
8:16	62
8:29	11, 176
12:2	11
13:10	132

1 Corinthians
15:9–10	12

2 Corinthians
3:6	9

Galatians
2:20	62
4:19	9, 11

Ephesians

1:4	167
4:15–16	132
4:24	179

Philippians

2:3–4	153
2:12–13	13, 143

Colossians

3:3	182
3:12	153

1 Timothy

6:19	34

2 Timothy

3:1–5	68

1 Peter

1:14–16	176

Revelation

1:1	183
13:1	117n2
21:18–22:21	184–85

"Harris's Hegelian approach in this volume introduces important connections between three church leaders who, at first, seem distant stars within the galaxy of the Spiritual Formation Movement. With Wesley's pietistic evangelicalism as thesis, Harris explores the 'faith in bands' which led early Methodists toward mutual contemplation for spiritual refinement. To this, he pairs the antithesis of Merton, a Trappist monk who viewed solitude as the place where God orders the mind of faith. Mulholland, who began teaching as American fundamentalists were regaining power in the latter half of the twentieth century, emerges as Harris's synthesis—as a skilled practitioner of spiritual formation which was both pietistic and evangelical but not fundamentalist, and contemplative but not quietist. Harris's approach is fresh and will please clergy and laity who have much to learn from these three giants in the history of the Spiritual Formation Movement."

—GREGORY TOMLIN, Director of PhD Programs,
East Texas Baptist University

"This book is a significant addition to the literature on spiritual formation! How wonderful to have the contributions of these three giants of our faith—Robert Mulholland, John Wesley, and Thomas Merton—in conversation with each other across the generations. My heart is strangely warmed."

—Ruth Haley Barton, Founder, Transforming Center

"Daniel Harris has brought us a hugely significant piece of work. We need this kind of parallel analysis that identifies common themes and shared influences when we study spiritual formation and what this means for the church. Harris has done this and done it so very well, giving us an invaluable resource."

—Gordon T. Smith, Executive Director,
Christian Higher Education Canada

"Daniel Harris has done the field of spiritual formation a great service! In this outstanding book he highlights the work of three giants of spiritual theology—John Wesley, Thomas Merton, and M. Robert Mulholland Jr.—revealing heretofore unrecognized points of overlap in the teaching of these seemingly disparate figures. Harris sheds light on the surprising connections among these teachers and their respective traditions, offering important insights into the history and future of the spiritual formation movement."

—Robert C. Pelfrey, author of *An Untold Story:
Heroism, Mysticism, and the Quest for the True Self*

"When I received the text from Daniel saying his work on this book was complete, I wept. I would not be the person I am becoming without the love, teaching, and mentorship of Dr. Bob Mulholland. And Dr. Bob, in turn, would not have become the towering figure he is in my life and in the spiritual formation movement without the influence of John Wesley and Thomas Merton. This story needed to be told—and Daniel tells it with such grace and depth that you will find yourself profoundly encouraged to be more fully conformed to the image of Christ for the sake of others."

—Steve Brooks, Pastor First Methodist Church Midland, Texas

www.ingramcontent.com/pod-product-compliance
Lightning Source LLC
Chambersburg PA
CBHW062017220426
43662CB00010B/1364